POSSIBLE SELVES:
THEORY, RESEARCH AND APPLICATIONS

POSSIBLE SELVES:
THEORY, RESEARCH AND APPLICATIONS

CURTIS DUNKEL

AND

JENNIFER KERPELMAN

EDITORS

Nova Science Publishers, Inc.

New York

LIBRARY OF CONGRESS CATALOGING-IN-PUBLICATION DATA

Possible selves : theory, research, and applications / Curtis Dunkel and Jennifer Kerpelman, editors.
        p. cm.
Includes bibliographical references and index.
ISBN 1-59454-431-X
1. Self. 2. Self-perception. 3. Identity (Psychology) I. Dunkel, Curtis. II. Kerpelman, Jennifer.
BF697.P69   2005
155.2'5--dc22   2005010806

Published by Nova Science Publishers, Inc. ✦ *New York*

CONTENTS

PREFACE

Jennifer L. Kerpelman
Auburn University
Curtis S. Dunkel
Illinois Central College

The concept of possible selves, first brought to life only a short time ago by Hazel Markus and Paula Nurius (1986) has grown into an exciting stream of research. A literature search using PsychInfo indicated that, between 1986 and 2004, approximately 90 published articles and over 40 dissertations focused specifically on possible selves. Scholars have examined possible selves with regard to a host of adolescent outcomes, including academic achievement, school persistence, career expectations, self-esteem, delinquency, identity development, and altruistic behaviors. Adults' possible selves have been associated with parenthood, physical and mental health, self-esteem, motivation, professional roles, coping, and aging. In addition, gender and ethnicity have been addressed in a number of possible selves studies. Although, most studies have focused on Caucasian, American samples, there has been notable attention given to ethnic minorities (African American, Latino, and Mexican) within the United States, and a handful of studies have addressed samples outside of the United States, from countries such as Greece, the United Kingdom, Japan, France, Canada, Italy, and Korea.

Empirical and theoretical articles have appeared in over 50 different journals, located in diverse disciplines, including psychology, sociology, nursing, business, social work, counseling, medicine, and education. Collectively the possible selves research base has grown in many directions and shows great promise for continuing to offer important contributions to a number of fields. In fact, one growing area of possible selves work is that of applying the concept of possible selves to therapeutic and educational goals. Educationally, what has been learned about possible selves offers a unique and viable approach to helping adolescents learn ways to identify and work toward attainable self-goals in the academic and career domains. Furthermore, possible selves offer avenues of intervention when working with both adolescents and adults in need of behavioral change, ranging from health risks, to addictions, to delinquent behaviors, to physical fitness. Also exciting, are the number of emerging scholars who have chosen to make possible selves central to their dissertations during the last

5 years. They are addressing new and important issues such as adolescent suicide, socio-economic status, disability, adult career change, immigrant experiences, life stress, and youth interventions.

Possible Selves: Theory, Research, and Application represents a sample of the current research being conducted in the area of possible selves. Each chapter was written by a scholar who is an expert in this developing field. The contributors to the book were chosen to represent a variety of perspectives, and to collectively illustrate some of the different ways that possible selves are being conceptualized, empirically examined, and used in interventions.

Strahan and Wilson (chapter 1) summarize a series of studies that demonstrate the effects of time perspective on the valence of possible selves. They also describe how the psychological closeness of past or future selves influences current self-evaluation. Oyserman and Fryberg (chapter 2) review a broad range of work addressing adolescents' possible selves, offering a useful summary of what is known about diverse groups of adolescents. They note important dimensions of possible selves, content, balance, and behavioral strategies. Frazier and Hooker (chapter 3) use Bronfenbrenner's ecological model to frame their discussion of possible selves in adult development. They add clarity to how possible selves fit within the developmental tasks across adulthood. Knox (chapter 4) offers an informative discussion of gender and possible selves construction. She also highlights gender differences in the ways that possible selves relate to a number of adolescent outcomes. Segal (chapter 5) explores the affective and cognitive nature of possible selves, noting the role of "fantasy" in development. He presents the Anticipated Life History method for capturing, qualitatively, projective aspects of self. Nurius, Casey, Lindhurst, and Macy (chapter 6) apply possible selves to an understudied group, adolescent mothers. They demonstrate the value of understanding the diversity of adolescent mothers when considering intervention efforts. Anthis (chapter 7) compares the possible selves of younger and older women, noting similarities across age. In her work she integrates the possible selves and the identity development literatures. Marshall, Young and Domene (chapter 8) use Action theory to describe the social construction of possible selves occurring within close relationships. They describe an alternative set of methods for examining possible selves, emphasizing issues of salience, balance, clarity, malleability and temporal orientation. Kerpelman (chapter 9) describes Q methodology as an alternative means for examining the relative importance of possible selves. Variation, within and across diverse groups of adolescents, is explored using this method. Dunkel, Kelts, and Coon (chapter 10) elaborate how possible selves offer a clinical tool to assess therapeutic change. They apply the Stages of Change model to illustrate the production, elimination and validation of possible selves as individuals address issues of drug addiction. Finally, Hock, Deshler and Schumaker (chapter 11) describe the use of possible selves as a means for enhancing student motivation. At the center of this intervention is the metaphor of a tree that adolescents draw, label and analyze in terms of their possible selves, considering how they might nurture their trees and protect them from harm. The compilation of these chapters represents an important slice of the research being performed in the area of possible selves. They demonstrate diverse ways that possible selves are being assessed among diverse groups of adolescents and adults, and the range of processes and outcomes that emerge when possible selves become the central focus. The hope is that this book not only provides a glimpse of some of this research, but also acts as a catalyst for further research.

We would like to extend our gratitude to the authors for making this book possible. Special thanks are extended to the originators of the possible selves concept, Dr. Paula Nurius and Dr. Hazel Markus, for their involvement. Finally, we would like to thank Nova Science for their patience and work in the publishing of this book

FOREWORD

I dwell in Possibility
A fairer House than Prose
More numerous of Windows
Superior – for Doors

Emily Dickinson, No. 657, 1862

The space of what might be is a uniquely human domain that is still to be fully mapped. Some is roughly charted, but much more remains to be surveyed. This fine volume brings together two decades of theory, research and application of possible selves. The chapters commissioned by Curtis Dunkel and Jennifer Kerpelman together convey a contagious sense of excitement with what has been discovered and promise of much that is still to be illuminated. I recognize the feelings. I believe they are similar to the ones that Paula Nurius and I, along with Daphna Oyserman and Susan Cross shared as we began exploring this concept. Possible selves, what we defined then individuals' ideas of what they might become, what they would like to become, and what they are afraid of becoming, opened up a window on psychology's most compelling problems.

Our excitement with the notion of possible selves had multiple sources. Focusing on possible selves gave us license to speculate about the remarkable power of imagination in human life. We also had room to think about the importance of the self-structure as a dynamic interpretive matrix for thought, feeling and action, and to begin to theorize about the role of sociocultural contexts in behavior. Finally, the concept wove together our mutual interests in social psychology, social work, and clinical psychology.

Most of all, and the same appears to hold for many of the authors in this volume, we were looking for a space in which to explore the ways people actively construct and invent themselves, and to think about how the content of these thoughts influences behavior. The 1980s was the height of the cognitive revolution in psychology and we all knew that thinking mattered. Processing information was a key, perhaps the key, psychological activity. Yet with respect to the self, we knew that *what* people thought was as important as *how* they were thinking. The creation of possible selves allows people to individualize more general goals and aspirations. We were impressed by the fact that people spend an enormous amount of time envisioning their futures. We now know that this imaginative work has powerful consequences. Possible selves can work to energize actions and to buffer the current self from everyday dragons and many less overt indignities as well. Unarmed with specific positive possibility or burdened by negative possible selves, we can suffer and fail to take the appropriate actions. The ability to generate and use possible as referents, anchors, incentives, and metaphors in the construction of current self-relevant experience affords people substantial agency, the sense of keeping their options open, even in relatively constrained circumstances. This is true for hoped for or expected possible selves, but even feared possible selves can be a spring for action, unless of course, people can devise a method to avoid their influence.

In the U.S., it is both a birthright and a moral imperative to tailor one's personal version of the American Dream. The notion that one should "dream on," "keep the dream alive," and that "if you dream it, you can become it" is a critical element in the world's cultural imagination about the U.S. Doing so is a source and a consequence of all good things-- freedom, choice, self-expression, control, and optimism-- at least from an American perspective. People across a wide array of contexts are capable and willing to generate possible selves. The number and content differs, but across cultural contexts, including those associated with social class, ethnicity, race, and national origin, they are similarly salient and serve to motivate behavior and provide an interpretive context for current behavior remains to be determined.

With the analysis of possible selves, we also hoped we could approach the study of meaning-making. People respond so variably and idiosyncratically to what appears as the "same" events or circumstances. Knowing how people think about themselves currently is of some help but knowing what they hope and fear should refine this understanding. If one has a self-schema as a good student or is identified with schooling and hopes to go to law school, a B has a different significance than it does for the person without these commitments. With an analysis of possible selves, we hoped to gain further understanding about the interpretive matrix of the self and the ways in which it confers form, meaning and significance to action. Possible selves then can provide some insight into intention and into what it is that a person is trying, or not trying to do, whether or not they, or others, judge themselves to be succeeding. Possible selves are not applied as frames after experience; rather they are used in the ongoing constitution of experience

A third source of our excitement with possible selves stemmed from the fact that peering inside the private and personal imaginary revealed the clear imprint of society and history. While dwelling alone in possibility can be pleasant and empowering, possible selves are not independently owned and controlled. As with all aspects of self and identity, possible selves are co-owned; they are socially contingent and conditioned. Whether or not other people validate, affirm and help realize them, or instead threaten or ignore them is a key to their power. Moreover, the social world, particularly peoples' relations with others, is very often the source of the materials for the creation of possible selves, and has a large hand in what, if anything, is done with them. We saw possible selves as sites of both individual agency and of social determination.

Now in chapters of this volume, I can see the impressive and far reaching results of psychologists who share a fascination with possibility and who seek to open as many doors and windows as they can while establishing a strong theoretical and empirical foundation. The book threads together studies on the behavioral outcomes of possible selves, new thinking about how they function within the self system, reports of innovative methods to measure and manipulate possible selves, careful theorizing about the role of others in developing and maintaining possible selves and many suggestions about how possible selves are shaped by a variety of sociocultural contexts.

As originally theorized, the possible selves one can imagine are powerful and shape educational, career and health outcomes. In the domain of schooling, Daphna Oyserman and Michael Hock have both created simple but cleverly designed interventions targeted at creating possible selves and guiding students as they think about hopes, fears and expectations. This is courageous work and these interventions have been successful in enhancing student motivation and are associated with staying in school, improved academic performance and higher rates of graduation. In the domain of psychological health, Paula Nurius and her colleagues, Erin Casey, Taryn Lindhorst and Rebecca Macy, have studied adolescent mothers and find that promoting possible selves, as well as challenging negative possible selves, is associated with higher levels of efficacy and control, more successful coping in stressful circumstances and better success in overcoming adverse circumstances. In the course of therapy, Curtis Dunkel, Daniel Kelts and Brian Coon find that possible selves are strongly associated with change in the self.

Another set of chapters extends theorizing on possible selves. Leslie Frazier and Karen Hooker ask how possible selves can be specifically used to understand adult development and examine the patterns of among developmental processes, possible selves and psychosocial outcomes. Harry Segal advocates for understanding how the imagination works in the self concept and explores the role early negative memories play in people's development and use of their adult possible selves. A chapter by Dunkel and colleagues examines in detail when in the self-change process, the generation of possible selves is likely to be most effective.

Other chapters highlight a variety of methodological innovations. Jennifer Kerpelman has designed a Q sort method that has many advantages over check lists or other listing methods. She uses it to examine the multitude of ways that adolescents think about their possible selves and identifies how these different types of thinking vary by demographic, personality and social context variables. Erin Strahan and Anne Wilson manipulate possible selves rather than measuring them. In a series of very innovative studies they manipulate how people think about their past and their future and show a very strong impact on the current self. When people feel their past possible selves are very recent, they feel better about themselves than when they are induced to feel that these possible selves are in the more distant past. Moreover, their studies importantly reveal that it is not the degree of elaboration of particular possible selves, but how they are used in the process of constructing the present self.

Chapters by Sheila Marshall, Richard Young and Jose Domena and also by Jennifer Kerpelman explore the role of other in possible selves and the very significant idea of how possible selves emerge, and may in fact require others, even though possibility presents itself as private and individual. Conflicts between children and parents, husbands and wives, and friends and colleagues often involve the failure of partners to account for and appreciate each others' possible selves, both hoped for and feared. Marshall and colleagues develop a theory and a systematic methodology that highlights how possible selves can be productively approached as joint projects between socially connected individuals.

Finally, other chapters focus on the sociocultural shaping of possible selves. Michele Knox explores the role of gender and finds that it plays a significant role. The feared possible selves of girls are more likely to be associated with disturbances in mood or self and girls are more likely to have their possible selves influenced by feedback from others than is the case for boys. She also argues for the importance of exploring the links among media, gender socialization and possible selves. Kristine Anthis explores how possible selves change by age and cohort. Daphna Oyserman and Stephanie Fryberg review studies of the possible selves of youth engaged in ethnically diverse cultural contexts (i.e., African American, Asian American, Latino, Native American and White). Their studies underscore the importance of the social context in developing possible selves. Minority and low income teens are at risk of developing few specific academic or occupational possible selves. Their studies also discuss the impact of stereotyped images of particular minority groups on possible selves. For examples, students exposed to charicatures of Indian or Indian themed mascots generated few possible selves.

The realm of what I might be has come under empirical and theoretical scrutiny and has yielded more than we might have imagined some twenty years ago. Within psychology, it is easy to despair over the fragmentation of our field and to be pessimistic about whether our findings have any significant or last impacting. Kerpelman and Dunkel have done a great service for those of us who are intrigued by the power of possibility. The volume provides reason for optimism. The types of studies collected here are typically published in a variety of outlets in separate subfields, but together they inform each other and create a solid platform for future research. I would hope that the volume serves to inspire others as it has me. I would like to see more strong tests of various theories of possible selves, more far-reaching interventions, and more attention to how to structure social environments and communities so that positive possible selves can be developed and fostered, while limiting or devaluing possible selves are discouraged. In particular, the role of the media in every form should be examined for its obvious and central role in the creation, validation and invalidation of possible selves.

I hope the volume succeeds in convincing other researchers not to be faint-hearted about the imaginative capacities of the human mind and our abilities to invent ourselves and our worlds. As humans our great evolutionary advantage is our capacity for self-making and world making. The individual advantages for education, for social relationships, for psychological health and well-being are now being formulated and many are spelled out in this volume. There are also significant collective consequences of our skills in thinking and rethinking ourselves. In fact, our futures may rest with our shared willingness to experiment with possible selves and possible worlds, and to redesign ourselves and our worlds so that there is room for all of us.

Hazel Rose Markus
Stanford University
June, 2004

In: Possible Selves: Theory, Research and Application   ISBN 1-59454-431-X
Editors: C. Dunkel and J. Kerpelman, pp. 1-15   © 2006 Nova Science Publishers, Inc.

Chapter 1

TEMPORAL COMPARISONS, IDENTITY, AND MOTIVATION: THE RELATION BETWEEN PAST, PRESENT, AND POSSIBLE FUTURE SELVES

Erin J. Strahan and Anne E. Wilson
Wilfrid Laurier University

ABSTRACT

Temporal self-appraisal (TSA) theory states that people are motivated to praise their psychologically recent past selves and criticize their psychologically distant past selves in order to feel good about themselves in the present (Wilson and Ross, 2001a). To date, evidence supporting TSA theory (Ross and Wilson, 2002; Wilson and Ross, 2001a; 2003) has focused primarily on individuals' views of their past and present selves and how they influence one another. In the present chapter, we extend the temporal focus to the future. We propose that people construct possible future selves in ways that parallel how they remember their past selves. We demonstrate that future selves which are experienced as psychologically close to the present are evaluated more positively than future selves which are more psychologically remote, that subjectively close futures selves have a greater impact on present identity than do distant selves, and that the temporal proximity of future possible selves has an impact on people's current motivation to act in ways to achieve their future goals. The implications of these findings are discussed in terms of the larger question of how the self is experienced in time.

In his famous novel 'A Christmas Carol,' Charles Dickens tells the story of Ebenezer Scrooge, a cranky old man who hates the warmth and generosity of the Christmas season. When Scrooge falls asleep on Christmas Eve, he is visited by three ghosts. First, the 'Ghost of Christmas Past' shows Scrooge images of his childhood and early adulthood and reminds Scrooge that he used to be a kinder, nicer person. The reader learns details of Scrooge's past that may have led to his eventual transformation. Next, the 'Ghost of Christmas Present' reveals Scrooge's present context, for example showing him the kindness present in his employee Cratchit's and in his nephew's houses. Finally, the 'Ghost of Christmas Yet to Come' shows Scrooge what his life will be like if he continues to be uncaring and cruel, revealing that he will die alone and that nobody will mourn his death. Overwhelmed by all of these elements of his temporal self, Scrooge breaks down and says "I will live in the Past, the Present, and the Future. The Spirits of all Three shall strive within me. I will not shut out the lessons that they teach" (p.98). Scrooge awakes on Christmas morning a changed man, and sets out to repair the damage he has done in the past.

In this novel, Scrooge is faced with his past, present, and possible future selves, and as a result is motivated to change his behavior and avoid an undesirable fate. In real life, of course, people are not faced with their former and future selves quite so dramatically, yet individuals' memories of past experiences and their constructions of possible future selves do affect their current identity and motivation in interesting and important ways. In this chapter, we will discuss research that examines a person's identity and motivation as it is influenced by both temporal directions in time.

Although understandably, many self researchers focus primarily on present identity, it is frequently recognized that the current self does not exist in a vacuum. A person's identity involves more than the thoughts, feelings and behaviors of the current self; it also includes reflections of what a person was like in the past and hopes and fears about what a person may become in the future (e.g., Sedikides and Skowronski, 1995; Taylor, Neter, and Wayment, 1995; Wilson and Ross, 2003). This broader conceptualization of identity extends the temporal focus into both temporal directions and suggests that a person's present identity is influenced by both their past and their possible future selves. In turn, present identity affects people's constructions of their remembered and predicted selves. Many researchers have typically focused on one temporal direction or the other, investigating either autobiographical memory (Conway and Pleydell-Pearce, 2000; Gergen and Gergen, 1988; Libby and Eibach, 2002; Ross and Wilson, 2002; Singer and Salovey, 1993; Wilson and Ross, 2001a) or predicted future selves (Cinnirella, 1998; Cross and Markus, 1991; Markus and Nurius, 1986; Markus and Ruvolo, 1989; Oyserman and Markus, 1990). Researchers have found evidence that both past and future selves exert an important influence on the present self (Markus and Nurius, 1986; Oyserman, Terry and Bybee, 2002; Singer and Salovey, 1993; Wilson and Ross, 2003).

PAST SELVES INFLUENCE PRESENT IDENTITY

Researchers have long recognized that the self is a product of an individual's personal memories (e.g., Albert, 1977; Conway and Pleydell-Pearce, 2000; James, 1890/1950; Klein, 2001). Anecdotal evidence suggests, for example, memory deficits (e.g., amnesia, Alzheimer's dementia) disturb one's sense of self (see Klein, 2001). Similarly, Schacter (1996) described the experiences of a head-injury patient: The patient lost his autobiographical memories and reported a consequent loss of his sense of self. Generally, people report that memories and comparisons with past selves are important sources of self-knowledge (Sedikides and Skowronski, 1995).

Other past research has demonstrated that memories can sometimes have a direct influence on current mood and well-being. For example, people's reported affect and life satisfaction often improve after they recall pleasant personal experiences and worsen when they remember distressing personal episodes (e.g., Martin, 1990; Salovey, 1992), and ruminating about negative events is typically detrimental to well-being (e.g., Holman and Silver, 1998; Nolen-Hoeksema and Morrow, 1991). However, memories can also be contrasted with present circumstances. As a result, positive memories can sometimes depress mood and lower self-view whereas unpleasant memories can boost current identity, affect or life satisfaction (e.g., Nolen-Hoeksema, 1987; Strack, Schwarz, and Gschneidinger, 1985; Tversky and Griffin, 1991; Wilson, 2000). Clark, Collins, and Henry (1994) identified a number of factors influencing whether direct or contrast effects occur. They suggested that direct effects occur when respondents: 1) recall *how* an event occurred, 2) vividly recall an event, 3) ruminate about an incident, or 4) recall an episode from the *recent* past. Conversely, they suggest that contrast effects will be more likely when people: 1) recount *why* an event happened, 2) recall an episode in only sketchy or brief detail, 3) are distracted from ruminating or thinking about an event, or 4) recall an incident from the *distant* past. In other words, the remembered past does influence people's current views of themselves; but *how* they remember former episodes or selves matters as much as *what* they remember in determining the impact of the event.

FUTURE SELVES INFLUENCE PRESENT IDENTITY

Researchers have found that future possible selves also affect one's current identity (Markus and Nurius, 1986). Possible selves are hypothetical images about one's future, including the ideal selves that we would like to become, such as 'the good parent,' 'the successful business person,' and 'the loving spouse;' as well as the selves that we are afraid of becoming, such as 'the alcoholic,' 'the college dropout,' and 'the lonely spinster.' Theorists believe that possible selves are important because they help people to evaluate their current selves and because they serve to motivate people to behave in ways that will help them to attain or avoid their hoped-for or feared possible selves. For example, someone who has a vision of herself as a varsity-level swimmer may be motivated to work hard to achieve that positive possible self. If the person is currently working hard to achieve her goal, this possible self will help her feel good about her present actions. However, if she has not been training to achieve this goal, this possible self might help her realize what she currently needs to work on. Research has shown that people do think about themselves in the future a great deal of the time and that people are more likely to endorse positive possible selves than negative ones.

Oyserman and her colleagues have also found that possible selves play an important role in distinguishing between well-adjusted and delinquent youths (Oyserman and Markus, 1990; Oyserman, Terry, and Bybee, 2002). Well-adjusted youths see a wide range of possible selves for themselves and are more likely to endorse positive possible selves. In contrast, delinquent youths are more likely to endorse negative possible selves and to believe that terms such as 'depressed,' 'alone,' and 'junkie' may describe them in the future. Based on these findings, Oyserman, Terry, and Bybee (2002) developed a possible selves intervention to target potentially delinquent youths. They helped these youths envision positive possible selves and taught them how to take the necessary steps to attain them. Youth in the intervention group showed more bonding to school and higher class attendance than those in a control group. These findings suggest that how people envision the future does have an impact on their current motivation and behavior (see also Hooker and Kaus, 1992).

PAST SELVES INFLUENCE FUTURE IDENTITY

Not only do the past and future exert an influence on the present, theorists have also speculated that individuals' remembered former selves might have an impact on who they think they could become in the future (Markus and Nurius, 1986). For example, Markus and Nurius (1986) suggested that "past selves, to the extent that they may define an individual again in the future, can also be possible selves" (p. 955). Wilson (2000) speculated that past selves may or may not be experienced as relevant to the present or to one's future direction, depending on how the past was recalled. Wilson tested this idea by manipulating how people remembered a past self and measuring the effect of this past self on people's predictions for the future.

First, Wilson (2000) reasoned that people might be more likely to experience a past self as relevant to their current and possible future identity if they re-experienced the emotions associated with that past self. William James (1890/1950) argued that a past event would be included in one's identity when it elicits a "self-feeling" (that is, it evokes the same emotions that it did originally), whereas it would be regarded as quite separate and irrelevant to self when no emotions were evoked. Drawing on this theory, Wilson reasoned that a past self might also only be seen as applicable to possible future selves when it continues to be regarded as a relevant aspect of identity. She predicted that people who recalled a superior earlier self might be more optimistic about their future prospects if they focused on and 'relived' the experience of their better past self. To test this notion, university students were asked to think about their grades in high school – which were superior to their current grades – and either vividly *re-experience* the emotions they felt in their last year of high school or focus on how they *currently* feel about their last year of high school. Participants in the control condition were instructed to recall their high school grades but were not asked to focus on emotions. Participants were then asked to look ahead to their final undergraduate year (approximately 3 years in the future) and rate their expected performance as students on a number of general evaluative items (e.g., very poor / very good student, etc.).

Wilson found that participants who were induced to re-experience the emotions associated with their past self in high school rated their expected future selves more favorably than participants who focused on their current feelings. Thus, it appears that those who experienced the past as relevant might have used this memory to convince themselves of their future potential: They expected to regain their former academic success in the future. In contrast, those who did not relive their past successes relegated their former glories to the past and did not apply them to their future expectations. This study demonstrates that past selves can have an impact on people's constructions of possible future selves; but only when past selves are experienced vividly and perhaps incorporated into present identity.

This study also demonstrates that although the past can influence the future, it is important to consider the conditions under which this impact will occur. Similarly, we suggest that the factors that might moderate the relation between present identity and possible future selves have received relatively limited attention in the possible selves literature and is ripe for investigation. Just as past selves sometimes have direct effects on the present and sometimes have contrasting effects, might it be that hypothetical future selves do not always exert the same influence on a person's current identity? Conversely, what factors determine the nature of the future selves that are predicted in the first place?

One factor that we suggest will moderate the relation between past or future selves and current identity is how subjectively close the past or future self *feels*, regardless of its actual temporal distance. Theorists and researchers have long recognized that although the subjective experience of temporal distance is influenced by actual time, the relation between these variables can be far from perfect (e.g., James, 1890/1950; Schacter, 1996). Sometimes, a long past episode is experienced as though it occurred yesterday (e.g., the birth of one's child), whereas another chronologically nearer event might feel like a lifetime ago. Similarly, an upcoming future event may seem like it is fast-approaching (e.g., a work deadline), while another chronologically nearer event might feel like it will never occur (e.g., a long-awaited trip). Ross and Wilson (2000; 2002) use the term *subjective temporal distance* to describe the psychological experience of closeness between one's current self and one's past and future selves, and have developed a theory of temporal self-appraisal to help explain how the subjective experience of closeness to or distance from a past self might influence a person's current identity. In this chapter, we will review some of the theory and research on past selves, and then discuss recent work which extends the temporal focus into the future.

TEMPORAL SELF-APPRAISAL THEORY

Temporal self-appraisal (TSA) theory begins with the tenet that people are motivated to think highly of themselves (Baumeister, 1998; Higgins, 1996; Sedikides, 1993). However, people do not simply pluck this view of themselves out of thin air. Instead, they search for evidence that supports this favorable impression (Kunda, 1990). One strategy that people may use to achieve this goal involves evaluating one's past in ways that maintain or enhance current self-regard. Sometimes, people will benefit from praising the past. However, TSA theory suggests that individuals will frequently benefit more from criticizing rather than from commending their former selves. Just as a downward social comparison – comparing to an inferior other person – can help people feel good about themselves (Wills, 1981; Wood, 1989; Wood and Taylor, 1991), a downward *temporal* comparison – comparing to a supposedly inferior past self – can cause people to feel happy with their new and improved current self (Albert, 1977; Greenwald, 1980; Wilson and Ross, 2001a).

More specifically, TSA theory suggests that people will prefer to praise their psychologically recent past selves and criticize their distant past selves. Wilson and Ross (2001a) argue that subjectively close past selves continue to have direct implications for present identity, resulting in people's motivation to glorify them. Conversely, psychologically distant past selves no longer have the power to directly flatter or taint former selves, instead they might be contrasted with current state. Hence, people are motivated to downplay those distant selves and highlight the degree to which one has improved.

In past research, Ross and Wilson (2002; Wilson and Ross, 2001a; Wilson and Ross, 2003) have demonstrated that subjectively distant past selves are remembered more critically than close past selves. They also find that negative past events are perceived as more psychologically distant than pleasant earlier episodes; and that past selves and events experienced as temporally recent have a greater impact on current self than do subjectively distant selves and events. They argue that these findings demonstrate people's general motivation to maintain a favorable view of present self by taking credit for past successes and relegating past failures to the distant past.

EXTENDING TEMPORAL SELF-APPRAISAL THEORY INTO THE FUTURE

To this point, temporal self-appraisal theory has dealt primarily with individuals' views of past and present selves and how they mutually influence one another. We suggest that there will be parallels between how people remember their past and how they predict their possible future selves. We will review a number of studies highlighting these parallels and comment on the larger question of how the self is experienced in time.

HOW DO PEOPLE EVALUATE CLOSE AND DISTANT PAST AND FUTURE SELVES?

First, we will briefly describe earlier research on past selves, and then detail more recent studies predicting parallel effects for possible future selves. In research examining past selves, Wilson and Ross (2001a) asked participants to rate their current self on a variety of attributes (e.g., socially skilled, satisfied with life, naïve). All participants were then asked to think back to a former self, approximately three months prior. Although everyone recalled the same actual period in time, participants were randomly assigned to feel like the past self was either recent or distant. Subjective temporal distance was manipulated by asking half of the participants to "think of a point in the *recent* past, the beginning of this term. What were you like then?" and asking the other half to "think *all the way back* to the beginning of this term. What were you like *way back* then?" Wilson and Ross found that when the beginning of the term was represented as recent, people's evaluations of former selves were as favorable as their present self-appraisals. However, when the identical point in time was portrayed as distant, people were significantly more critical of their past than their current selves (see Table 1). This study supports TSA theory's contention that people will praise subjectively recent past selves more than distant selves, because psychologically close selves and events still have direct implications for current identity whereas distant selves are no longer included in current self and may be contrasted instead.

According to TSA theory, people's predictions for future selves should parallel their memories of former selves: Future selves which are experienced as psychologically close to the present should be evaluated more positively than future selves which are more psychologically remote. One difference in our predictions for past and future selves is that unlike the past, we do not expect that people will derogate even their more distant future selves, because they expect to become those selves someday. However, we expect that close future selves will be more enthusiastically praised. Great expectations that are just around the corner may offer immediate gratification for current identity: One can start taking credit for these predicted accomplishments immediately. However, although people may enjoy looking forward to more distant glories, the experience may be bittersweet: The remoteness of those future successes may highlight how the present pales in comparison.

Table 1: Participants' Evaluations of Past and Present Self

Self	Past Self Feels Recent	Past Self Feels Distant
Past	6.1	5.6
Present	6.1	6.2

Recently, Wilson, Lawford, and Buehler (2003) tested whether this TSA-predicted pattern of results would occur for future possible selves. In one study, participants rated their current self on a variety of attributes, and then were randomly assigned to feel that a future self was either in the near or distant future. In this study, subjective temporal distance was manipulated with the use of a time line. The time line functions to alter the psychological perception of time by altering people's spatial representation of time. People in both conditions were asked to think about a point in time 2 months into the future. To help them think about this point they were asked to place this point on a time line. People were given one of 2 versions of the time line. In one version, the end points were labeled "today" and "spring break" (several *months* away) and in the other version the end points were labeled "today" and "graduation" (several *years* away) (see Figure 1). Participants were asked to place the target period, 2 months in the future, on the time line. Participants whose time line spanned only a few months would be led to place the future time point spatially much further from the present than those whose time line spanned several years, creating the illusion of temporal distance or proximity. Following the manipulation of temporal distance, participants rated their expected future self on the same dimensions on which they had rated current self. Results showed that when the future self was induced to feel close, participants expected a significantly more favorable future self than when the same point in the future felt far off in the distance. Wilson and her colleagues interpret this finding to indicate that people are more motivated to glorify their subjectively close possible selves because they offer immediate gratification to current identity. This interpretation was supported in a second study, where the pattern of findings was replicated when people predicted their own future selves, but not when people predicted the future attributes of an acquaintance. Presumably, people are not motivated to enhance the near future prospects of other individuals.

HOW DO CLOSE AND DISTANT PAST AND FUTURE SELVES AFFECT CURRENT IDENTITY?

According to TSA theory, people rate close past and future selves more positively than distant ones because close selves in either temporal direction are included in current identity and people are motivated to see their current selves in a favorable light. In the following two studies, Wilson and her colleagues tested whether people do feel more positively about themselves in the present when they feel close to, rather than distant from, a successful past or future self.

Future Self Feels Distant		
Today	↑	Spring Break
(Nov 01)	target date	(Feb 2002)

Future Self Feels Close		
Today	↑	Graduation
(Nov 01)	target date	(April 2005)

Figure 1: Time-line Manipulation

In the first study, Wilson and Ross (2001b) asked participants to report their past academic success in high school. All of the participants had been more academically successful in high school than they currently were. Participants were then randomly assigned to feel like this superior past self was recent or distant, using a time line manipulation similar in principle to the one discussed previously. After being induced to feel close or distant from their former, more successful, academic selves, participants reported on their *current* perceived academic success. Students currently felt more successful in school when their former accomplishments felt recent, relative to when past glories seemed far away. Thus, people do feel more positively about themselves when they reflect on a past success that feels psychologically close to their present self.

In a second study, Schmidt, Buehler, and Wilson (2003) tested whether people would also feel better after feeling close to an expected future success. Participants were all asked to describe a very positive future self or event that they expected to occur in a few months and that would make them feel good about themselves. Participants were then randomly assigned to a time line condition making that feel that the very positive future event was in the close or distant future. Then they rated their *current* self on a variety of attributes (e.g., socially skilled, smart). Results revealed that participants who felt that their expected positive event was in the near future rated their present selves more favorably than participants who felt the positive event was in the distant future. Comparisons with a control condition revealed that participants' present selves were boosted above baseline in the close future condition but not significantly different from control in the distant condition. In other words, people appear to benefit particularly from close future glories, whereas distant successes have neither beneficial nor detrimental effects.

Taken together, these two studies demonstrate that people do benefit in the present from feeling psychologically close to a positive past or future self. The past and the future can have significant implications for individuals' present identity, but their impact is not always straightforward: It is important to consider factors that might moderate the relation between people's various temporal selves.

HOW DO PEOPLE PERCEIVE THE DISTANCE OF PAST AND FUTURE SELVES AND EVENTS?

The previously described studies demonstrate that people will praise a temporally close past or future self more than a temporally distant one. Moreover, praising close past or future selves has positive effects on one's present self. In the final set of parallel studies we will describe, Wilson and her colleagues tested another prediction of TSA theory: That people will regard past and future experiences which have favorable implications for their current self-appraisals as temporally closer than experiences which have unflattering implications. Thus, in these two studies, subjective distance was the dependent variable, as opposed to the independent variable as it was in the previous sets of parallel studies.

First, Ross and Wilson (2002) examined how people perceived the temporal distance of past events: They asked participants to record either their best or their worst final grade of the previous academic term. Next, participants reported the subjective distance of the course in which they received that grade. This was assessed by having participants indicate how far away the course felt on a 10-point scale with endpoints labeled *feels like yesterday* (1) and *feels far away* (10). Ross and Wilson found that participants felt farther away from the course in which they received their worst grade than the course in which they received their best grade, even after controlling for the actual passage of time (see Figure 2). Thus, people appear to distance negative past events and keep their earlier successes close. This should allow them to reduce the threat to current identity posed by former failings while continuing to take credit for earlier glories.

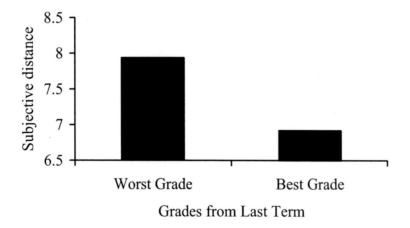

Figure 2: Subjective Distance as a Function of Grade Received

In the next study, Wilson and Ross (2002) and their colleagues tested whether this pattern of distancing would be true of future events. Specifically, they tested whether people's expectations about a specific future event (i.e., a midterm exam) would affect how close to the present the event felt. Participants were first contacted by phone approximately two weeks before their mid-term exam in Introductory Psychology. The researchers asked participants to predict the grade they most reasonably expected to receive on the midterm, then asked participants how far away the midterm currently felt to them on a 10-point scale with endpoints labeled *feels like tomorrow* (1) and *feels far away* (10). Results revealed that participants who expected to do poorly on the exam indicated that the exam felt further away to them than participants who expected to do well on the exam (see Figure 3), suggesting that students might be inclined to distance their expected failures to reduce the threat to current identity.

Wilson and Ross also wondered whether the pattern of distancing might be associated with actual outcome on the exam, so they obtained participants' actual grades on the exam. Interestingly, the more students had distanced their future exam, the more poorly they actually performed ($r = -.22, p < .05$). This study demonstrates that students who expected to do well on a midterm exam felt that the exam was coming up fairly quickly, whereas students who expected to do poorly on the exam felt that the exam was still in the remote future. It may also suggest that pushing the exam off into the distance was associated with worse performance, perhaps because these people also put off preparing for the midterm which still felt very far away.

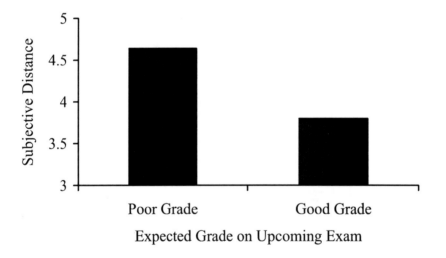

Figure 3: Subjective Distance as a Function of Expected Grade

The results from this study, though very preliminary, could suggest a self-fulfilling prophecy in which students might regularly engage. Students who expect to do well on a test are more motivated to feel that an upcoming exam is in the near future. Because the exam feels close, these students may start studying for the exam fairly early, increasing their chances of success on the test. In contrast, students who expect to do poorly on an exam are inclined to feel that the exam is in the distant future. Because the exam feels far away, these students may put off studying for the test, thereby decreasing their chances of success on the test.

THE IMPACT OF CLOSE AND DISTANT
FUTURE SELVES ON MOTIVATION

We were intrigued by the findings from the last study and wanted to test whether people actually do feel more currently motivated by a possible future self when that self feels temporally close to the present, as compared to temporally distant. The possible selves literature suggests that well-elaborated future selves play a role in motivating people to take steps to achieve their goals. However, little is known about whether all possible selves would have this similar effect: Do possible selves in the psychologically close future exert more of a motivating influence than psychologically more remote future selves? We conducted a study in which we manipulated how far away a future possible self felt to participants and then examined how motivated they were to achieve success in the future (Strahan and Wilson, 2003).

In this study, we asked participants to think about themselves graduating from university which would occur in approximately 3 years time. All participants were instructed to spend a moment picturing their graduation day and thinking about the person they expected to be at that future point in time. Next, we manipulated participants' apparent distance from graduation using the timeline procedure. Both time-lines began with "Today" as the starting point, and all participants were asked to place graduation on the line. Participants in the 'graduation feels distant' condition completed a time-line that stretched only 5 years into the future, and participants in the 'graduation feels close' condition completed a time-line that spanned 25 years into the future. Participants whose time line spanned 5 years would be led to place the future time much further from the present than participants whose time line extended 25 years, creating the illusion of temporal distance or proximity. After completing the time line manipulation (hence feeling close to or distant from their future possible selves related to graduating from university), participants were asked to generate their hoped for and feared selves by listing who they expected to be and who they would like to avoid being at graduation. Then, they were asked to write in an open-ended format about the strategies they planned to implement to achieve academic success at graduation. Finally, participants filled out a questionnaire designed to assess their current academic motivation (Lockwood, Jordan and Kunda, 2002). This measure contained items such as "I plan to put more time into my schoolwork" and "I plan to focus more on my studies."

First, we examined whether feeling close or far away from graduation influenced people's current academic motivation. Our analysis of the closed-ended measure of motivation revealed that participants who felt that graduation was in the near future were more motivated to currently work hard at their studies than participants who felt that graduation was in the distant future. Thus, the relation between participants' possible future selves and their level of current motivation was moderated by the temporal distance manipulation.

The possible selves literature suggests that *well-elaborated* possible selves will be particularly motivating (Markus and Nurius, 1986; Markus and Ruvolo, 1989; Schouten, 1991). Therefore, we next investigated whether participants differed in the extent to which they elaborated upon their possible future selves. First we counted the number of expected possible selves and the number of to-be-avoided possible selves that participants listed. We also assessed the number of open-ended statements that participants generated concerning their plans to achieve success at graduation. We found that the close and distant conditions did not differ in the extent to which participants elaborated upon their future self at graduation. Both conditions wrote about fairly elaborated possible future selves, but they did not differ in the number of expected or to-be-avoided possible selves listed. The extent to which they elaborated on their plans to achieve these possible future selves also did not differ by condition. Furthermore, the degree of elaboration of possible selves and plans did not correlate with how motivated participants were in the present.

These findings suggest that elaboration per se may not determine the degree to which a possible self motivated current action. However, we reasoned that the *type* of elaboration might be important. Drawing on the work of Taylor and her colleagues who have found that process-based mental simulations are more motivating than outcome-based mental simulations (Pham and Taylor, 1999; Taylor and Schneider, 1989), we re-examined participants' elaboration of their plans to achieve future goals, and distinguished between statements describing the *process* of achieving goals versus statements depicting the end goal or *outcome*. Process-based mental simulations involve thinking about the steps that one needs to take to achieve a given end state, whereas outcome-based simulations involves envisioning the desired end state. We coded open-ended descriptions of participants' plans to achieve success by identifying specific action plans (e.g., "I plan to attend lectures every week," "I am going to study harder for exams), mentions of the outcome only (e.g., "I plan to have high grades when I graduate"), and mentions of plans for other things in life unrelated to graduation (e.g., "I plan to spend more time with my friends," "I want to have a balance in my life"). The content analysis of the open-ended data revealed that participants who were induced to feel that graduation was close spontaneously listed more concrete action plans describing the *process* of achieving goals than did participants who were induced to feel that graduation was in the distant future. In contrast, participants who felt that graduation was in the distant future tended to list more end goals and plans for other things in life than participants who felt that graduation was near. These results suggest that feeling close to graduation induced participants to focus more on the actual actions or strategies they should start taking now, in order to achieve their future goals. We also found that the more concrete action plans people spontaneously listed, the more motivation they reported (r = .30). These findings suggest that elaboration per se may not determine the motivational impact of a possible self, but rather that a specific type of elaboration – making concrete action plans, or focusing on the *process* by which a goal would be attained – seems to be a key component in explaining why a close possible self is more motivating than a distant one.

Possible selves have long been thought to motivate people's current actions (Markus and Nurius, 1986). The results from this study suggest that not all possible selves will have the same effect: A future possible self which feels psychologically close is more motivating than a future possible self which feels psychologically distant. Students who felt that graduation was in the near future were more motivated to work hard on their current academic studies than students who felt that graduation was in the more distant future. In addition, students who felt that graduation was near listed more specific action plans for academic success and fewer plans for other things in their lives than students who felt graduation was far away. Finally, the more specific action plans students listed, the more motivated they were to work hard in the present. Thus, a psychologically close future self may have motivated students to do well in the present by helping them to think of specific steps that they could take to achieve success at graduation. These findings support the notion that possible selves are motivating, and help to explain how possible selves might work as motivators. When a possible self feels close, people may feel that swift action is needed to reach desired goals. Hence, they focus on the specific steps to take *in the present* that are necessary to achieve success in the future, thereby increasing their motivation and possibly also increasing their chances of success.

THE TEMPORALLY EXTENDED SELF

In sum, we have argued that people's past and future selves have important implications for present identity and motivation, and in turn present self-goals can influence how people construct their past and possible future selves. We have demonstrated that past and future selves can demonstrate parallel effects and are both influenced by subjective temporal distance. Another element that is shared by both past and future selves is that there are relatively malleable: Memories are ephemeral, and future selves are by their very nature hypothetical. Hence, individuals have some freedom to construct their present identity by adjusting their views of the past and predictions for the future in a way that helps to support their desired conclusions about current self.

REFERENCES

Albert, S. (1977). Temporal comparison theory. *Psychological Review, 84,* 485-503.

Baumeister, R. F. (1998). The self. In D. T. Gilbert, S. T. Fiske and G. Lindzey (Eds), *Handbook of Social Psychology* (4th edition, pp. 680-740). New York: McGraw-Hill.

Cinnirella, M. (1998). Exploring temporal aspects of social identity: The concept of possible social identities. *European Journal of Social Psychology, 28,* 227-248.

Clark, Collins, and Henry (1994). Biasing effects of retrospective reports on current self-assessments. In N. Schwarz and S. Sudman (Eds.), Autobiographical memory and the validity of retrospective reports. (pp.291-304). New York: Springer-Verlag.

Conway, M. A. and Pleydell-Pearce, C. W. (2000). The construction of autobiographical memories in the self-memory system. *Psychological Review, 107,* 261-288.

Cross, S. and Markus, H. (1991). Possible selves across the life span. *Human Development, 34,* 230-255.

Gergen, K. J., and Gergen, M. M. (1988). Narrative and the self as relationship. In Berkowitz, L. (Ed.). *Advances in Experimental Social Psychology, Vol.21: Social Psychology Studies of the Self: Perspectives and Programs* (pp.17-56). San Diego, CA: Academic Press, Inc.

Dickens, C. A. (1995). *A Christmas Carol and Other Stories.* Random House, Inc., 1995.

Greenwald, A. G. (1980). The totalitarian ego: Fabrication and revision of personal history. *American Psychologist, 35,* 603-618.

Higgins, E.T. (1996). The "self digest": Self-knowledge serving self-regulatory functions. *Journal of Personality and Social Psychology, 71,* 1062-1083.

Holman, E. A. and Silver, R. C. (1998). Getting "stuck" in the past: Temporal orientation and coping with trauma. *Journal of Personality and Social Psychology, 74,* 1146-1163.

James, W. (1950). *Principles of psychology*. New York: Dover. (Originally published in 1890).

Kunda, Z. (1990). The case for motivated reasoning. *Psychological Bulletin, 108,* 480-498.

Libby, L. K., and Eibach, R. P. (2002). Looking back in time: Self-concept change affects visual perspective in autobiographical memory. *Journal of Personality and Social Psychology, 82,* 167-179.

Lockwood, P., Jordan, C. H. and Kunda, Z. (2002). Motivation by positive or negative role models: Regulatory focus determines who will best inspire us. *Journal of Personality and Social Psychology, 83,* 854-864.

Markus, H. and Nurius, P. (1986). Possible selves. *American Psychologist, 41,* 954-969.

Markus, H. and Ruvolo, A. (1989) Possible selves: Personalized representations of goals. In L. A. Pervin (Ed), *Goal concepts in personality and social psychology* (pp. 211-241). Hillsdale, NJ, England: Lawrence Erlbaum Associates, Inc.

Martin, M. (1990). On the induction of mood. *Clinical Psychology Review, 10,* 669-697.

Nolen-Hoeksema, S. (1987). Sex differences in unipolar depression: Evidence and theory. *Psychological Bulletin, 101,* 259-282.

Nolen-Hoeksema, S. and Morrow, J. (1991). A prospective study of depression and posttraumatic stress symptoms after a natural disaster: The 1989 Loma Prieta earthquake. *Journal of Personality and Social Psychology, 61,* 115-121.

Oyserman, D. and Markus, H. (1990). Possible selves in balance: Implications for delinquency. *Journal of Social Issues, 46,* 141-157.

Oyserman, D., Terry, K. and Bybee, D. (2002). A possible selves intervention to enhance school involvement. *Journal of Adolescence, 25,* 313-326.

Pham, L.B. and Taylor, S. E. (1999). From thought to action: Effects of process- versus outcome-based mental simulations on performance. *Personality and Social Psychology Bulletin, 25,* 250-260.

Ross, M. and Wilson, A. E. (2000). Constructing and appraising past selves. In D. L. Schacter and E. Scarry (Eds.), *Memory, brain and belief* (pp. 231-258). Cambridge, MA: Harvard University Press.

Ross, M. and Wilson, A. E. (2002). It feels like yesterday: Self-esteem, valence of personal past experiences, and judgments of subjective distance. *Journal of Personality and Social Psychology, 82,* 792-803.

Salovey, P. (1992). Mood-induced self-focused attention. *Journal of Personality and Social Psychology, 62,* 699-707.

Schacter, D. L. (1996). *Searching for memory: The brain, the mind and the past*. New York, NY: Basicbooks, Inc.

Schmidt, C., Buehler, R., and Wilson, A. E. (2003). *How do close and distant future successes influence present self-appraisals?* Unpublished honours thesis, Wilfrid Laurier University.

Schouten, J. W. (1991). Selves in transition: Symbolic consumption in personal rites of passage and identity reconstruction. *Journal of Consumer Research, 17,* 412-425.

Sedikides, C. (1993). Assessment, enhancement, and verification determinants of the self-evaluation process. *Journal of Personality and Social Psychology, 65,* 317-338.

Sedikides, C. and Skowronski, J. J. (1995). On the sources of self-knowledge: The perceived primacy of self-reflection. *Journal of Social and Clinical Psychology, 14,* 244-270.

Strack, F. Schwarz, N. and Gschneidinger, E. (1985). Happiness and reminiscing: The role of time perspective, affect, and mode of thinking. *Journal of Personality and Social Psychology, 49,* 1460-1469.

Strahan, E. J. and Wilson, A. E. (2003). Possible selves and motivation: Exploring the role of temporal distance. Raw data, Wilfrid Laurier University.

Taylor, S.E., Neter, E. and Wayment, H.A. (1995) Self-evaluation processes. *Personality and Social Psychology Bulletin, 21,* 1278-1287.

Taylor, S.E. and Schneider, S. K. (1989). Coping and the simulation of events. *Social Cognition, 7,* 174-194.

Tversky, A. and Griffin, D. (1991). Endowment and contrast in judgments of well-being. In F. Strack, M. Argyle (Eds.), *Subjective well-being: An interdisciplinary perspective. International series in experimental social psychology, Vol. 21* (pp. 101-118). Elmsford, NY, US: Pergamon Press, Inc.

Wills, T. A. (1981). Downward comparison principles in social psychology. *Psychological Bulletin, 90,* 245-271.

Wilson, A.E. (2000). *How do people's perceptions of their former selves affect their current self-appraisals?* Unpublished doctoral dissertation, University of Waterloo.

Wilson, A. E., Lawford, H., and Buehler, R. (2003). *The effect of temporal distance on future self-appraisals.* Manuscript in preparation.

Wilson, A. E., and Ross, M. (2000). The frequency of temporal-self and social comparisons in people's personal appraisals. *Journal of Personality and Social Psychology, 78,* 928-942.

Wilson, A. E., and Ross, M. (2001a). From chump to champ: People's appraisals of their earlier and present selves. *Journal of Personality and Social Psychology, 80,* 572-584.

Wilson, A. E., and Ross, M. (2001b). *How do people's perceptions of their former selves affect their current self-appraisals?* Paper presented at the Society for Personality and Social Psychology Annual Convention, San Antonio, TX.

Wilson, A. E., and Ross, M. (2002). *Students' predictions and recall for their exam performance.* Raw data, University of Waterloo.

Wilson, A. E., and Ross, M. (2003). The identity function of autobiographical memory: Time is on our side. *Memory: Special Issue Exploring the Functions of Autobiographical Memory, 11,* 137-149.

Wood, J. V. (1989). Theory and research concerning social comparisons of personal attributes. *Psychological Bulletin, 106,* 231-248.

Wood, J. V. and Taylor, K. L. (1991). Serving self-relevant goals through social comparison. In J. Suls and T. A. Wills (Eds.), *Social comparison: Contemporary theory and research* (pp. 23-49). Hillsdale, NJ: Erlbaum.

In: Possible Selves: Theory, Research and Application   ISBN 1-59454-431-X
Editors: C. Dunkel and J. Kerpelman, pp. 17-39   © 2006 Nova Science Publishers, Inc.

Chapter 2

THE POSSIBLE SELVES OF DIVERSE ADOLESCENTS: CONTENT AND FUNCTION ACROSS GENDER, RACE AND NATIONAL ORIGIN

Daphna Oyserman
Univeristy of Michigan
Stephanie Fryberg
The University of Arizona

ABSTRACT

This chapter provides an overview of what is known about content of possible selves and implications of possible selves for outcomes for male and female teens differing in race/ethnicity (African American, Asian American, Latino, Native American, and white teens). Although findings are somewhat ambiguated by heterogeneity in time focus (e.g. 'next year', 'when you are an adult', 'in five years'), it appears that expected possible selves for the near future most commonly focus on academic and interpersonal domains, while fears are more diverse. There is some evidence that number of academic possible selves declines across the transition to middle school and from middle to high school. Low income, rural and Hispanic youth are at risk of having few academic or occupational possible selves, or having such general possible selves in these domains that they are unlikely to promote self-regulation. For a number of reasons, possible selves of girls may function more effectively as self-regulators. Moreover, there is at least some evidence that content of possible selves and especially the existence of strategies to attain these selves is predictive of academic attainment and delinquent involvement.

Self-concepts are what we think about when we think about ourselves. They are semantic, but also visual and affective representations of who we were, who we are, and who we can become. Although children develop some sense of self in the early years of life, with increased abstract reasoning ability in adolescence, youth begin to establish a sense of the selves they can become in addition to already developed sense of self based on current appearance, skill and competencies (e.g., Harter, 1982; Marsh, 1989; Oyserman, 2001). In adolescence these possible or imagined future selves become increasingly central to self-regulation and well-being (for similar perspectives see Cantor and Kihlstrom, 1987; Csikszentmihalyi and Larson, 1984).

The idea that the self is temporal and that the future-oriented components of the self are critical to understanding well being can be traced to William James (1890/1950). According to James, individuals narrow down various possibilities for the selves they might become only as needed, having a natural tendency to incorporate as much as possible into the self. Thus developing a sense of the self one might become involves choices- some voluntary, others forced. While individuals might *wish* to be all things simultaneously, they cannot *strive* be all things – because the activities involved in different selves conflict. The 'bon vivant' self and the 'quiet scholar' self would not be able to agree on how to spend the evening. The popular girl would want to hang out while the 'A' student would want to be home studying. Choice or at least compromise is necessary between these competing visions of the self one could be – both cannot be the most important self-goal at the same time. While painful, these are voluntary choices between selves one may equally likely attain.

Choices may also be less voluntary when individuals find themselves unable to attain a possible self. Striving and persistently failing to become like a desired self is painful, and so, James suggests, we eventually drop desired selves we had once striven to attain when it becomes clear that they will never be attained. Childhood wishes to become an Olympic gymnast or professional ballerina fade and practicing the cello falls to the wayside in part because it is much less painful *not* to become something one is uninterested in than to not become something one wishes to be. Thus, according to James (1890) we all have to give up on some aspirations and stake a claim on the person we will become. Over time, and with accumulating failure feedback, we eventually give up on becoming those aspects of our desired selves that are too painful to keep striving for in the face of repeated failures. We do this because our sense of worth or self-esteem is a dynamic proportion, the ratio of our aspirations (the selves we wish to attain) divided by actual attainments (the selves we are); self-esteem is battered unless aspirations are periodically pruned to come into line with attainments. Thus, following from James' perspective, the selves we strive to become focus motivational attention, guide behavior and are an important sources of positive self-regard.

Despite the assumed importance of present, past, and future selves on understandings of the self-concept, future selves were not the focus of research until the mid-1980s when Markus and Nurius (1986) refocused attention on future or possible selves. At the same time, other social and personality psychologists interested in personal strivings and personal projects and life tasks (e.g. Cantor 1990; Kennon and Emmons, 1995), gave new life to the future-oriented elements of the self-concept and to the modern perspective that these future selves are critical to motivation. Since then, a body of empirical evidence has accumulated on the content and the consequences of possible selves in adolescence, the linkage between possible selves and self-esteem, and the influence of possible selves on the self-regulation of behavior.

Although much of the research evidence is based on single studies, is correlational and involves small scale samples and qualitative methods, not all of it is and across studies there is evidence both for the postulated link between self-esteem and possible selves and for the postulated link between possible selves and behavior. Thus, adolescents who believe that *positive* possible selves *are likely* to be attained have higher self-esteem than those who do not (Knox et al, 1998); adolescents with both academically oriented possible selves and strategies are significantly more likely to attain improved grades than those without these possible selves (Oyserman, Bybee, Terry, and Hart-Johnson, 2004). Moreover, experimental evidence indicates that shifts in possible selves can lead to shifts in academic behavior (e.g. Oyserman, Terry, and Bybee, 2002).

Following James, in the current chapter, we assume that possible selves play a motivational and self-regulatory role in shaping future behavior. This chapter begins with a definition of possible selves and a brief overview of how possible selves are measured. We then fit possible selves into a developmental context as an aspect of self-concept susceptible to contextual influences and outline why it is important to study possible selves of minority youth. Using this as our structure, we review the literature on content of possible selves and implications of possible selves for outcomes for male and female teens differing in race/ethnicity (African American, Asian American, Latino, Native American, and white teens).

We used the on-line Psychlit and the key words: Possible selves and each of the following adolescence, African American, Black, Hispanic, Latino, Mexican American, Asian American, Asian, American Indian, and Native American to search for literature as well as adding any additional research we were aware of. The literature on possible selves is limited by use of somewhat different measures of possible selves, differing reference periods for possible selves, correlational or qualitative designs and use of either mono-racial ethnic samples or small samples. However, enough literature has accumulated to make a summary valuable and to allow for some tentative conclusions. To foreshadow our conclusions, although somewhat ambiguated by heterogeneity in reference period for possible selves (e.g. 'next year', 'when you are an adult', 'in five years,' 'in the future'), our review suggests that expected possible selves most commonly focus on academic and interpersonal domains, while fears are more diverse. There is at least some evidence that content of possible selves and especially the existence of strategies to attain these selves is predictive of academic attainment and delinquent involvement.

WHAT ARE POSSIBLE SELVES?

Possible Selves are the Future-Oriented Component of a Multifaceted Self-Concept

Possible selves are the selves we imagine ourselves becoming in the future, the selves we hope to become, the selves we are afraid we may become, and the selves we fully expect we will become. Possible selves can be distally imagined – 'the self I will become as an adult', or more short term – 'the self I will become next year'. The source of these selves is varied. Possible selves can be rooted in one's own experience and past behavior or accomplishments. Thus, high performing students may have an easier time imagining positive academic possible selves than low performing students (e.g. Leondari, Syngollitou, and Kiosseoglou, 1998). Possible selves can be rooted in what important others believe one should become. They can also be rooted in one's own values, ideals and aspirations. Thus, low performing students who come to believe that they can succeed in spite of obstacles or that they are obligated to improve their performance given family expectations may be able to create and sustain academic possible selves in spite of lack of previous academic successes. In many ways, it is this latter group, the low performers, that are the more interesting cases in which to study possible selves since it is in this case that possible selves have to be created from something other than simple repetition of current and past outcomes.

Positive, expected selves, and feared or to be avoided selves are often studied separately, either as summaries or counts of the number of positive and negative possible selves over all, or in terms of content (e.g. academic, interpersonal). Expected and feared possible selves can also be studied in conjunction. *Balance* refers to the construal of both positive expectations and fears in the same domain (e.g., I expect to be popular and have lots of friends and I am afraid that I'll be alone, that other kids' parents won't let them hang out with me). Youths with balanced possible selves have both a positive self-identifying goal to strive for and are aware of the personally relevant consequences of not meeting that goal. This balance may preserve motivation to attain the positive possible self and therefore avoid the negative self, leading these youths to make more attempts to attain expected selves and avoid feared ones. Balance may also decrease the range of strategies deemed acceptable in attempting to attain positive possible selves. Strategies that may both increase the possibility of attaining a positive self and reduce the possibility of avoiding the negative self with which it is balanced will be discarded. Only strategies that simultaneously increase the possibility of attaining the positive self and avoiding the negative self will be attempted (Oyserman and Markus, 1990b).

Lack of balance in possible selves may mean that youths are more likely to act without taking into account possible negative consequences for a possible self. This oversight is likely to result in surprise and bewilderment when attempts to attain a positive possible self result in unforeseen negative consequences for the self. Thus, a youth with expectations of becoming accepted by his peers at school who is lacking feared possible selves focused on rejection may think that breaking into school after hours and marking his initials on the walls will help him attain this possible self without taking into account that this behavior is illegal and that youth involved in delinquency may not be socially accepted. By writing his initials on the walls he imagined promoting social possible self without taking into account that he is also providing officials with clues as to who to prosecute. Being expelled and getting into trouble may not be an intended consequence, particularly if the result is that he becomes less accepted.

In addition to measuring balance, possible selves can differ in whether they are linked with behavioral strategies. Possible selves linked with strategies should be better able to promote behavior change. Thus the difference between a youth whose possible self is to pass the eighth grade and one whose possible self is to pass the eighth grade by coming to school on time each day and not cutting class with friends is that one has a possible self linked to action sequences while the other does not. For one youth, evoking the goal automatically evokes strategies, actions to be taken and avoided. For the other youth, evoking the goal may simply evoke an image of the self at the end state, necessary but perhaps not sufficient, for movement toward the goal to occur (Oyserman, Bybee, Terry, and Hart-Johnson, 2004).

Possible Selves are Social Constructions

Possible selves are always importantly social. When possible selves are based on one's own past successes and failures, they are social, because these successes and failures are frequently successes and failures *relative* to the attainments of comparable others. Grades are relative to the extent that teachers standardize grading to fit actual accomplishments of students. Similarly, when possible selves are based on one's own values, ideals and aspirations, they are social, because these values, ideals and aspirations are also importantly shaped by social contexts (Oyserman, 2002). For example, aspirations are importantly shaped by consensual stereotypes about what people like me (a girl, a rural kid, an American Indian) can become. As social contexts shift, so too may possible selves. The same rural kid can develop a 'college bound' possible self with appropriate feedback and role models. Further, although possible selves are based on past successes and failures, they are not limited to them. For example, although in general, academically successful high school students will find it easier to sustain possible selves focused on school success than academically failing high school students, not all students will translate proximal academic possible selves into adult career-related possible selves. Thus, in a relatively large scale study of adult possible selves of highly academically successful adolescent boys and girls in Northern Ireland, Curry and colleagues (1994) found that highly academically successful girls were significantly less likely to form career-oriented possible selves than boys. Instead, girls were more likely to imagine a future either at home raising children, or a career based not on ability but on balancing home and some sort of job. Simply knowing academic track and past attainment was not sufficient; gender also influenced content of possible selves.

Both specific others and social contexts more generally play an important role in the creation and maintenance of possible selves. Significant others (e.g. parents), role models, and media images are examples of the models used to instantiate possible selves, but so too are important socio-cultural identities. That is, we can become the kind of person that people of our group can become; we fear disappointing important groups by failing to attain group norms and standards. In our own research with African American youth in Detroit, this can be seen clearly in possible selves such as "Become a proud Black woman" in which adherence to group values *is* the possible self. In this way, possible selves are tightly connected to racial, ethnic, gender and cultural identities, and perceived in-group norms. Individuals learn not only who people like them can become, but also who people not like them can become, creating both a series of possible 'me's' and a series of 'not me's', selves one does not strive for or actively tries to avoid. For example, in a series of interviews urban high school students reported common stereotypes of Asians and Latinos, with Latinos linked to manual labor and Asians linked to doing well in school (Kao, 2002). It is reasonable to assume that teens surrounded by pro or anti academic expectations for their group are likely to find development of academic possible selves facilitated in the former and impeded in the latter case since for former but not the latter teens, others will help sustain and maintain the possible self. Because local norms can be changed or shifted, possible selves are also open to change when norms are perceived to change.

Possible Selves are Shaped By Social Context

Adolescents learn about what is possible and what is valued through engagement with their social context (Oyserman and Markus, 1993). When social contexts lack images of possible selves for 'people like us' in a particular domain, possible selves in this domain are likely to be missing entirely or will be so global as to be useless as a self-regulatory mechanism. Feedback can be reinforcing or restrictive and undermining. In studying minority youths, low socio-economic status youths, and girls, the issue of social contextual undermining and restricting is of particular interest. For example, youth in rural or urban inner-city settings may experience a restriction of possibilities both because specific role models for a range of academic and occupational outcomes are missing and because important social identities may be felt to conflict with certain possible selves. In rural settings, given lack of occupational opportunities, a youth might lack role models of choosing a career rather than simply settling for a job. Thus, in a qualitative interview study (Shepard, 2001), the adult hoped for and feared possible selves generated by rural 17-19 year old adolescent girls in British Columbia did not focus on education and fewer than 10% mentioned occupations, with even these few mentions being vague and general (e.g., "I want a job."). Instead, possible selves focused on personal attributes ("Someone people can like and trust"), relationships ("develop closer relationships with my brother and sister"), and possessions ("I want a jeep"). Similarly, in inner city contexts with high unemployment rates, it may be hard to instantiate specific and detailed occupational possible selves and media images of occupational possible selves for one's racial group may be equally limiting, leaving the implied message that one cannot be both a member of one's racial group and also a member of various professions.

Social contexts also provide important feedback to adolescents and young adults about whether a possible self is positively or negatively valued. Thus, the same possible self can be a positive expected possible self or a dreaded and to-be avoided feared possible self, depending on social contextual feedback. Graduating medical students in primary care specialties were more likely to view becoming a primary care physician as a positive possible self if they had a mentor whose professional and personal life refuted negative stereotypes about people in their specialty (Burack, Irby, Carline, Ambrozy, Ellsbury, and Stritter, 1997).

Similarly, social contexts can shift the perceived likelihood that an expected or feared possible self is likely. Teens whose parents divorced are more likely to have feared possible selves focused on problems in marriage (Carson, Madison, and Santrock, 1987). Similarly, teens are more likely to generate feared possible selves focused on developing mental health problems when they have experienced maternal separations due to maternal mental health problems (Oyserman, Bybee, and Mowbray, 2005). These effects of situations are also found in experimental manipulations of likelihood of attaining a possible self: College undergraduates rated career as compared to marital, and parental possible selves as more (or less) likely to be attained when they received false feedback that their personality matched (did not match) the personality of people who attained career success (or were successful parents) (Kerpelman and Pittman, 2001). The link between possible selves and congruent behavior has also been shown experimentally: College undergraduates primed to think of 'success after hard effort' possible selves were more persistent as compared to undergraduates primed to think of 'success due to stroke of luck' possible selves (Ruvolo and Markus, 1992).

Because it is a context central to attainment of both academic and social possible selves and because youths spend a large portion of their day at school, school as a social context has been a particular focus of possible self research. Although school transitions have not been the explicit focus of possible self research, content of academic or school-focused possible selves are likely to shift focus across school transitions because these transitions result in changing social contexts (from more personalized to more regimented, from learning to outcome focused). As contexts shift, the meaning of academic success shifts from trying and improving to attaining successful outcomes. Thus, from early adolescence on, becoming a successful student should increasingly focus on grades, performance, and comparisons with others rather than personal mastery or involvement. For these reasons, we assume that adolescents' academic possible selves are less likely to focus on learning (e.g. "I expect to learn new things in school", "I want to avoid being bored in class") and more likely to focus on outcomes (e.g. "I expect to get good grades," "I want to avoid failing."). Indeed, in our own lab, when we ask Detroit middle school students to generate possible selves, they commonly mention passing, getting good grades, avoiding failing or getting good grades, but rarely mention expecting to learn new things, or wanting to avoid not learning.

There is also some evidence that school and academic success may become less salient possible selves as youth move from elementary to middle and high school. Anderman and colleagues report that in elementary school, boys' possible selves were more likely to focus on being a good student than in middle school, with likelihood of 'good student' possible selves declining across the middle school years (Anderman, Hicks, and Maehr, 1994 as described in Anderman, Anderman and Griesinger, 1999; Anderman et al., 1999). In our own lab, our longitudinal research on the middle to high school transition in Detroit also shows an overall decline in the number of academic possible selves. However, the data do not appear linear, each fall students generate more academic possible selves than they do by the end of the academic year.

Yet if students are actively engaged, positive academic possible selves can also be increased across these years. This is shown in a small group based brief universal intervention with urban African American middle school youth. The intervention increased academic possible selves and balanced possible selves in the year after the intervention (in comparison with intervention and control youth and controlling for previous year's GPA) (Oyserman, Terry, and Bybee, 2002). This effect was replicated in a larger experimental trial that also documented that change in possible selves mediated significant change in school behavior, grades, and depression (Oyserman, Bybee, and Terry, 2005). Effects may not be easy to attain – another intervention did not find effects on possible selves when African American elementary and middle school youth received mentoring for various lengths of time (Lee and Cramond, 1999).

WHY STUDY POSSIBLE SELVES OF MINORITY YOUTH?

There are two key reasons why a focus on possible selves of minority youths is needed. First, because possible selves mediate between values and actual behavior, understanding possible selves is critical to narrowing the gap between Mexican American, African American, American Indian and white youth. Possible selves are critical to understanding the gap when it is in the opposite direction as well – such as the case with Asian Americans. That is, higher achieving and lower achieving groups may differ systematically in the nature of their possible selves. Because possible selves are socially constituted and maintained, it is likely that racial/ethnic groups differ systematically in their possible selves so that a second reason to study possible selves of racial/ethnic minority youth is to gain better understanding of the interface between possible selves and content of racial/ethnic identity. Such understanding would allow for development of effective interventions to reduce the achievement gap and decrease risk of other negative outcomes contained in stereotypes. Stereotypes about minorities are focused on the important domains of adolescence – academic achievement, interpersonal and relational style, and engagement with risky activities. When minority youths imagine what is possible for them, preformed images in these domains are likely to be highly accessible. Thus, for example, part of the answer to the question 'am I likely to do well in school?' comes from group images. Are 'we' stereotyped as a model minority or as dumb and lazy?

For minority youth, shared ideas about who one is, where one belongs, what is possible for the self and what is not, are reflected in culturally significant metaphors, images, stories, proverbs, icons, and symbols (Oyserman and Harrison, 1998). These shared ideas or images are shaped by contact and interface with American society (Oyserman, Kemmelmeier, Fryberg, Brosh, and Hart-Johnson, 2004) and carry with them socially contrived messages about what targets of those messages can and cannot do. Hence, what it means to be American Indian, African American, Asian American or Mexican American is particularized by culture of origin, and its interface with both mainstream American culture, and mainstream America's views of one's group. Studying the possible selves of minority youth provides a window into the motivational world of these youths.

WHY FOCUS ON ADOLESCENCE?

Following Erikson's (1968) model of psychosocial development, adolescence is the life phase focused on identity development. Adolescence is a *psychosocial moratorium*, during which time youth are free to try on possible selves without suffering sanctions from misbehavior related to their conception of how a person with such a self would act. Erikson defines active identity seeking as a moratorium phase in which youth try out, without commitment, various roles. Once roles have been tried, young adults *achieve* a sense of identity, picking a smaller set of possible selves to commit to becoming. Erikson recognized that not all youth went through a phase of trying on or actively seeking an identity, either because they decided on adult identities to strive to become early in adolescence without much seeking (what Erikson termed *foreclosure*) or because they are neither searching for adult selves nor settled on future selves, but were simply unsure (what he termed *identity diffusion*). While the possible self model does not require that Erikson be correct, it is compatible with his model of phases of identity development. Specifically, during moratorium youth should have more and more varied possible selves, though not necessarily strategies to attain them. During achievement and foreclosure phases, youth should rate their possible selves as more certain to be attained and should have few possible selves that are vague or lack strategies. The difference in possible selves of achievement and foreclosure youth should be in their content not their number or their perceived certainty of occurring. Given that foreclose and achievement phases differ in how much youth engaged in active seeking prior to choosing, with foreclosure youth seeking less, the possible selves of achievement youth should be more diverse and less likely to simply mirror the content of in-group stereotypes than the possible selves of foreclosure phase youth.

We did not find many empirical tests of the connection between possible selves and identity development phase. Those we found focused on Marcia's (1980) operationalization of Erikson's phases of identity formation – with the assumption that as youth pass through the moratorium phase on the way to identity resolution of some type, they should be actively imagining more possible selves than prior (e.g. identity diffusion) or later identity phases (e.g. identity achievement), and that those who do not seek an adult identity at one time point (e.g. identity foreclosure), may do so at another. Dunkel (2001) tested whether possible self construction is indeed related to adolescent identity development phase using the EOM-EIS2 operationalization of identity status (Marcia, 1980) with 17-25 mostly white psychology undergraduates. Students who scored in the 'Moratorium' phase and 'low profile' respondents (who did not score high in any of the identity phase subscales) reported more positive possible selves than students who scored in the 'Foreclosure' or 'Diffusion' identity phase. Not only did 'Moratorium' phase students have more positive possible selves, they also endorsed more neutral and more negative possible selves than did individuals in the other four groups. In addition, students who had either completed an identity seeking phase (coded as Identity Achieved) or had never sought an identity (coded as Identity Foreclosed) rated their positive and neutral possible selves as more certain and likely to be achieved than did students who scored in the Moratorium, Diffusion or low profile groups. These findings, though focused on somewhat older adolescents and young adults, lend support to the relevance of developmental phases of identity development to the construct of possible selves.

HOW ARE POSSIBLE SELVES MEASURED?

Three general formats appear in the published literature, a close-ended format yielding sum scores of positive and negative possible selves across domains, an open format content coded for domain, a closed-format focusing on a specific type of possible self (typically academic possible selves). Markus and Nurius (1986)[1] introduced a close-ended measure to assess the number of positive and negative possible selves in their research with college students, subsequent use of this measure also typically involves college students (e.g. Dunkle, 2001; Leondari, Syngollitou, and Kiosseoglou, 1998). Open-ended measures suitable for use with children and adolescents are reported for children as young as 10 or 11 (Lobenstine et al., 2001; Shepard and Marshall, 1999). We also found a number of close-ended measures[2]

---

[1] Markus (1987) provides one week stability and reliability information for this measure, describing positive, negative and neutral selves.

[2] Anderman, Anderman & Griesinger (1999) studied academic and social possible selves in white Midwestern 7th graders and a separate sample of African American and European American Southeastern high school students. Using a five year time horizon, students rated the likelihood that they would attain Academic Positive Possible Selves (rating the likelihood of being a good student, being smartest in class, doing better than other students, being on the honor roll, and get rewarded for doing well), Social Positive Possible Selves (rating the likelihood of being popular, chosen first for teams and groups, having lots of friends and being competitive), and of Academic Negative Possible Selves (rating the likelihood of doing as little school work as possible, being interested in school work (reversed), wanting to quit school, getting good grades (reversed), and being a poor student). Academic positive possible selves were reliable in both samples, Chronbach's α = .73 (white sample), .62 (mixed sample), social possible selves were reliable only in the white sample, Chronbach's α = .69, and negative academic possible selves were reliable only in the mixed race sample, α =.71 (other than stating unreliable, no further α information available for the other sample for social or negative academic selves). Briefer scales of academic possible selves were developed in the work of Oyserman and her colleague, Markus Kemmelmeier. In a study with primarily white college students they asked "How do you think you will do in

for teens and college students focused specifically on academic (Anderman, Anderman and Griesinger, 1999, Kemmelmeier and Oyserman, 2001b; Kemmelmeier, Oyserman, and Brosh, 2003) and social (Anderman, Anderman and Griesinger, 1999) possible selves.

A detailed description of an open-ended possible selves measure and coding schema for Black and White adolescents is provided by Oyserman and Markus (1990), the measure they developed in their study with low-income high school and institutionalized youth is also used by others focused on risky behaviors in the middle and high school years (e.g. Aloise-Young, Hennigan, and Leong, 2001). This initial format was later modified to include questions about strategies to attain possible selves in subsequent research with African American, Hispanic and low-income white middle and high school students (Oyserman and Saltz, 1993; Oyserman, Gant and Ager, 1995, Study 1; Oyserman, Bybee, Terry, and Hart-Johnson, 2004). An alternative open-ended format focuses on hoped for and feared possible selves, elicits ratings of likelihood of attaining each possible self and ratings of how much each possible self is hoped for or feared (Cross and Markus, 1991), although initially used in research with middle to older aged adults, this format is also used in research with white middle class high school students (Knox, Funk, Elliott, and Bush, 2000).

Across research, possible self measures also differ in their reference point. Some measures refer to "the future" with no further specification; other measures specify a reference point in terms of chronological ("next year") or developmental ("as an adult") time. Clearly measure and reference point influence findings, though we only found one study (Oyserman and Markus, 1990) that explicitly compared results from one reference point to another. These authors found that use of the "adult" reference point resulted in results that were more similar across youth and did not distinguish among youth differing in delinquent involvement while use of a "next year" reference point result in more heterogeneous responses that were significantly related to delinquent involvement.

WHAT DO WE KNOW ABOUT THE RELATIONSHIP BETWEEN POSSIBLE SELVES AND IMPORTANT OUTCOMES IN ADOLESCENCE?

Possible Selves and Academic Outcomes

Possible selves have been linked to academic attainments. At the middle school level, Midwestern mostly white seventh graders with positive academic possible selves had improved GPA from 6th to 7th grade, especially when their academic possible selves were more positive than their current academic self-concept (Anderman, Anderman and Griesinger,

---

school next year, overall what are your chances of being successful in the future, how easy or hard will it be for you to find a really good job when you finish school, how confident are you that you will succeed in the future" Cronbach's α = .78 (Kemmelmeier & Oyserman, 2001b), with the Chronbach α reliable (.71) in a subsequent study with Arab Israeli and German high school students (Kemmelmeier, Oyserman, & Brosh, 2005). Similarly, in a study with mostly white college students, they asked students to rate the likelihood of the following academic possible selves: do well in school, get good grades, understand the material in my classes (Cronbach's α = .88), and strategies to attain these possible selves: using my time wisely, handling problems that come my way successfully, coping well with distractions, and striving persistently toward my goals (Cronbach's α = .80), moreover, since the two scales correlated at r = .45, they were averaged as a single score for subsequent analyses (Kemmelmeier & Oyserman, 2001b).

1999). In a mixed raced sample of 6th-8th graders, positive academic possible selves predicted higher endorsement of performance goals - wanting to do schoolwork in order to prove one's competence or to appear more able or competent than other students (Anderman et al, 1999). Even in samples at high risk of academic problems due to high poverty concentration, when youth had more academically focused possible selves and strategies to attain them, they had significantly improved grades (controlling for previous year GPA) compared with youth lacking these possible selves (Oyserman, et al., 2004).

With regard to college, students (male and female) who were math/science schematic took and planned to take more math and science courses than their peers (Lipps, 1995, Study 2). Female college students with a positive math/science self-schema performed better on a math test than those who were either aschematic or had negative math/science self-schemas (Lips, 1995, Study 1).

Possible Selves and Delinquent Involvement

Possible selves have also been linked with delinquent involvement. Youth may initially view a delinquent lifestyle as a means to create possible selves such as "independent," "daring," "competent," or "fun-loving and adventurous." The negative self-definitional consequences of delinquency may not be taken into account, especially by youths who lack balanced possible selves (Oyserman and Markus, 1990a; 1990b). In a study of four subgroups of primarily African American adolescent males who varied in level of official delinquent involvement from the state maximum security lockup facility for juveniles to high school students attending the schools most commonly cited as the last school attended by these youth, with midrange levels of delinquent involvement including youth in living in group homes after delinquent adjudication and youth attending schools of attention after more minor involvement with police or school infractions, Oyserman and Markus (1990a; 1990b) find differences in content of next year expected possible selves, next year feared possible selves and extent that expected and feared selves are 'balanced' or represent what the youth wants to attain and avoid in a specific domain. For public school and community placement youth, the most common expected possible self generated focused on doing well in school and accounted for nearly a third of responses. For the two most delinquent groups, however, "getting along in school" is only the third or fourth most frequent response, accounting for only 13.9% of the responses given by the training school youth. Similarly, the achievement-related response of "having a job," which is the third or fourth most frequently generated possible self for the public school and community placement youth does not appear at all for the two most delinquent groups. Instead, what appears in these positions is a variety of *negatively* valued possible selves: "junkie," "depressed," "alone," "flunking out of school," "pusher," "criminal." Note that these negative selves are generated not in response to the query about feared selves, but in response to expected possible selves. The amount of official delinquency predicted greater likelihood of generating these kinds of negative selves as expected next year possible selves. Lower likelihood of generating next year expected selves focused on doing well or getting along in school, and higher likelihood of materially focused next year expected possible selves (e.g. expecting to have a car or nice clothes).

With respect to the possible selves that are hoped for in the next year, there is more homogeneity among the four groups, all groups indicate with about equal frequency the hope to "have friends" and, indeed, this is the most frequently generated hoped-for possible self of the two most delinquent groups. In contrast with the expected selves, "having a job" is a commonly hoped-for possible self for all the groups including the two most delinquent groups. "Getting along in school" is a frequently generated hoped-for self by all but the training school youth, where it is replaced by the material hoped for selves (e.g. having certain types of clothes or cars). Feared possible selves show striking differences across the four groups. By far the most frequently generated feared possible self of the public school youth is that of "not getting along in school." It accounts for nearly a quarter of all responses to this question. For the other three groups, however, the most frequently generated response is the fear of being criminal–a "thief," a "murderer." For the two most delinquent groups this fear explains a third of all their responses. In contrast, the fear of being criminal does not appear at all among the five most frequent responses of the public school youth and only 8% mentioned this self at all. The amount of official delinquency predicted fearing criminal selves and fearing school failure. Generally, the percentage of youth generating school failure selves decreased, whereas the percentage of youth generating criminal selves increased across groups from public school to training school youth.

When the balance between the expectations and fears of the four groups of youth was examined, the officially nondelinquent youth showed significantly more balance between their expectations and fears than did the most officially delinquent youth. More than 81% of nondelinquents had at least one match between their expected and feared selves, whereas this was true for only 37% of the most delinquent groups. Of the most officially delinquent youth in this sample, 33% to 37% feared becoming criminal. Yet, these feared selves were not balanced by expectations that focused on avoiding crime and attaining conventional achievement. The two most delinquent groups do not expect to "have a job" and only 14% to 19% of them expect to "get along in school." Although these delinquent youth have the type of feared selves that might be associated with the avoidance of delinquent activity, many of them seem to be missing the expected possible selves that could provide the organizing and energizing vision of how they might avoid criminal activity, and what they might expect if they do.

Self-reported delinquency data (collected 2-3 months after the self-concept measures) were available for the least officially delinquent youth – the public school and community placement youth. Controlling for sex, race, and sample source, balance significantly predicted self-reported delinquency among these youth. This effect remained even when controlling for the impact of expecting negative selves. The relationship between self-esteem and delinquent involvement was non-linear and not significant, (Oyserman and Markus, 1990a; 1990b).

These findings were substantively replicated in a subsequent study with another African American sample showing that controlling for other factors, youth who were in public school (officially nondelinquent youth) were more likely to have balanced possible selves, to believe that they were attempting to attain expected selves and avoid feared selves, and to view individuated and achievement-oriented selves as important than youth in detention after felony arrest, these differences were replicated when the public school sample only was used and youth were compared in their level of self-reported delinquent involvement (Oyserman and Saltz, 1993). Using a somewhat different approach, Newberry and Duncan counted number of positive and negative possible selves among high school students and found that having fewer positive and more negative possible selves correlated with self-report delinquent involvement (Newberry and Duncan, 2001).

Possible Selves and Health Risk Behaviors

Balance in possible selves is also related to substance use in junior high school aged youth. Aloise-Young, Hennigan, and Leong (2001) looked at the relationship between possible selves, cigarette and alcohol consumption among 6th-9th grader in a large sample (n=1606) of Los Angeles youth, about 45% Anglo, with most of the other students being Hispanic. Youth who smoked and drank more had significantly fewer balanced possible selves, no gender or ethnicity interaction effects were found. The relationship between balance and substance use was stronger after 6th grade because in 6th grade relatively few of these behaviors were reported. By the 9th grade, a quarter of youth without any positive expected selves reported heavy substance use, as compared with only 1% of those with three positive expected selves. These results substantively replicate an earlier study examining self-schemas, possible selves, and risky behavior (alcohol use/misuse, tobacco use, and sexual activity) in 8th graders and then a year later after they had transitioned to high school (9th grade) (Stein and Markus, 1998). A bi-directional relationship indicated that 8th grade popularity self-schema scores were predictive of 9th grade risky behaviors and that engagement in risky behaviors in 8th grade contributed to the conceptualization of the self as currently deviant and positively predicted the deviant self-schema scores in the 9th grade. Involvement in risky behaviors increases subsequent negative possible selves and the reverse, negative possible selves predict subsequent risky behaviors. Thus possible selves have been implicated in both promoting positive outcomes – academics and in increasing risk of negative outcomes – delinquency, alcohol and tobacco use, and early sexual activity. The next sections use the framework laid out to focus on gender, race and ethnicity.

GENDER DIFFERENCES IN POSSIBLE SELVES

In adolescence, girls and boys differ in self-esteem, in the extent that self-concept contains others and relationships to them, and in their cognitive and emotional maturity. All of these gender differences may relate to differences in possible selves. With regard to self-esteem, on average, girls have lower self-esteem than boys. Indeed, higher self-esteem is associated with greater confidence that positive possible selves will be attained (Knox et al., 1998). Thus on average, girls should be less sure that they will attain their possible selves and more certain that negative possible selves may occur – taken together, these perceptions may reduce their commitment to any particular positive possible self while focusing energies on avoiding negative possible selves. Those with lower self-esteem may be more prone to give up on possible selves, following James' (1890) notion that low self-esteem stimulates pruning of possible selves that are deemed unattainable. Second, with regard to social or relational content of self-concept, those with more social content may be more open to contextual influence, both because obligations to important others may be perceived as more central to self-concept and because others' successes and failures are more likely to be incorporated into self-concept. This means that girls may be more susceptible to contextual influences – taking on as their own both successes and failures of related others. Third, with regard to gender differences in cognitive development, the self may have more influence on the behavior of girls than of boys to the extent that girls are better able to develop 'if-then' consequential strategies related to their possible selves. While remaining confident that one's possible selves can be attained and being less influenced by context may seem positive, to the extent that the self is not engaged or turned on in everyday behavioral situations, this confidence may have little effect on actual behavior. In our own research, we found boys' possible selves less influenced by social contextual information about likelihood of academic failure while also being at higher risk of academic failure themselves, it was as if girls took information about other's failure as a cautionary tale to increase vigilance, boys did not (Oyserman, Gant, and Ager, 1995, Study 3). In this section, we review evidence of gender differences in these three areas as they relate to possible selves.

SELF-ESTEEM

With regard to self-esteem and content of possible selves, we found little evidence to explain why gender differences occur. Male and female college students do not differ in the number of balanced possible selves they generate (Oyserman, Gant and Ager, Study 1). Boys and girls do not differ in the number of positive possible selves they have. No gender differences in number of expected possible selves were found in a 6th-9th grade sample, with 2.4-2.6 expected possible selves generated across each grade and gender (Aloise-Young et al., 2001). No gender differences were found in positive possible selves in a sample of 14-15 year old high school students although girls had significantly lower self-esteem than boys (Leondari, Syngollitou, and Kiosseoglou, 1998).For girls, the likelihood of attaining negative possible selves is also negatively associated with higher self-esteem (Knox et al, 1998). However in a large scale study with predominantly white Ohio high school students, gender differences in feared possible self content and likelihood were found (Knox, Funk, Elliott, and Bush, 2000). Specifically, high school girls rated feared possible selves as more likely than boys (overall $M = 5.4$, range = 1-19) and described more feared relational possible selves whereas boys generated more feared possible selves related to occupation, general failure, and inferiority (Knox et al., 200). No gender differences in likelihood or content of hoped-for possible selves were found ($M = 8$ range = 1-19), though girls rated hoped for selves on average as more hoped for than boys. The three most frequently mentioned hoped for possible selves for boys and girls (in descending order of frequency) were occupation, relationship, and education. Physical illness, general failure, relationships were the most frequent feared possible selves for boys, for girls, relationships, illness, failure were the order. Boys were more likely to have occupation and general failure fears while girls were more likely to have relationship fears.

SENSITIVITY TO SOCIAL CONTEXT

Another possibility is that girls' possible selves are more sensitive to social contextual feedback – incorporating both negative and positive possible selves more easily into self-concept. We already noted Curry et al.'s (1994) finding that girls took into account their likely need to take on parenting roles in imagining possible selves related to careers, however, this research did not directly address sensitivity to contextual feedback, since both boys and girls in this research could be seen to be responding to social norms about appropriate gender roles in adulthood. In our lab, we addressed these issues more directly by assessing the response of teenaged girls and boys to social comparison information, finding that girls were more likely to shift up their academic possible selves when they thought of someone their same gender who was succeeding in school, and more likely to shift down these possible selves when they thought of someone they knew who was failing in school (Kemmelmeier and Oyserman, 2001a; 2001b, Kemmelmeier, Oyserman, and Brosh, 2005).

In these studies with Arab Israeli high school students, German high school students and mostly European American university students– girls were more likely to assimilate outcomes of significant others to their own academic possible selves, whether the other that was brought to mind is successful or a failure. We speculated that this effect was at least partially mediated by differences between boys and girls in how the self-concept is organized. That is, is self-concept a way of clarifying how one is unique, agentic, different and separate from others (an 'independent self-focus'), or a way of clarifying how one is connected and related to others, embedded in relationships, and responsible for others (an 'interdependent' self-focus) (Markus and Oyserman, 1989). Indeed, girls' assimilation of others outcomes into their own possible selves was due in part to interdependence, as shown in a set of mediation analyses (Kemmelmeier et al., 2005).

COGNITIVE DEVELOPMENT

In addition to self-concept differences in possible self content, certainty, and susceptibility to social influence, gender differences may occur due to differences in cognitive and social development. In adolescence, girls are faster to develop self-awareness, self-reflection and abstract reasoning; their self-concepts contain more relational content, and by mid-adolescence, are they are more likely to begin thinking about the integration of future work and family roles. Curry, Trew, Turner and Hunter (1994) provide a useful review of gender differences in adolescence. They note that adolescent girls attain ego-development milestones earlier than boys and so may be both more concerned about future selves and concerned at earlier ages than boys. In terms of possible selves, these differences imply first, that possible selves will have less self-regulatory power for boys than for girls and second, that girls are less likely to develop strictly task-focused possible selves and will attempt to juggle more numerous possible selves connecting the self to others. For example, rather than choose between school and family focused possible selves, girls may remain torn between their personal desire to do well in school, and their belief that they are expected to also be a good family member. Following James' model, girls may have lower self-esteem because they are unable to give up or prune low likelihood possible selves, resulting in relatively modest ratios of current successes compared with domains of aspiration.

CONTENT OF POSSIBLE SELVES
AMONG ETHNIC/RACIAL MINORITIES

In our review of the literature, we found studies describing content of possible selves among African American, American Indian, Asian American, and Hispanic youth, with little information on possible selves of other ethnic, racial or national minorities. In this section we review what is known about content of possible selves in these groups.

African American Adolescents

Academic or school-related possible selves predict positive change in grades (controlling for previous grades) even among low income African American middle school students when the possible selves are linked with strategies (Oyserman et al., 2004). There is evidence that academic and occupational possible selves are common among African American youth, although between race differences have not been fully explored, whites and blacks may differ in the cultural values associated with academic or school-related possible selves and in whether emphasis is on attaining positive academic possible selves or avoiding negative academic possible selves. Oyserman and Markus (1990) find African American public high school students are more likely to generate doing well in school as a hoped for self than white students; in a middle school sample Anderman and colleagues report African American 6th - 8th graders are less likely to report positive academic possible selves than other (primarily white) youth (Anderman et al, 1999). In a college sample (Oyserman et al., 1995, Study 1) no between race difference was found in total number of balanced possible selves, but Black and White undergraduates differed significantly in the number of balanced possible selves that were in the academic domain of school and/or work, with Black students having fewer such balanced school-related pairs of possible selves. Although they had fewer balanced possible selves focused on the academic or occupational domain, Black students described significantly more strategies they were currently using to *attain* their school-related possible selves (no race differences were found in the number of currently used strategies generated to avoid feared achievement-related possible selves).

Moreover, whereas for white students balance in academic possible selves positively correlated with generating strategies to approach positive possible selves, balance was correlated with generating strategies to avoid negative possible selves for Black students. Among White students, Individualism and the Protestant Work Ethic were positively correlated with generating strategies to approach academic possible selves. The relationship between cultural values and strategies was sharply different for African American students. For Black students, the Protestant Work Ethic did not relate to possible selves, instead, those who were lower in Individualism, higher in Collectivism, and higher in endorsement of a positive Racial Identity generated more strategies to approach academic possible selves (see also Oyserman and Harrison, 1998). This positive relationship between Collectivism and academic possible selves was also found in a study with male African American high school students, those who valued interconnection generated more balanced academic possible selves (Oyserman and Saltz, 1993 high school subsample). These studies are important because they link academic possible selves with racial/ethnic identity of minority youth.

Given the importance of academic possible selves, we looked for evidence of that malleability among African American students and found that academic possible selves are amenable to change, as documented in a brief small group based after school program for low-income, urban African American eighth graders. Controlling for previous grades, gender, and levels of possible selves, youth in the 6-week after-school intervention group had significantly more balanced academic possible selves and significantly more concrete strategies to attain these academic possible selves by the end of the academic year than control group youth (Oyserman, Terry, and Bybee, 2002). We have now replicated this effect showing improved academic outcomes two full years after the possible selves focused intervention. There is also evidence that academically oriented possible selves may not always be the most central or important possible selves for African American youth. In an open-ended interview with a small sample of rural African American mother-daughter pairs about teen's desired selves, academic and occupational possible selves were the most frequently mentioned, but not necessarily described as one's most central possible self – for some teens attainment of personality attributes rather than attainment of occupational and academic possible selves was the most central self (Kerpelman, Shoffner, Ross-Griffin (2002).

American Indian Adolescents

Although school and relationship possible selves are most common among American Indian students, possible selves about poverty and material things were also quite common. Fryberg and Markus (2005) examined the content of possible selves in three samples of American Indian students -- American Indian high school students who live on a reservation, but attend school off the reservation, American Indian university students at a mainstream university, and American Indian university students attending an American Indian university (half who grew up on Indian reservations and half who did not). When asked to think about their possible selves in the coming year the most common hoped for possible self across samples was to be successful in school and to get good grades, the most common feared possible self focused on school failure. All three samples mentioned having relationships and material things and feared not having relationships and living in poverty as the next most common possible selves. However, American Indian high school students and the American Indian university students from the reservation were less likely to mention relationships and were more likely to mention poverty than were the other American Indian samples. A second study (Fryberg and Markus, 2005) compared American Indian junior high, high school, and college students and found that junior high and high school students generated more expected possible selves about success in school and more feared selves about poverty and deviance than did American Indian college students. These descriptive studies provide evidence that academic possible selves are common among high risk American Indian youth in junior high and high school. A final experimental study focused on consequences of social contexts on academic possible selves. Compared to no prime control, students asked to rate American Indian-themed mascots later generated fewer academic possible selves (Fryberg, Markus, Oyserman, and Stone, 2005). Making salient thoughts about Indian mascots reduced salience of academic future selves. This study is important because it focuses directly on the impact of stereotyped images in the social context of minority youths on their possible selves.

Asian American Adolescents

Compared with African American and American Indian youth, considerably less research attention has focused on the possible selves of Asian American youth. One small scale qualitative study suggests that academic possible selves are likely to be common among Asian Americans (Kao, 2000). Using focus groups and interviews with African American, Hispanic, Asian American, and white youth at an urban high school, Kao (2000) found that all students (including Asian Americans) associate Asian American students with doing well in school, in particular high achievement in math and sciences. The author uses qualitative, content analyses to contend that the expectation by others and one's own group to do well in school help to facilitate the development of academic possible selves for Asian Americans.

No other research on Asian American adolescents was available; however, one study (Fryberg and Markus, 2005) using college students provides some empirical evidence for the prevalence of achievement related possible selves in this racial/ethnic group. In terms of content of possible selves, the majority of Asian American college students sampled reported at least one expected or hoped for self related to success in school (88.5%). The second most common responses included having relationships (70%) and positive psychological attributes (57.7%). Asian Americans did not differ from European American college students in the frequencies of these responses (although sample sizes were relatively small). In terms of feared selves psychological attributes were the most common feared possible self of Asian American and European American students (84.6% and 81.1% respectively), with failing in school (61.5% and 75.7%) and lacking relationships (65.4% and 67.6) the second and third most common possible selves respectively.

Hispanic American/Latino Adolescents

We found six studies that explicitly focused on possible selves among Latino youth. Controlling for previous grades, academic possible selves and strategies to attain them predict improved academic outcomes even in high poverty Latino youth (Oyserman et al., 2004). A number of studies suggest that having such academic possible selves may not be common among Latino youth. In a descriptive study of ninth graders, feared, not hoped for educational and occupational possible selves related to risk status for student dropout (Yowell, 2002). A third study with a smaller sample of 13-14 year old Latino youth, found boys more likely to report occupational possible selves as central than girls and girls more likely to report constrained possible selves. Both genders showed high but vague educational and occupational hoped for possible selves and global feared selves that focused more on about well-being than either academics or occupation (Yowell, 2000). Potentially the lack of specificity has to do with negative stereotypes about the likely attainments of Latinos. Among urban African American, Asian, Hispanic and white 9th -12th grade high school students, stereotypes about Hispanics focused less on their current academic performance and more on their future likely occupational concentration in manual labor, influencing the nature of their possible selves (Kao, 2000). The notion that academics may not be central to Latinos possible selves was underscored in the findings from a small qualitative study (Lobenstine, et al., 2001) that focused on adult hoped for and feared possible selves among teenaged mostly Puerto Rican (raised in the U.S.) girls recruited from youth agencies. While career and education were central hoped for selves, failing to attain career and educational goals were not common fears. The three most common hoped for selves (with at least 60% of respondents generated these) were family, career and education, with feared possible selves, the four most common (at least 60% of respondents generated these) feared selves were be a victim of violence, drug/alcohol abuse, be lonely/broken hearted, be poor/homeless, in addition, almost half of teens for feared dying young. The only feared self focused on occupation/education was high school dropout with 20% of teens generating this (Lobenstine et al., 2001). Day, Borkowksi, Punzo, and Howsepian (1994), utilizing a sample of 83 3rd-5th graders, showed that a brief intervention focusing on the vividness and salience of both proximal and distal possible selves could increase links between current academic performance and future occupational as well as academic possible selves. Comparing three intervention conditions (child-only, parent and child, or no instruction), they found that participants in the child-only intervention group hoped for more prestigious jobs than children in the no-instruction control group and that children in both instructional groups expressed increased expectation that they could become doctors, lawyers, or pilots after having been exposed to more specific information about these occupations. In our own lab, we find that a brief intervention focused on increasing salience and specificity of next year academic possible selves (and strategies to attain them) increases academic outcomes, especial school attendance, for Hispanic youth and that the effects are maintained two years post intervention, through the transition to high school.

CONCLUDING COMMENTS

In the current chapter, we reviewed what is known about the relationship between possible selves and attainment of important life tasks (e.g. school success) or avoidance of risky behavior (e.g. delinquency, early initiation of sexual activity, smoking, alcohol or drug use during adolescence, showing that academic possible selves, balanced academic possible selves, and strategies to attain these possible selves have positive influence on academic outcomes and are related to reduced risk of negative outcomes in adolescence. We reviewed the literature on content of possible selves for diverse youth during this life phase and explored whether gender, racial/ethnic differences were found. Gender differences were found, girls' possible selves are more susceptible to social context and girls feel more certain that negative possible selves may indeed occur, susceptibility to social context is at least in part mediated by girls' higher interdependence. Given the literature showing between ethnic group differences in interdependence among racial and ethnic groups within the U.S. (Oyserman, Coon, and Kemmelmeier, 2002), this means that possible selves of Hispanic and Asian American youth may also be more susceptible to social context – although to date no research has been carried out on this issue. The literature on race/ethnicity is composed mostly of single group studies so that direct comparisons between groups are not possible. However, the available evidence points to similarities across quite different youth – arguing that possible selves can be viewed as the personalized expression of the life tasks of adolescence – because all teens must figure out who they can become in the important social domains of adolescence – school/work, family, and friends, these possible selves dominate content of future oriented self-images. Moreover, teens must also articulate for themselves how to handle risks – of school failure, involvement with drugs or other substances, loneliness, and where relevant, poverty or mental health problems, and these are articulated in feared possible selves. African American and American Indian youth appear similar to white youth in envisioning possible selves that include academic or school-related outcomes; while less research is available for Asian Americans, this appears to be the case for this group as well. With regard to Hispanic youth, academic possible selves may be less common, though when they are part of the self, they have the same beneficial effects. Evidence suggests African American and Hispanic youths' possible selves are amenable to change from structured intervention, with positive effects lasting through the transition to high school. For American Indian youth, there is no evidence of the efficacy of structured intervention but there is evidence of the pernicious effects of stereotypes on salience of academic possible selves. Finally, there is some evidence that academic possible selves and strategies are related to cultural values – Individualism, Collectivism, and Racial/Ethnic Identity. This is an important tack for future research because it holds promise for development of culturally sensitive intervention.

REFERENCES

Aloise-Young, P., Hennigan, K., and Leong, C. (2001). Possible selves and negative health behaviors during early adolescence. *Journal of Early Adolescence, 21,* 158-181.

Anderman, E.M., Anderman, L. H., and Griesinger, T. (1999). The relation of present and possible academic selves during early adolescence to grade point average and achievement goals. *Elementary School Journal, 100,* 3-17.

Anderman, E. M., Hicks, L. H., and Maehr, M. L. (1994, February). *Present and possible selves across the transition to middle grades school.* Paper presented at the biannual meeting of the Society for Research on Adolescence, San Diego, CA.

Anderman, E. M., and Midgley, C. (1997). Changes in achievement goal orientations, perceived academic competence, and grades across the transition to middle-level schools. *Contemporary Educational Psychology, 22,* 269-298.

Burack, J. H., Irby, D. M., Carline, J.D., Ambrozy, D. M., Ellsbury, K. E., and Stritter F. T. (1997). A study of medical students' specialty-choice pathways: Trying on possible selves. *Academic Medicine, 72,* 534-541.

Cantor, N. (1990). From thought to behavior: "Having" and "doing" in the study of personality and cognition. *American Psychologist, 45,* 735-750.

Carson, A. D., Madison, T., and Santrock, J. W. (1987). Relationships between possible selves and self-reported problems of divorced and intact family adolescents. *Journal of Early Adolescence, 7*(2), 191-204.

Cross, S., and Markus, H. R. (1991). Possible selves across the life span. *Human Development, 34,* 230-235.

Curry, C., Trew, K., Turner, T., and Hunter, J. (1994). The effect of life domains on girls' possible selves. *Adolescence, 29,* 133-150.

Day, J., Borkowksi, J., Punzo, D., and Howsepian, B. (1994). Enhancing possible selves in Mexican American students. *Motivation and Emotion, 18,* 79-103.

Dunkel, C. (2000), Possible selves as a mechanism for identity exploration. *Journal of Adolescence, 23,* 519-529.

Erikson, E. (1968). *Identity, youth, and crisis.* New York: Norton.

Fryberg, S. A. & Markus, H. R. (2005). Cultural models of education in American Indian, Asian American, and European American contexts. Unpublished manuscript.

Fryberg, S. A., Markus, H. R., Oyserman, D., & Stone, J. M. (2005). Honor or harm? The impact of using American Indian mascots on American Indian selves.

James, W. (1890/1950). *The principles of psychology* (Vol. 1). New York: Dover.

Kao, G. (2000). Group images and possible selves among adolescents: Linking stereotypes to expectations by race and ethnicity. *Sociological Forum, 15,* 407-430.

Kemmelmeier, M., and Oyserman, D. (2001a). Gendered influence of downward social comparisons on current and possible selves. *Journal of Social Issues: Special Issue: Stigma: An insiders perspective, 57,* 129-148.

Kemmelmeier, M., and Oyserman, D. (2001b). The ups and downs of thinking about a successful other: Self-construals and the consequences of social comparisons. *European Journal of Social Psychology, 31,* 311-320.

Kemmelmeier, M., Oyserman, D. , & Brosh, H. (2005). Gender, interdependence and the effects of upward comparison on self-concept" for review in Social Cognition. Unpublished manuscript. Ann Arbor, MI: The University of Michigan.

Kerpelman, J., and Pittman, J. (2001). The instability of possible selves: Identity processes within late adolescents' close peer relationships. *Journal of Adolescence, 24,* 491-512.

Kerpelman, J., Shoffner, M., and Ross-Griffin, S. (2002). African American mothers' and daughters' beliefs about possible selves and their strategies for reaching the adolescents' future academic and career goals. *Journal of Youth and Adolescence, 31,* 289-302.

Knox, M., Funk, J., Elliott, R., and Bush, E. G. (1998). Adolescents' possible selves and their relationship to global self esteem. *Sex Roles, 39,* 61-80.

Knox, M., Funk, J., Elliott, R., and Bush, E. (2000). Gender differences in adolescents' possible selves. *Youth and Society, 31,* 287-309.

Lee, J., and Cramdon, B. (1999). The positive effects of mentoring economically disadvantaged students. *Professional School Counseling, 2,* 172-178.

Leondari, A., Syngollitou, E., and Kiosseoglou, G. (1998). Academic achievement, motivation, and future selves. *Educational Studies, 4*(2), 153-163.

Lips, H. (1995). Through the lens of mathematical/scientific self-schemas: Images of students' current and possible selves. *Journal of Applied Social Psychology, 25,* 1671-1699.

Lobenstine, L., Pereira, Y., Whitley, J., Robles, J., Soto, Y., Sergeant, J., Jimenez, D., Jimenez, E., Ortiz, J., and Cirino, S. (2001, month not listed). *Possible selves and pastels: A truly socially contextualized model of girlhood* [On-line]. Paper presented at "A New Girl Order: Young Women and Feminist Inquiry Conference", London, England. Retrieved August, 3, 2003, from *http://whatkidscando.org/shorttakes/Holyoke GirlsPaperdoc.pdf*

Markus, H., and Nurius, H. (1986). Possible selves. *American Psychologist, 41,* 954-969.

Marsh, H. (1990). Causal ordering of academic self-concept and academic achievement: A multivariate, longitudinal panel analysis. *Journal of Educational Psychology, 82,* 646-656.

Newberry, A., and Duncan, R. (2001). Roles of boredom and life goals in juvenile delinquency. *Journal of Applied Social Psychology: Special Issue, 31,* 527-541.

Oyserman, D. (2001). Self-concept and identity. In A. Tesser, and N. Schwarz (Eds.), *Blackwell Handbook of Social Psychology* (pp. 499-517). Malden, MA: Blackwell Press.

Oyserman, D. (2002). Values, psychological perspectives on. In N. Smelser, and P. Baltes (Editors-in-chief), *International Encyclopedia of the Social and Behavioral Sciences* (Vol. 22, pp. 16150-16153). *Developmental, Social, Personality, and Motivational Psychology* (N. Eisenberg, Volume Ed.). New York: Elsevier Science.

Oyserman, D., Bybee, D., and Mowbray, C. (2005). *When your mother has a mental health problem: Antecedents of mental health feared possible selves in adolescence.* Manuscript in preparation. Ann Arbor, MI: The University of Michigan.

Oyserman, D., Bybee, D., Terry, K., and Hart-Johnson, T. (2004). Possible selves as roadmaps. *Journal of Research in Personality, 38,* 130-149.

Oyserman, D., Bybee, D. & Terry, K. (2005). Possible selves, strategies, social identity and meta-cognitive experience.Unpublished manuscript. Ann Arbor, MI: The University of Michigan.

Oyserman, D., Coon, H., and Kemmelmeier, M. (2002). Rethinking Individualism and Collectivism: Evaluation of Theoretical Assumptions and Meta-Analyses. Psychological Bulletin, 128, 3-73.

Oyserman, D., Gant, L. and Ager, J. (1995). A socially contextualized model of African-American identity: Possible selves and school persistence. *Journal of Personality and Social Psychology, 69,* 1216-1232.

Oyserman, D., and Harrison, K. (1998). Implications of cultural context: African American identity and possible selves. In J. Swim and C. Stangor (Eds.), *Prejudice: The target's perspective* (pp. 281-300). San Diego, CA: Academic Press.

Oyserman, D., and Markus, H. (1990a). Possible selves in balance: Implications for delinquency. *Journal of Social Issues, 46,* 141-157.

Oyserman, D., and Markus, H. R. (1990b). Possible selves and delinquency. *Journal of Personality and Social Psychology, 59,* 112-125.

Oyserman, D., Terry, K., and Bybee, D. (2002). A possible selves intervention to enhance school involvement. *Journal of Adolescence, 25,* 313-326.

Oyserman, D., and Markus, H. R. (1993). The Sociocultural self. In Jerry M. Suls (Ed.), *Psychological perspectives on the self: Vol. 4. The self in social perspective* (pp. 18-220). Hillsdale, NJ, England: Lawrence Erlbaum Associates.

Oyserman, D., and Saltz, E. (1993). Competence, delinquency, and attempts to attain possible selves. *Journal of Personality and Social Psychology, 65,* 360-374.

Ruvolo, A., and Markus, H. (1992). Possible selves and performance: The power of self-relevant imagery. *Social Cognition: Special Issue: Self-knowledge: Content, structure, and function, 10,* 95-124.

Sheldon, K., and Emmons, R. (1995). Comparing differentiation and integration within personal goal systems. *Personality and Individual Differences, 18,* 39-46.

Shepard, B. (2003). Creating selves in a rural community [On-line]. In W. M. Roth (Ed.), *Connections '03* (pp 111-120). Retrieved August 3, 2003, from the University of Victoria, Faculty of Education Research Web Site: *http://www.educ.uvic.ca/Research/conferences/connections2003/07Shepard102.pdf*

Shepard, B., and Marshall, A. (1999). Possible selves mapping: Life-career exploration with young adolescents. *Canadian Journal of Counselling, 33,* 33-54.

Stein, K. F., Roeser, R., and Markus, H. R. (1998). Self-schemas and possible selves as predictors and outcomes of risky behaviors in adolescents. *Nursing Research, 47*(2), 96-106.

Yowell, C.M. (2000). Possible selves and future orientation: Exploring hopes and fears of Latino boys and girls. *Journal of Early Adolescence, 20,* 245-280.

Yowell, C.M. (2002). Dreams of the future: The pursuit of education and career possible selves among ninth grade Latino youth. *Applied Developmental Science, 6,* 62-72.

In: Possible Selves: Theory, Research and Application   ISBN 1-59454-431-X
Editors: C. Dunkel and J. Kerpelman, pp. 41-59   © 2006 Nova Science Publishers, Inc.

Chapter 3

POSSIBLE SELVES IN ADULT DEVELOPMENT: LINKING THEORY AND RESEARCH

Leslie D. Frazier
Florida International University
Karen Hooker
Oregon State University

ABSTRACT

In this chapter we explore the theoretical relevance of possible selves for understanding adult development. We first describe the theoretical anchors that have influenced the way we conceptualize and examine possible selves. Next, we discuss the importance of understanding development in adulthood in terms of adults' possible selves and psychosocial outcomes. We then introduce Bronfenbrenner's (1977, 1979) contextual-ecological model of development, which states that human development is best understood within the ecological settings in which it unfolds. We use this model to present nearly two decades of research in our laboratories examining the structure and function of possible selves and to highlight the inter-related, contextual, and ecologically-relevant nature of our work on possible selves. Finally, we articulate some potential avenues for future research on possible selves in adulthood.

"I see myself at the summit of Denali, arms out-stretched, turning in circles, taking in the views, I'm totally euphoric. In the back of my mind, I hear the refrain *"The hills are alive…"* I'm not really Julie Andrews, more like 40-year-old Julie Andrews with the endurance of Chantal Mauduit. Anyway, I think about this every day as I train for my next climb." (Female, age 40)

"I just want to be well-enough to bake cookies for my grandchildren." (Female, age 67).

"Most important…I want to be a good father. Not mean and angry like my father was. I want to be able to provide for my wife and kids and have a loving family life. First, though, I have to get my degree, find a wife, then buy a home, and that will set the plan in motion." (Male, age 19).

Almost 20 years have passed since Markus and Nurius (1986) published their groundbreaking paper in the *American Psychologist*, introducing the concept of *possible selves* – the hoped-for and feared future self-representations that guide behavior. Their paper has been the impetus for nearly two decades of research in our laboratories. The goals of our empirical work have been to gather descriptive and explanatory data on the influence of possible selves for developmental outcomes in adulthood. Nevertheless, as we approach the anniversary of this important paper we must ask; "what is the theoretical relevance of possible selves for understanding adult development?"

In this chapter, we begin by describing the theoretical anchors that have influenced the way we conceptualize and examine possible selves. Next, we discuss the importance of understanding the development in adulthood in terms of adults' possible selves. Then, we utilize Bronfenbrenner's (1977, 1979) contextual-ecological model of development to structure the presentation of our work examining the structure and function of possible selves. Finally, we articulate some potential avenues for future research on possible selves in adulthood.

THEORETICAL ANCHORS OF POSSIBLE SELVES

The quotes above illustrate several theoretical anchors that guide our conceptualization of possible selves. First, individuals create their own developmental pathways toward the future. The quote from the young man who wants to be a good father shows that he sees the steps along the pathway to becoming one. Possible selves demonstrate the self-directed nature of development and are consistent with the contemporary theories of intentional self-development (e.g., Baltes and Schaie, 1973; Lerner and Busch-Rossnagel, 1981b; Nesselroade and Reese, 1973). One such theory, the developmental action theory (e.g., Brandtstädter, 1998; Carver and Scheier, 1998; Heckhausen and Schulz, 1995), articulates how the "life course" of developmental goals play out within the context of life transitions. The emphasis of this approach is on understanding how individuals adapt their developmental goals to the changing opportunities and constraints presented by their unique developmental trajectories, and more importantly, understanding the processes promoting pursuit of, and the processes promoting disengagement from, developmentally-relevant goals (Heckhausen and Dweck, 1998). With this solid foundation in life span developmental theory, possible selves allow greater insight and understanding of the processes of continuity and change across the life span.

Second, as the quotes illustrate, an individual's possible selves are grounded within developmental, interpersonal, and sociohistorical contexts. The grandmother who wants to be able to bake cookies for her grandchildren is articulating aspects of aging, health, family, and her role as the nurturing grandmother. Consistent with developmental systems theory (Ford and Lerner, 1992) and developmental contextualism (Lerner, 1979; Lerner and Kauffman, 1985), possible selves are the product of normative, non-normative, and historical forces that become integrated into self and motivate behavior in the present. They reflect both intra- and inter-personal influences and the interaction among the self, family, community, sociocultural, and global/historical forces. More importantly, possible selves are embedded within the ecology (i.e., the reciprocal relationship between the organism and it's environment) of the individual (Bronfenbrenner, 1977, 1979), and reflect their real-world and practical developmental strivings.

Third, as the first and third quotes show, possible selves are important motivational forces on present behavior. The quote from the female mountain climber illustrates how her visions of the successful future climb depend on her training in the gym today. From a developmental systems perspective, the action-oriented nature of development is captured in the self-regulatory processes enacted to help achieve or avoid certain selves in the future. These self-regulatory processes are conceptualized as the cognitive expectations of self-efficacy and outcome expectancy (Bandura, 1989), that determine the actions, plans, and behaviors that facilitate the achievement of one's possible selves. The focus from this perspective is on the creative, anticipatory, selective, "feed forward" developmental processes that influence self-directed behavior (Hooker, 1999). Possible selves then, are the generative, dynamic, and contextually sensitive personal embodiment of self-development.

Fourth, as the quotes illustrate, possible selves reflect personality. Without even seeing the subjects who provided the quotes one can imagine who they are and what they are like. Possible selves are conceptualized as existing in the part of personality known as "personal action constructs" (Hooker and McAdams, 2003; Little, 1983). In the *Six Foci Model of Personality* (Hooker, 2002) there are three different levels (McAdams, 1995) with personality structures of traits, personal action constructs, and life stories being continually produced and recreated by parallel processes of states, self-regulatory processes, and self narrative processes at each of the three levels (see Hooker and McAdams, 2003 for a detailed explanation). Seeing possible selves in the overall model of personality allows us to more clearly articulate and delineate linkages between possible selves and other personality constructs, as well as outcome measures of health and well-being. We believe that possible selves and the self-regulatory processes associated with each possible self have the potential to drive personality development throughout adulthood.

ADULT DEVELOPMENT AND POSSIBLE SELVES

Developmental processes, certainly those that are self-directed and action-oriented, depend crucially on the complex construct of *self* (Hooker, 1999). But what is the *self?* We argue that the self embodies human agency and directs volitional processes and goal-directed behaviors, especially those that are central to itself. We view possible selves as a lens that brings into focus salient developmental purposes in adulthood. Our focus on adulthood is important because during adulthood the temporal and contextual frames that influence developmental growth and change are not as neatly linked to biological and maturational phenomena as they are at other points in the life-span. Consequently, Hooker (1999) and others (e.g., Baltes, 1987) have argued that a major challenge for developmental theory, especially in adulthood, is to distinguish among *change in general* from *developmental change*. Change has been conceptualized in terms of gains/loss processes (e.g., Baltes, 1987). Whereas, others argue that change must be adaptive, or elaborative to the individual to be considered developmental change (see Ford and Lerner, 1992; Kaplan, 1983).

If change appears to be teleonomically-relevant to the individual, that is, it is adaptive and moves the individual closer to his or her personally- or developmentally-relevant goals, then it can be considered developmental change. The notion of the teleonomic trend is an expression of "what an individual is trying to do" (Allport, 1937). Hooker (1999) argues that by understanding what adults are *trying to do* and the extent to which they are successful at their purposeful strivings, we gain one standard for evaluating whether or not development has taken place. Possible selves provide an individually articulated image of exactly what an individual is trying to do, and with our recent initiation of longitudinal studies of possible selves across adulthood we will be able to see the success of possible selves in helping individuals reach their developmental goals.

OUR CONCEPTUALIZATION OF POSSIBLE SELVES

Most of the contributors to this book share the same basic conceptualization of possible selves, which is based on Markus and Nurius' (1986) original articulation of the concept. Consistent with their view, we believe that self-knowledge develops and changes across the life-span through the process of symbolic interactions with others, self-reflexive thought, and one's unique personal strivings (Breytspraak, 1984). The sense of self that develops becomes operationalized, to some degree, in one's unique cognitive-behavioral and psychosocial ways of being. The self-system is both stable and enduring and yet contextually sensitive and dynamic (Frazier, Hooker, Johnson, and Kaus, 2000; Hooker, 1999; Markus and Herzog, 1992; Smith and Freund, 2002). The most developmentally responsive component of the self-system is the amalgamation of future-oriented representations of self -- or *possible selves* (Cross and Markus, 1991; Hooker, 1992; Markus and Herzog, 1992). Possible selves can take the form of the visions we hope to achieve (i.e., hoped-for selves) or the visions of self we fear becoming (i.e., feared selves), and as such, they are conceptualized as the motivational component of the self-system (Hooker, 1992; Hooker and Kaus, 1994).

Research that is focused on present-oriented conceptions of self (e.g., self-constructs, schemas, identity), and asks adults to consider the question "Who am I?" yield a "snap-shot" of development that is static in time. We have argued elsewhere (Frazier, Johnson, Gonzales, and Kafka, 2002) that it is more useful to examine adults' personal strivings and subjective developmental goals by posing the question "What do you hope to become?" This approach yields a clear picture of the psychosocial influences that shape 'who I am' now as well as the identity-relevant goals that shape how one wants to grow older. Thus, we have found possible selves to be the best way to glean information about adult development.

POSSIBLE SELVES AND ADULT DEVELOPMENT:
A DECADE OF RESEARCH FROM OUR LABORATORIES

Over the past decade work in our laboratories has focused on understanding how adults interpret, experience, and adapt to their changing developmental landscapes. Our interests have ranged from the experience of becoming a parent to adjusting to a diagnosis of chronic illness. We have examined the role of age, gender, and cohort effects as well as the role of social norms and cultural influences. Given the varied interests of our research agendum, an organizational framework for presenting the findings is necessary. As Bronfenbrenner (1977,

1979) has noted, human development is best understood within the ecological settings in which it unfolds. His model delineates four inter-related settings in which action and development occur: a) the microsystem (or immediate setting such as family, friends); b) the mesosystem (interactions among specific settings including community); c) the exosystem (external influences on immediate settings such as social and institutional influences); and d) the macrosystem (comprised of cultural values and historical events). In this section we have organized the presentation of our findings along these levels to illustrate the inter-related, contextual, and ecologically relevant nature of our work on possible selves.

The studies we report are grounded in the same methodological framework. These studies were aimed at uncovering the content of possible selves and understanding linkages among the self-regulatory processes associated with those selves and various developmental periods, outcomes, and psychosocial mediators. To investigate these issues we use the interview protocol initially designed by Cross and Markus (1991), and modified by Hooker (1992) for use with older adults. Detailed description of the protocol and coding format is in the Appendix. We have found this protocol to be useful in generating rich qualitative data that lends itself easily to quantitative analyses. In all studies from our laboratories inter-rater reliability for coding is consistently high (i.e., above .85) and is consistent across time (see Frazier et al., 2000).

MICROSYSTEMIC INFLUENCES – INTRAPERSONAL AND SELF-DIRECTED INFLUENCES ON POSSIBLE SELVES

Bronfenbrenner (1977, 1979) conceptualized the microsystem as the individual's immediate ecological setting. This includes the individual's biological, cognitive, emotional, and psychosocial experiences, all of which we have found to interact with possible selves.

POSSIBLE SELVES, AGING, AND HEALTH

As developmentalists interested in successful aging, we have sought to understand how older adults make meaning of their lives and experiences as they age. We have argued that possible selves reflect this meaning-making process (Waid and Frazier, 2003), that is, the meaning of aging can be seen in older adults' visions of their future selves, which domains are important and which are not, especially when compared to other age groups. Moreover, successful aging can be seen in the structure of the possible selves repertoire, when compared to other age groups, and especially when viewed over time. Our findings show a winnowing in the number of domains reported suggesting that older adults slough-off future goals and images of self that are not centrally-relevant in order to concentrate on those that are (Frazier et al., 2000; Frazier et al., 2002; Hooker, 1992).

As one moves from mid-life to later life issues concerning health become increasingly important (Hooker, 1992). These changes are often normative and reflect the variation of maturational and psychosocial processes. In fact, individuals are likely to have at least one hoped-for or feared health-related possible self by the time they are in their forties (Hooker, 1999). This emphasis on health continues during the later years, is clearly present in many domains of self, and is a strong influence on actual behaviors motivated to achieve better health or offset undesirable health outcomes (Frazier, 2002; Frazier et al., 2000; Frazier et al., 2002; Hooker, 1992; Hooker and Kaus, 1992; 1994). For example, our earlier work (Hooker, 1992; Hooker and Kaus, 1992; 1994) showed that compared to young and middle-aged adults, older adults had more hoped-for and feared selves in the domains of health, physical functioning, and the ability to maintain one's independence. The presence of these possible selves influenced older adults' actual perceptions of their health (Hooker, 1992), and older adults with hoped-for health-related selves reported better perceived health than those with feared selves in this domain (Hooker, 1992). In later life, consistent with the Selective Optimization with Compensation (i.e., Successful Aging) model of aging that emphasizes the importance of avoidance of losses (Baltes, 1997), our findings show that future self-representations reflect a desire to maintain good health as well as a desire to avoid health events or downturns.

How successful older adults are at preserving their perception of good health is apparent in the linkages among possible selves and the self-regulatory functions of these selves (i.e., self-efficacy for achieving/avoiding the self; outcome expectancy for the self). Our research shows that when older adults have hoped-for or feared health-related selves that they feel capable of achieving in the future, they are more likely to be engaged in health promoting behaviors such as monitoring cholesterol, eating well, getting exercise, having regular contact with their physicians, as well as avoiding nicotine, alcohol, and other health-compromising behaviors in the present (Hooker and Kaus, 1992; 1994).

In piecing together the puzzle of how possible selves might serve to motivate behavior we have also considered the role of perceived control over health. Those findings showed that older adults who reported hoped-for and/or feared health-related selves reported greater internal perceptions of control over health (Frazier and Hooker, 1993; Frazier, 2002).

Our findings had shown us that health is an instrumental aspect of self for older adults and plays a motivational role in behavior. But we wondered why health is so important to sense of self. In a recent study that compared three cohorts of older adults we examined *when* and *why* health emerges in the possible selves of older adults (Frazier et al., 2002). Specifically, we wanted to know whether health becomes salient as a response to normative biological and maturational processes; as a motivational influence for preserving good health and preventing poor health. Or, whether health emerges in response to a significant health downturn, event, or pathological change; such as being diagnosed with a chronic condition. Based on our earlier work (Frazier et al., 2000; Hooker, 1992; Hooker and Kaus, 1992; 1994) we expected that there would be a greater frequency of reporting health-related selves in the oldest old. We also anticipated that health-related selves would emerge in response to health events as opposed to normative changes in health with age. This hypothesis was based on evidence that older adults are able to maintain positive perceptions of health despite age-related changes and some degree of disability. We reasoned that with advancing age there would be an increase in normative, and perhaps pathological, health changes that would impact functional ability. This would make it more difficult for older adults to maintain a positive perception of health and this change would be reflected in their hoped-for and feared selves. Finally, we hypothesized that older adults in poor health (i.e., self-reported health, reported medically-diagnosed conditions), who perceived less control over their health, and who report poorer quality of life would be more likely to report health-related selves.

Participants were 151 older adults in their 60s, 70s, and 80s or older (Frazier et al., 2002). Across the whole sample the content of their possible selves was consistent with our prior work with older adults (e.g., emphasis on health, physical, family, independence). However, when we compared cohorts we found some interesting differences. As we predicted, the oldest group was more likely to report health-related selves (45%) compared to those in their 70s (16%) or those in their 60s (11%). Yet, compared to the oldest group (4%), those in their 60s (53%) and 70s (45%) were more likely to report leisure-related selves as their most important possible selves. We also found that the oldest group had poorer physical health and functioning, and was more likely to attribute control over their health to external sources (i.e., powerful others, chance). These psychosocial variables and age were significantly predictive of the presence of health-related selves. Conversely, better physical functioning and better emotional well-being were predictive of the absence of health-related selves. Thus, our findings show that health emerges as a salient possible self in the 8th or 9th decade and most likely in response to health downturns or events that impact perceptions of health and physical functioning.

These findings show a different trend from our earlier work, reflecting perhaps, the changes in social, historical, and demographic characteristics of older adults in the United States today. To elaborate, the shift in emphasis to leisure may reflect that those over 60 are enjoying more years of better health, better health care, and greater economic resources than previous cohorts of older adults. Moreover, as a society our aging population is breaking outdated stereotypes of aging and creating new ones that emphasize good health, vitality, and new frontiers during the "golden" years.

CONTINUITY AND CHANGE IN POSSIBLE SELVES

When facing normative changes in health status, middle-aged and older adults' concerns for their health are reflected in domains of self that are important to them. The presence of these future self-representations relates to health perceptions, perceptions of control over health, and ultimately, health behaviors. Moreover, what we find is that when older adults are followed over time, the domains of self that are most important to them remain so over time. In one study, we followed a group of older adults over a five-year period. Our findings showed that continuity in possible selves was the norm. When change occurred it was generally emergent in nature, with domains such as health and physical functioning emerging in the repertoire with advancing age (Frazier et al., 2000).

This study also examined the issue of balance in possible selves. Oyserman and her colleagues (Oyserman and Markus, 1990a; 1990b; Oyserman and Saltz, 1993) have articulated balance in possible selves as the presence of a hoped-for and feared self in the same domain. Building on their work, we wondered whether balance in domains of self would be present and maintained over time. Our findings showed that balance in the possible selves repertoire of older adults was significantly more common than disparity, especially in the domains of physical functioning and family. We conclude that maintenance of the most central and salient domains of self are important for navigating the changes experienced in later life. We also conclude, consistent with Oyserman and her colleagues, that balance is important as a motivational force for possible selves, perhaps especially so in later life when the realities of aging make negative outcomes appear more likely.

To summarize thus far, our earlier cross-sectional work showed that health emerges in middle age and grows in importance in later life reflecting age-related changes in what is central to self. The longitudinal findings, consistent with other work (Smith and Freund, 2002) show a winnowing down of the number of domains that are important and a continuity and balance in the presence of health over time in later life. When we look more closely at differences among older adults, we find that health is significantly more important to those in their late 70s and older, and those who have poor health and physical functioning. Our findings have begun to illuminate some of the psychosocial variables that influence the presence of certain domains of self and the influence of those selves on psychosocial outcomes and behaviors. These findings were derived from samples of community-dwelling seniors who were still reasonably engaged in life. Thus, the challenges they face are the typical challenges that most older adults might encounter as they grow older. Our findings reflect the integration of normative developmental concerns into the possible selves repertoire. Because possible selves are the motivational aspect of self, this integration may demonstrate how possible selves serve to guide developmental goals.

POSSIBLE SELVES AS MARKERS OF ADAPTATION

Up to this point, the research findings we have discussed relate to the interplay among self and normative age-related developmental processes that provide opportunities for growth and change (Hagestad and Neugarten, 1985; Havighurst, 1972; Hooker, 1991; 1999; Kling, Ryff, and Essex, 1997). However, given that growth and change in self often occur in response to critical challenges and transitions, we wanted to explore how possible selves would reflect non-normative, stressful, life-altering events such as becoming chronically ill, or becoming a caregiver for a chronically ill spouse. We were interested in possible selves as markers of adaptation in the context of developmental challenges such as these.

Building on the idea that adjustment stems from the process of making meaning of a challenging situation, we wanted to know the extent to which these challenges would be integrated into future self-representations. We also wanted to know whether integration of the life challenge into sense of self would represent better adaptation. Our reasoning was that if the illness or caregiving status was not represented in the possible selves repertoire it might reflect denial (or other psychological defense mechanisms), poorer coping, and poorer adjustment.

Thus, in one study we compared healthy older adults and chronically ill older adults to determine the frequency of reporting health-related selves and the degree to which future selves were articulated with regard to health and illness (Frazier, Cottrell, and Hooker, 2003). Yet, living with chronic illness is not a monolithic experience (Shifren, 1996). Different illnesses create different contexts for coping and adaptation, thus we proposed that illness contexts might differentially influence possible selves. So, we compared older adults diagnosed with early-stage Alzheimer's disease (AD) and older adults diagnosed with Parkinson's disease (PD) with a control group of relatively healthy older adults. We expected that the experience of living with progressive, degenerative cognitive dysfunction would influence different domains of self than living with a progressive, degenerative physical dysfunction. Our findings supported this notion. Although there were no significant differences in the total number of domains reported by the three groups, specific domains were differentially reported by patient groups. As expected, AD patients were more likely to report cognitive-related selves and PD patients were more likely to report physical-related selves. Secondary coding for the presence of "illness-related selves" (i.e., an reference to illness) across domains revealed even greater differences among the patient groups. Almost all the PD patients (97%) reported selves related to their illness as opposed to just over half (59%) of the AD patients. In the AD sample, greater awareness of symptoms of AD related to greater reporting of illness-related selves. In the PD sample, patients were more likely to report less temporal distance among the current and future feared self, and that might explain the greater infusion of illness into all domains of self within this group. Although these findings are somewhat intuitive, this was the first study to examine possible selves within the context of chronic illness and the influence of developmental challenges on sense of self. One weakness of this study is that we did not explicitly examine the link among illness-related selves and mental or physical health outcomes. Rather, this study was designed to describe and explore the degree to which possible selves may embody a life-altering event such as living with chronic illness. Nevertheless, our goal is to continue this work in order to identify markers of adaptation in the context of coping with chronic illness.

As we have seen, chronic illness presents a challenge that significantly influences the sense of self of the patient. It may also have a profound effect on loved ones as well. In a study of the spouse caregivers of patients with AD or PD, approximately half the sample (49%) reported caregiving possible selves (Hooker, Monahan, Frazier, DeHart, and Lamp, 1997). Future self-representations concerned with caregiving were the most frequently listed hoped-for selves, and second only to health for feared selves. Caregivers hoped-for selves were often expressed in terms of being able to continue giving care to their spouses in the future, and their feared selves were focused on maintaining their health so that they would be able to do so. We also found that those who reported caregiving possible selves reported more positive mental health outcomes. Perhaps reflecting realistic but optimistic goals for the future. Thus, for older caregivers, incorporating caregiving into their goal structures may be a cognitive adaptation that allows them to find meaning and challenge in their efforts to support their spouses. Taken together, these findings shed light on possible markers of adaptive responses to changes such as these, as well as the importance of phrasing interventions in terms of self-enhancing, reconstructing, and future oriented visions of self.

MESOSYSTEMIC INFLUENCES – INTERPERSONAL CONTEXTS FOR THE DEVELOPMENT OF POSSIBLE SELVES

The mesosystem includes the individual and those closest to the individual who may influence the ecological setting (Bronfenbrenner, 1977, 1979). Although anecdotally we were quite aware that possible selves are often articulated in reference to significant others, as the second and third quotes above illustrate, the role of others on possible selves had not been systematically investigated.

THE ROLE OF OTHERS IN POSSIBLE SELVES

Possible selves, as an outgrowth of symbolic interaction theory (Cooley, 1902; Dewey, 1896; James, 1890; Mead, 1934), are to some degree, co-constructed through interaction with others, and thus responsive to interpersonal, sociocultural, and historical forces.

In order to explore the co-constructed nature of self, we undertook a study that examined the role of others in the emergence of possible selves across adulthood (Frazier, Montgomery, Barreto, and Perez, 2003; Frazier and Barreto, 2004). The study involved identifying the moment in time when a particular self emerged (e.g., through an epiphany experience, after deep self-reflection, as a circumstance of a planned or unplanned life change, or in anticipation of a life change). In addition, because of our interest in social comparison theory, we wanted to know to whom people compare themselves when striving towards or seeking to avoid particular selves. Moreover, we wanted to know whether upward comparisons (comparing yourself to someone more accomplished), downward comparisons (comparing yourself to someone worse off), or temporal comparisons (comparing yourself to yourself at another point in time) would lead to greater self-efficacy and outcome expectancy for achieving/avoiding possible selves. The study was comprised of 235 young, middle-aged, and older adults. Presented here are the preliminary correlational analyses from the young sample (aged 18-30), adults navigating the transition to adulthood (Frazier et al., 2003).

Across the life-span, the importance of others may wax and wane, but during adolescence and young adulthood, family, peers, and other social forces are especially influential in shaping development (Brofenbrenner and Morris, 1998; Furman and Burhmester, 1985; Payne, 2002; Steen, Kachorek, and Peterson, 2003). The transition to adulthood has both social and developmental significance for sense of self (Arnett, 2000). Thus, we expected that the role of social comparisons would be most salient for domains of self that were most psychologically central to the individual (see Beach and Tesser, 2000).

The domains of hoped-for self that were most salient to this age group were occupation (34%), education (18%), family (17%), and success (14%). The most salient feared domains were family (12%), success (12%), dependence (9%), and occupation (9%). These results replicate earlier studies on domains of possible selves in this age group (Hooker, 1992; Oyserman, 1990). Across all domains of self, the most common target person was a family member (70%), the self (13%), or a close friend (6%). When young adults make comparisons among themselves and their target person with respect to their most important hoped-for selves, they most often engage in upward comparisons. However, for feared selves, upward processes are only slightly more frequent than downward processes.

Next, we examined how the self-regulatory processes (i.e., centrality, importance, self-efficacy, outcome expectancy) associated with possible selves would relate to engagement in social comparisons. We found that for hoped-for selves, less distance between current self and hoped-for self was associated with temporal comparisons. Self-efficacy for achieving hoped-for selves was associated with downward comparisons, which is consistent with expectations based on the social comparison literature. For feared selves, the more central the self is to one's core self the more likely one is to make upward or temporal comparisons. Self-efficacy for avoiding feared selves was associated with temporal comparisons whereas outcome expectancy was associated with upward comparisons. These findings demonstrate the influence of others on future self-representations and the influential role that others play in shaping goals and behavior. Moreover, these findings also illustrate one mechanism (i.e., influential others) through which larger sociocultural and historical forces may influence developmental goals and sense of self.

We also examined social comparison processes in concert with other psychosocial variables and mental health outcomes (Frazier et al., 2003). Briefly, findings showed that upward social comparisons were associated with traditionally masculine gender roles, self-efficacy, mastery, and life satisfaction for both men and women. Downward social comparisons related to greater anxiety, depression, and lower satisfaction with life. We are currently testing some models to determine the directions of influence among intrapersonal psychosocial variables, possible selves, social comparison processes, and mental health outcomes.

EXOSYSTEMIC INFLUENCES – SOCIAL NORMS AND EXPECTATIONS AND POSSIBLE SELVES

Just as individuals are embedded within the context of their close relationships, they are embedded within their neighborhood, community, and social network (Bronfenbrenner, 1977, 1979). Thus the exosystem is comprised of the social and institutional forces that create an ecological context. Based on a body of empirical evidence demonstrating that identity is shaped by social forces, we expected to see that possible selves would be articulated in terms of the social forces influencing development at different points in adulthood.

THE ROLE OF SOCIAL FORCES ON POSSIBLE SELVES

The most obvious link we have found among the self and development is illustrated in the way socially recognized normative developmental tasks are integrated into possible selves. These findings are important for understanding development because growth and change in sense of self is often linked to transitional periods (Hagestad and Neugarten, 1985; Havighurst, 1972; Hooker, 1991; 1999; Kling, Ryff, and Essex, 1997).

Rosow (1985) predicted that the influence of socially-structured developmental tasks would be more apparent in young adulthood, when roles and tasks are more structured, than in later adulthood, when there is more flexibility in social roles and tasks are fewer. Hooker, Kaus, and Morfei (1993) used Havighurst's (1972) developmental task framework and "mapped" possible selves onto tasks with samples of young, middle-aged, and older adults. The young adult sample, 228 men and women in their late twenties to early thirties, were participating in a study on the transition to parenting (Hooker, Fiese, Jenkins, Morfei, and Schwagler, 1996). As one might expect, findings showed that the developmental tasks of this period; *starting a family, raising children, learning to live with a marriage partner*, were clearly present in their possible selves repertoire. In fact, the hoped-for selves reflected these life tasks for 73% of the sample. Moreover, 65% of the sample mentioned feared selves that were concerned with failure in these tasks. Outside of the family domain, this age group also reported possible selves, both hoped-for and feared, that pertained to *getting started in an occupation, taking on civic responsibilities, and finding a congenial social group*, and *managing a home.*

In another study focused specifically on the transition to adulthood, Frazier et al. (2003) found that young adults' possible selves reflected developmental tasks as well. Specifically, for hoped-for selves, completing one's education (18%) and choosing an occupation (34%) were the most important domains of self, followed by finding a suitable marriage partner and starting a family (17%) and being successful (14%). These young adults' feared selves did not parallel the developmental tasks reflected in their hoped-for selves, rather they were more likely to reflect feared failures in the domains of personal and material goals (28%), family (12%), and success (12%). These data converge with the findings from Hooker et al.'s (1993) young adult sample.

In Hooker's (1993) middle-aged sample, findings showed that adults between the ages of 40 and 59 reported selves that pertained to the generative tasks of: *assisting teenage children to become responsible and happy adults, relating oneself to one's spouse as a person, adjusting to aging parents.* In fact, 52% of the hoped-for family-related selves reported specifically referenced these tasks. The realistic developmental challenge to *accept and adjust to physiological changes of middle-age* was also clearly present in this sample's hoped-for physical selves, over 67% reported selves associated with this task. Similarly, 56% of the hoped-for occupational selves pertained to the developmental task of *reaching and maintaining satisfactory performance in one's occupational career.* Although the possible selves reflecting the task of *achieving social and civic responsibility* did not emerge, as a whole, most of the possible selves in this sample related to developmental tasks of this phase of life.

In the sample of older adults, findings showed that possible selves were not related to developmental tasks in the same straight-forward fashion as they were in the younger age groups. This sample, composed of adults over age 60, reported possible selves pertaining to only 3 salient developmental tasks. Consistent with most of our studies that show that health is the most important domain of self for older adults (Frazier, 2002; Frazier et al., 2003; Frazier et al., 2000; Frazier et al., 2002; Hooker, 1992; Hooker and Kaus, 1992, 1994), Hooker et al. (1993) found that the developmental task of *adjusting to decreasing physical strength and health* was reflected in 55% of the older adults' hoped-for selves and 50% of their feared selves. The tasks of *establishing satisfactory living arrangements* and *adjusting to retirement* were also present in the possible selves repertoire. However, the remaining developmental tasks associated with later life, *(adjusting to death of a spouse, establishing an explicit affiliation with one's age group; adopting and adapting social roles in a flexible way)* were not clearly represented. Developmental tasks may appear less salient in later life because with increasing age individual development becomes more strongly influenced by unique characteristics as opposed to normative and socially influenced characteristics (Hooker, 1999; Rosow, 1985). Alternatively, the developmental tasks of old age half a century ago may no longer reflect the developmental tasks of older adults today.

Further exploration of the role of sociocultural forces is found in a number of studies that show the influence of gender and sex role on possible selves (Frazier et al., 2003; Hooker, et al., 1996; Morfei and Hooker, 1997; see also Knox, this volume). Ongoing work in our laboratories will illuminate how social forces such as these shape possible selves.

The findings reported thus far demonstrate the role of significant others (i.e., family) and the co-constructed nature of possible selves. We have drawn attention to the importance of gender roles and sex role identification in shaping possible selves. And, we have uncovered the role of culture as a prominent influence on possible selves.

MACROSYSTEM INFLUENCES – THE ROLE OF CULTURE IN POSSIBLE SELVES

Global cultural and historical forces have also been found to influence development. Thus, Bronfenbrenner (1977, 1979) conceptualized that individuals were also embedded within the macrosystem, and therefore influenced by the cultural and historical influences that they were exposed to.

Possible selves that individuals have are, to some degree, created in the context of a particular culture (Markus and Kitayama, 1991; Oyserman and Harrison, 1998; see also Oyserman, this volume). For example, following the work of Markus and Kitayama (1991), the role of culture was examined in older adults' possible selves (Waid and Frazier, 2003). Significant cultural differences emerged among the Hispanic and Non-Hispanic (primarily European-American) sample. The possible selves of older Hispanics clearly reflected the collectivistic nature of their culture, 82% of their hoped-for selves and 80% of their feared selves were collectivistic in nature. Consistent with a collectivistic orientation, Hispanic older adults were most likely to report family as their most important domain of self. In comparison, the Non-Hispanic older adults' possible selves were individualistic in nature and reflected their culture's emphasis on individual pursuits and goals such as abilities/education, physical functioning, and independence from others. In fact, 92% of their hoped-for selves and 89% of their feared selves were individualistic in nature. A secondary coding process was employed to explore theoretically-relevant sub-elements of individualism/collectivism in possible selves, and findings show that regardless of domain of self reported, the Hispanics articulated future self-representations in terms of familial -relations, -roles, and –duties, whereas the Non-Hispanic older adults possible selves reflected sub-elements of autonomy, social relations, and quality of life. These findings illustrate the dynamic interplay among social, cultural, and developmental context in shaping older adults' future self-representations.

THEORETICAL ADVANCES FOR POSSIBLE SELVES RESEARCH

In this paper we have presented the life-span developmental framework that our research on possible selves in adulthood has been grounded within. We have drawn on Bronfenbrenner's model of human ecology (1977, 1979) to present the findings from over a decade of work in our laboratories. We have found this model useful for examining the myriad developmental contexts and factors that influence possible selves. We argue that this framework, and our findings, demonstrate some of the important ways that possible selves shed light on developmental processes across adulthood.

The research we have discussed in this chapter has significantly advanced our understanding of the developmental influences and teleonomic relevance of possible selves in adulthood. In addition to providing descriptive data that relates sense of self to developmental tasks, transitions, sociocultural roles, and life events, we have found possible selves to motivate health beliefs and behaviors, to influence control processes, and social comparison processes. We have systematically examined a variety of psychosocial antecedents that may influence possible selves, as well as the mental and physical health outcomes related to particular domains of self. Although our work has begun to assess continuity and change in possible selves over time in adulthood, more work needs to be done to clearly articulate how developmental processes across the life-span become embodied in possible selves. Thus, we argue that for the field to advance, further research efforts need to begin testing theoretical models of self-development that may be useful for identifying patterns of optimal self-development. We argue that these models, once empirically tested, will provide blueprints for markers of successful aging, identifying individuals at risk for negative adaptive outcomes, and psychotherapeutic approaches grounded in the developmental context of self that would be helpful for promoting positive adjustment.

We have been working on developing a theoretical model that applies directly to possible selves and delineates the developmental processes that may influence possible selves and the patterns of influence that relate to optimal mental health outcomes (Frazier, 2004).

REFERENCES

Allport, G. W. (1937). The functional autonomy of motives. *American Journal of Psychology, 50*, 141-156.

Arnett, J. J. (2000). Emerging adulthood: A theory of development from the late teens through the twenties. *American Psychologist, 55*, 469-480.

Baltes, P. B. (1987). Theoretical proposition of life-span developmental psychology: On the dynamics between growth and decline. *Developmental Psychology, 23*, 611-626.

Baltes, P. B. (1997). On the incomplete architecture of human ontogeny: Selection, optimization, and compensation as foundation of developmental theory. *American Psychologist, 52*, 366-380.

Baltes, P. B., and Schaie, W. K. (1973). *Life-span developmental psychology: Personality and socialization.* New York: Academic Press.

Bandura, A. (1989). Regulation of cognitive processes through perceived self-efficacy. *Developmental Psychology, 25*, 729-778.

Beach, S. R. H., and Tesser, A. (2000). Self-evaluation maintenance and evolution: Some speculative notes. In J. Suls and L. Wheeler (Eds.), *Handbook of social comparison: Theory and research,* (pp. 123-140). New York: Kluwer Academic/Plenum Publishers.

Brandstädter, J. (1989). Personal self-regulation of development: Cross-sequential analyses of development-related control beliefs and emotions. *Developmental Psychology, 25*, 96-108.

Brandstädter, J. (1999). The self in action and development: Cultural, biosocial, and ontogenetic bases of intentional self-development. In J. Brandstädter and R. M. Lerner (Eds.), *Action and Self-development: Theory and research through the life span,* (pp. 37-66). Thousand Oaks, CA: Sage Publications Inc.

Breytspraak, L. M. (1984). *The development of the self in later life.* Boston, MA.: Little Brown.

Bronfenbrenner, U. (1977). Toward an experimental ecology of human development. *American Psychologist, 32*, 513-531.

Bronfenbrenner, U. (1979). *The ecology of human development*. Cambridge, MA: Harvard University Press.

Bronfenbrenner, U., and Morris, P. A. (1998). The ecology of developmental processes. In W. Damon, and R. M. Lerner (Eds.), *Handbook of child psychology: Vol. 1. Theoretical models of human development*. New York: Wiley.

Carver, C. S., and Scheier, M. F. (1982). Control Theory: A useful conceptual framework for personality-social, clinical, and health psychology. *Psychological Bulletin, 92*, 111-135.

Cooly, C. H. (1902). *Human nature and the social order*. New York: Charles Scribner's sons.

Cross, S., and Markus, H. (1991). Possible selves across the lifespan. *Human Development, 34*, 230-255.

Dewey, J. (1896). The reflex arc concept in psychology. *Psychology Review, 3*, 357-370.

Ford, D. H., and Lerner, R. M. (1992). *Developmental systems theory: An integrative approach*. Newbury Park, CA: Sage Publications.

Frazier, L. D. (1993). *The possible selves of people with Parkinson's disease*. Unpublished manuscript, Syracuse University.

Frazier, L. D. (2002). Perceptions of control over health: Implications for sense of self in healthy and ill older adults. In S. P. Shohov (Editor) *Advances in Psychology Research (vol 10.)* pp 145-164. New York: Nova Science Publishers.

Frazier, L. D. (2004). The developmental processes that shape the emergence and maintenance of possible selves across adulthood: A model of development. Manuscript in preparation.

Frazier, L. D., and Barreto, M. L (2004). Possible Selves: The role of past selves and significant others in shaping young adults' self-representations. Manuscript under review.

Frazier, L. D., Cotrell, V., and Hooker, K. (2003). Possible selves and illness:
A comparison of individuals with Parkinson's Disease, Alzheimer's Disease, and healthy older dults. *International Journal of Behavioral Development, 27(1)*, 1-11.

Frazier, L. D., Hooker, K., Johnson, P. M., and Kaus, C. R. (2000). Continuity and change in possible selves in later life: A 5-year longitudinal study. *Basic and Applied Social Psychology, 22(3)*, 237-243.

Frazier, L. D., Johnson, P. M., Gonzalez, G. K., and Kafka, C. L. (2002). Psychosocial influences on possible selves: A comparison of three cohorts of older adults. *International Journal of Behavioral Development, 26(4)*, 308-317.

Frazier, L. D., Montgomery, M., Barreto, M. L., Perez, A., Hinton, H., and Jauregui, J. (2003). *Who shapes the future? The role of others in young adults' possible selves*. Paper presented at the 56th Annual Scientific Meeting of the Gerontological Society of America. San Diego, CA. November 2003.

Furman, W., and Buhrmester, D. (1985). Children's perceptions of the personal relationships in their social networks. *Developmental Psychology, 26*, 227-233.

Hagestad, G. O., and Neugarten, B. L. (1985). Age and the life course. In R. H. Binstock and L. K. George (Eds.) Handbook of Aging and the Social Sciences (2nd ed., pp 35-61). New York: Van Nostrand Reinhold.

Havighurst, R. H. (1972). *Developmental tasks and education* (3rd ed.). New York: David McKay.

Heckhausen, J., and Dweck, C. S. (1998). *Motivation and self-regulation across the life span.* New York: Cambridge University Press.

Heckhausen J., and Schulz, R (1995). A life-span theory of control. *Psychological Review, 102*, 284-304.

Hooker, K. (1991). Change and stability in self during the transition to retirement: An intraindividual study using P-tenchnique factor analyses. *International Journal of Behavioral Development, 14*, 209-233.

Hooker, K. (1992). Possible selves and perceived health in older adults and college students. *Journal of Gerontology: Psychological Sciences, 47*, P85-95.

Hooker, K. (1999). Possible selves in adulthood: Incorporating teleonomic relevance into studies of the self. In F. Blanchard-Fields and T. Hess (Eds.), *Social cognition and aging* (pp. 97-122). New York: Academic Press.

Hooker, K. (2002). New directions for research in personality and aging: A comprehensive model for linking levels, structures, and processes. *Journal of Research on Personality, 36*, 318-334.

Hooker, K., Fiese, B. H., Jenkins, L., Morfei, M. Z., and Schwagler, J. (1996). Possible selves among parents of infants and preschoolers. *Developmental Psychology, 32*, 542-550.

Hooker, K., and Kaus, C. R. (1992). Possible selves and health behaviors in later life. *Journal of Aging and Health, 4,* 390-411.

Hooker, K., and Kaus, C. R. (1994). Health-related possible selves in young and middle adulthood. *Psychology and Aging, 9,* 126-133.

Hooker, K., Kaus, C. R., and Morfei, M. Z. (1993) *The function of possible selves in linking personal goals to developmental tasks.* Paper presented at the 46th Annual Scientific Meetings of the Gerontological Society of America. New Orleans, LA.

Hooker, K., and McAdams, D. P. (2003). Personality reconsidered: A new agenda for aging research. *Journal of Gerontology: Psychological Sciences, 58*, P296-P304.

Hooker, K., Monahan, D. J., Frazier, L. D., DeHart, K., and Lamp, D. (1997). *Caregiving possible selves.* Paper presented at the 50th Annual Scientific Meeting of the Gerontological Society of America. Cincinnati, OH.

James, W. (1890). *Principles of psychology.* New York: Holt.

Kaplan, B. (1983). A trio of trials. In R. M. Lerner (Ed.), *Developmental psychology: Historical and philosophical perspectives (pp. 185-228).* Hillsdale, NJ: Lawrence Erlbaum Associates.

Kling, K. C., Ryff, C., D., and Essex, M. J. (1997). Adaptive changes in the self-concept during a life transition. *Personality and Social Psychology Bulletin, 23*, 981-990.

Lerner, R. M. (1979). The life-span view of human development: The sample case of aging. *Contemporary Psychology, 24*, 1008-1009.

Lerner, R. M., and Busch-Rossnagel, N. A. (1981b). Individuals as producers of their development: Conceptual and empirical bases. In R. M. Lerner and N. A. Busch-Rossnagel (Eds.), *Individuals as producers of their development: A life-span perspective,* (pp. 1-36). New York: Academic Press.

Lerner, R. M., and Kauffman, M. B. (1985). The concept of development in contextualism. *Developmental Review, 5*, 309-333.

Little, B. R. (1983). Personal projects: A rationale and method for investigation. *Environment and Behavior, 15*, 273-309.

McAdams, D. P. (1995). What do we know when we know a person? *Journal of Personality, 63*, 365-396.

Markus, H., and Herzog, A. R. (1992). The role of the self-concept in aging. In K. W. Schaie and M. P. Lawton (Eds.), *Annual Review of Gerontology and Geriatrics* (Vol. 11, pp. 110-143). New York: Springer.

Markus, H. R., and Kitayama, S. (1991). Culture and the self: Implications for cognition, emotion, and motivation. *Psychological Review, 98*, 224-253.

Markus, H., and Nurius, P. (1986). Possible selves. *American Psychologist, 41*, 954-969.

Mead, G. H. (1934). *Mind, self, and society*. Chicago: University of Chicago Press.

Morfei, M. Z., and Hooker, K. (1997 May). *Generative possible selves in the parents of young adults*. Paper presented at the annual meeting of the Midwestern Psychological Associatiohn, Chicago, Il.

Nesselroade, J. R., and Reese, H. W. (1973). *Life-span developmental psychology: Methodological issues*. Oxford, England: Academic Press.

Nurmi, J. E. (1991). How do adolescents see their future? A review of the development of future orientation and planning. *Developmental Review, 11*, 1-59.

Oyserman, D., and Harrison, K. (1998). Implications of cultural context: African American identity and possible selves. In J. Swin, and C. Stangor (Eds.), *Prejudice: The target's perspective*, (pp. 281-300). San Diego, CA: Academic Press.

Oyserman, D., and Markus, H. R. (1990). Possible selves and delinquency. *Journal of Personality and Social Psychology, 59*, 112-125.

Oyserman, D., and Saltz, E. (1993). Competence, delinquency, and attempts to attain possible selves. *Journal of Personality and Social Psychology, 65*, 360-374.

Payne, M. A. (2002). Adolescent decision-making: A comparison of adult and teenage perspectives in New Zealand. *International Journal of Adolescence and Youth, 10*, 277-295.

Rosow, I. (1985). Status and role change through the life cycle. In R. H. Binstock and E. Shanas (Eds.), *Handbook of aging and the social sciences* (2nd ed., pp. 62-93). New York: Van Nostrand Reinhold.

Shifren, K. (1996). Individual differences in the perception of optimism and disease severity: A study among individuals with Parkinson's disease. *Journal of Behavioral Medicine, 19*, 241-271.

Smith, J., and Freund, A. M. (2002). The dynamics of possible selves in old age. *Journal of Gerontology: Psychological Sciences, 57B*, P492-P500.

Steen, T. A., Kachoreck, L. V., and Peterson, C. (2003). Character strengths among youth. *Journal of Youth and Adolescence, 32*, 5-16.

Waid, L. D., and Frazier, L. D. (2003). Cultural differences in possible selves during later life. *Journal of Aging Studies, 17*, 251-268.

APPENDIX

POSSIBLE SELVES INTERVIEW PROTOCOL

Interviewers introduce the concept of possible selves by reading the following to participants:

Now I'm going to ask you some questions about your future. Probably everyone thinks about their future to some extent. When doing so, we usually think about the kinds of experiences that are in store for us and the kinds of people we might possibly become. Sometimes we think about what we hope we will be like.

One way researchers have of talking about this is to talk about possible selves -- selves we hope to become in the future. Some of these possible selves seem quite likely; for example, one of my hoped for selves is {interviewer mentions one pertaining to career}. Others seem quite farfetched but are still possible, for example, one of mine is to win the lottery and become a millionaire.

I want you to take a few minutes now and think about all your hoped-for possible selves -- you may have just a few or you may have many. What are the hoped-for possible selves you imagine for yourself at this point in time? This might be difficult to think about on the spur of the moment, so TAKE YOUR TIME.

You may begin listing your hoped-for possible selves whenever you feel ready.

In addition to having hoped-for possible selves, we may have images of ourselves in the future that we fear or dread or don't want to happen. Some of these feared possible selves may seem quite likely. For example, one of my feared selves {interviewer mentions one pertaining to career}. Other feared possible selves may seem quite unlikely, for example, one of mine is "being a homeless person." Some of us may have a large number of feared possible selves in mind, while others may have only a few.

Please take a few minutes and think about all of your feared possible selves. TAKE YOUR TIME. What are the feared or unwanted possible selves that you imagine for your self at this point in time?

POSSIBLE SELVES CODING SCHEME

01 *Personal*: included references to personal attributes or attitudes, ("independent," "intelligent," or "harried," "dissatisfied with my life") and to philosophical or spiritual issues.

02 *Physical:* included references to fitness ("in good shape"), attractiveness ("thin" or "fat") or a physical problem (e.g., "disabled").

03 *Abilities and Education:* included references to creative or artistic expression ("to be a good artist", to education ("to have an advanced degree," "flunking out of school"), and to general knowledge ("becoming fluent in another language," "being well-read").

04 *Lifestyle*: included geographical references ("to live on the east coast"), references to living in a nursing home, and references to quality of life ("living a simpler lifestyle," "having children more far away").

05 *Family*: included all references to marriage or divorce, spouse, grandparenting, relating to one's own parents, and family illness. Anything family related.

06 *Relationships:* included all references to friendship ("being a sympathetic friend," "being alone and lonely") and opposite sex relationships not clearly indicated as family.

07 *Occupation:* included all references to jobs ("having a job I truly enjoy," "having a boring job"), careers ("to be an effective ...therapist"), and retirement.

08 *Material*: included all references to financial security ("self-supporting," "poor"), and to specific possessions ("having a medium-sized, comfortable home").

09 *Success*: included all references to achieving goals ("to finish the story of my family," " to be a failure"), and to recognition or fame ("becoming a dominant authority in my field").

10 *Social Responsibility*: included all references to volunteer work, community involvement, and activity relating to other social issues ("a leader in eliminating the threat of nuclear war").

11 *Leisure*: included all references to travel or vacations ("traveling with my husband as semi-retirees"), hobbies and recreational sports ("a good tennis player and runner"), and other leisure time activities (e.g., "a music appreciator").

12 *Health*: included all references to general health ("in poor health," "long-lived"), specific diseases ("having Parkinson's disease"), substance abuse ("being an alcoholic"). Anything pertaining to illness. 13   *Independence/Dependence:* included all references to being dependent on others for activities of daily living ("couldn't take care of myself," "not being able to cook for myself"). A hoped-for self could include independence ("maintaining my independence"), feared selves could include not being a burden to others.

14 *Death*: included are any references to personal death ("having a prolonged death," "having a terminal illness").

15 *Bereavement*: included all references to death of a loved one ("losing my spouse," "widowed," "child's death").

16 *Threats*: included all references to events which were perceived to be threatening to the individual ("being raped," "having my house broken into," being stranded on the highway with a broken down car").

17 *Caregiving*: included explicit references to giving care or assistance to spouse (e.g., hoped-for self - "to continue to caring for my wife" or feared self - "to be too sick to care for my husband"). Note that the last example makes reference to health, but is coded as caregiving because the reason she fears poor health is that she would no longer be caregiving for her husband.

18 *Cognitive*: included all references to loss of cognitive functions or processes ("to loose my memory," "to become senile," "to loose my mind").

In: Possible Selves: Theory, Research and Application   ISBN 1-59454-431-X
Editors: C. Dunkel and J. Kerpelman, pp. 61-77   © 2006 Nova Science Publishers, Inc.

Chapter 4

GENDER AND POSSIBLE SELVES

Michele Knox
Medical University of Ohio

ABSTRACT

The purpose of the chapter is to review the literature on possible selves and gender, and to examine how the functions, development, and characteristics of possible selves may differ by gender. The chapter reviews emerging research addressing how these differences may be relevant to gender differences in self-concept, self-esteem and other aspects of functioning. A review of the literature on this topic indicates that males and females may develop and maintain self-esteem and perhaps other related aspects of well-being in disparate ways. Whereas males' possible selves may serve to define them as unique and separate them from others, females may be more likely to incorporate the views of others or representations of others in forming possible selves and in determining self-worth. Gender roles may limit the possible selves that females and males develop, and this may result in constricted behaviors and functioning in areas traditionally characteristic of the opposite gender. The paucity of research in this area suggests the need for caution in making strong conclusions; however, a number of research directions are identified that, when addressed, have the potential to illuminate our understanding of gender-related aspects of multiple domains of human functioning.

"Possible selves" (Markus and Nurius, 1986) are a type of self-conception and refer to conceptions of the self in future states. Possible selves represent not only what one aspires to, but also what an individual fears or otherwise feels he/she could become. Possible selves make up a context by which the real self is evaluated, thereby shaping self-esteem. A second function is to motivate behavior toward personally-defined goals (hoped-for possible selves) and away from personally meaningful negative outcomes (feared or undesired possible selves). The purpose of the present chapter is to review the literature on possible selves and gender, and to explore how the functions, development, and characteristics of possible selves might differ by gender.

POSSIBLE SELVES, GENDER AND SELF-VIEWS

A primary function of possible selves is to provide a context in which to evaluate the current or real self. Individuals feel good about themselves, or experience high self-esteem, when they feel they can achieve their positive self-conceptions. Thus, when positive self-conceptions are accessed and experienced as likely or possible with respect to the present self, individuals experience heightened levels of self-esteem. On the other hand, when negative possibility pervades the working self-concept, low self-esteem results. Cross and Markus (1991) assert that substantial or continuous discrepancies between hoped-for possible selves and real selves tend to negatively affect life satisfaction and self-esteem. The discrepancy between real and undesired possible selves is closely related to depression and life satisfaction (Ogilvie and Clark, 1992). Conversely, hoped-for possible selves that are not discrepant from the real self can elicit feelings of self-efficacy, control, competence, and effectance (Oyserman and Markus, 1990).

GENDER AND POSSIBLE SELVES

The development and content of possible selves may differ by gender, and these differences may be relevant to gender differences in self-concept, self-esteem and other aspects of functioning. A theoretical perspective that may provide insight into such issues is the "self-in-relation" (Jordan, Kaplan, Miller, Stiver and Surrey, 1991) perspective. This model asserts that traditional views of the self that emphasize autonomy and separateness are based on men's experience. In contrast, female sense of self tends to be acquired through relations with others; the self is established in terms of important relationships. For females, self-esteem is viewed as the degree to which one feels that one is engaged in and fostering relationships with important others. According to this perspective, it is by way of emotional connections to others that competence and effectiveness are realized.

Jordan et al. (1991) maintain that two distinct representations of the self exist, and that the tendency to have such self-representations differs by gender and culture. Specifically, they assert that individuals influenced by American and European cultures tend to emphasize and strive toward an *independence* of self that is characterized by a separateness from others as well as a focus on unique achievements and attributes. Individuals influenced by Asian culture, however, often adopt a representation of the self based on *interdependence*. In contrast to the independent construal of the self, this orientation emphasizes connectedness to others, communal achievements, attending to others, and an interdependence with others. Interdependent self-esteem is based on the "ability to adjust, restrain (the) self, (and) maintain harmony with (the) social context" (Markus and Kitayama, 1991, p. 230). This view is expanded by Cross and Madson (1997), who propose the "interdependent self-construal," in which representations of others are part of the self. This type of self-construal is hypothesized to be more characteristic of women in the United States than men in the U.S. Many men (particularly White, middle-class men) in the U.S. are said to be likely to maintain a more independent self-construal, in which representations of others are separate from the self (Markus and Kitayama, 1991). Results of research addressing possible selves indicates that these gender differences are apparent in the characteristics of possible selves. For example, a study addressing young adults' feared and ideal selves suggests that young men's ideal and feared selves are characterized by instrumentality. On the other hand, 90% of young women (as compared to 30% of males) referred to interpersonal qualities when defining their feared selves (Ogilvie and Clark, 1992).

Research indicates that female self-esteem is related to qualities involved in interpersonal relationships, such as humor, sympathy, generosity, and overall social competence (Block and Robins, 1993; Nottelman, 1987; Walker and Greene, 1986). Females place great emphasis on their emotional connectedness to others, and social competence tends to be valued highly (Cross and Madson, 1997). Furthermore, research (e.g., Segal, DeMeis, Wood and Smith, 2001) clearly indicates that, when considering the future, women tend to emphasize interpersonal issues such as interpersonal conflict, family roles, and self-description, whereas men are more focused on goal attainment and agency. Therefore, females' possible selves, both hoped-for and feared, may be likely to be characterized by interpersonal qualities. For example, a woman may maintain a "generous and helpful" hoped-for possible self and a "stingy, self-centered" feared possible self, and behavior therefore may be motivated toward helping others. In contrast, men's possible selves may tend to be characterized by personal goals, such as attaining a promotion or completing a marathon.

Gender differences in sources of self-esteem may have implications for gender-related aspects of possible selves. According to Goethals, Messick and Allison (1991), higher self-esteem in men relates to a belief of oneself as unique and superior to others in a given domain; in contrast, women seem to feel better about themselves when they perceive their peers to be performing equally well. The results of a study by Josephs, Markus, and Tafarodi (1992), using a college sample, were similar. They found that high self-esteem in men was related to the traditionally masculine quality of seeing oneself as having "uniquely superior abilities" (Josephs et al., 1992, p. 394). Uniqueness of ability was assessed in this study by asking participants to report their greatest skill and to estimate the percentage of students at their university who were also good at the same skill. Self-esteem in women appeared unrelated to the capacity to see oneself as having uniquely superior abilities. In contrast, a high degree of interconnectedness with others appeared to be related to higher levels of self-esteem in women.

A better understanding of males' possible selves may improve our understanding of how male self-esteem is developed and maintained. Postulating from these views, males may tend to formulate hoped-for possible selves that are more extreme and perceived to be uniquely superior to others. Females may be more likely than males to develop and maintain hoped-for possible selves that are commensurate with the performance of others in their environment. For example, under similar circumstances, a male may develop a "billionaire" possible self, whereas a female's possible self may be characterized by hopes for more moderate wealth. If in fact males' hoped-for selves tend to be more unattainable, this would have significant implications for self-esteem. It is also possible that males' possible selves may reflect the social comparison necessary in establishing superiority; that is, males' possible selves may be more likely to include comparative concepts such as "best" as in "the best salesperson in the company." Very little research is available on male possible selves, and clearly much more is needed to better understand these issues.

Information used in forming possible selves may differ by gender. The symbolic interactionist perspective maintains that self-concept and associated self-esteem are related closely to the appraisals of others (Demo, Small and Savin-Williams, 1987). According to this perspective, a global sense of self is not formulated solely through introspection and self-observation, but through the understanding of others' views of the self. This approach to self definition may be particularly relevant for females who place importance on relatedness to others and the empathic understanding of others' views (Jordan et al., 1991). Females' possible selves may be formulated based in part on the perceived aspirations and views of others. That is, compared to males, females may be more likely to incorporate, for example, the hopes that others have for them into their repertoire of hoped-for possible selves. Likewise, others' negative views of females may be likely to be considered in the formation of feared possible selves. For example, a female adolescent whose parents frequently speak of high academic potential may be more likely to formulate an "A student" possible self than would a male adolescent in similar circumstances. The views of peers who tease the same female adolescent about being too committed to academics may harbor a "nerd" feared possible self. Findings of a recent study addressing African-American mothers' and daughters' academic and career possible selves (Kerpelman, Shoffner and Ross-Griffin, 2002) emphasized the importance of the validation of possible selves by significant others, a process that is hypothesized to lead to elaboration and likelihood of success in possible selves domains. Further, research by Kemmelmeier and Oyserman (2001) demonstrates that, particularly in individualistic cultures, women are more likely than men to assimilate the failure of a similar person into their own self-views when developing their own self-conceptions. Because this tendency interferes with the development and maintenance of certain positive possible selves, it may have a negative impact on women's achievement in domains such as academic and occupational functioning.

The content of possible selves also may differ by gender, and this may have implications for gender differences in self-concept and self-esteem. Research on the possible selves of adolescents revealed that the domains related to adolescent self-concept and self-esteem differ markedly by gender. Adolescent male and female possible selves appeared to be markedly different in their salience, likelihood and hopedforness/fearedness. Further, the domains related to global self-esteem differed according to gender. Although no gender differences were found on global self-esteem, ratings within domains of possible selves varied a great deal according to gender (Knox, Funk, Elliott and Greene Bush, 1998; Knox, Funk, Elliott and Greene Bush, 2000). Wylie (1974) had similar findings, and concluded that relatively weak gender differences in global self-esteem may mask gender differences within specific domains of self-esteem. These findings also support previous findings (e.g., Byrne and Shavelson, 1987; Dusek and Flaherty, 1981) that indicate that male and female self-concept and self-esteem are derived from different domains.

It should be noted that gender differences in possible selves are likely influenced by development. In the Knox et al. (1998) study, female adolescent self-esteem was related to the likelihood of self-oriented (e.g., "happy"), material/financial, educational, occupational, relational, and physical appearance possible selves. Male adolescent self-esteem was related to the likelihood of relational possible selves. Overall, the relational possible selves category emerged as the most pertinent category of possible selves for both male and female adolescents. This is consistent with the fact that interpersonal functioning (and in particular peer relations) is highly important to adolescents. Adolescents are acutely aware of and sensitive to how others perceive them. Although a great deal of past research suggests that relational functioning is more closely related to female than male self-esteem, the degree of this difference may have been overstated for adolescents. During this developmental period, this aspect of functioning may be important to boys' as well as girls' self-views.

Gender role socialization around aspects of perceived attractiveness may relate to the development of hoped-for and feared possible selves, and in turn to self-esteem and related pathology in females. Extreme emphasis is placed on attractiveness for females in U.S. culture (Thornton and Ryckman, 1991), and girls and women learn early in life that "looks" are very important. Self-esteem researchers concur that perceived attractiveness is related to females' overall self-esteem (AAUW, 1992; Block and Robins, 1993; Hagborg, 1993; Lavitt, 1992; Simmons and Rosenberg, 1975) or social self-esteem (Thornton and Ryckman, 1991). Through the media, girls are repeatedly exposed to many images of attractive females and are persuaded to emulate them. Wolf (1991) contends that this feminine ideal, established by the media and advertisers, serves to lower the self-esteem of girls and women who find the ideal unreachable.

This may, in part, explain why females often rate themselves poorly on measures of perceived attractiveness (Lavitt, 1992; Simmons and Rosenberg, 1975), while concurrently placing great importance on success in this domain (AAUW, 1992; Orenstein, 1994; Simmons and Rosenberg, 1975). Lavitt (1992) found that females rated themselves lower on appearance than on any other domain. She also found that appearance was the strongest predictor of female self-esteem. In accordance with Harter's (1985) view, this combination of low self-rating and high value placed on one variable is likely to have a strong negative effect on self-esteem. Very often, females' hoped-for possible selves in the domain of attractiveness may be so remote that success in this domain is virtually impossible, resulting in lowered self-esteem.

The American Association of University Women's (1992) study on elementary school-age and adolescent girls found that, not only was "the way I look" the strongest determinant of self-esteem for Caucasian girls, but the number of girls who said they like the way they look dropped dramatically between elementary and middle school. Similarly, adolescent girls' perceived attractiveness has been found to be much lower than that of adolescent boys (Simmons and Rosenberg, 1975; Thornton and Ryckman, 1991). This difference was nonexistent in Simmons and Rosenberg's (1975) 8 to 11 year old age group. Similarly, Marsh, Byrne and Shavelson (1992) found that, prior to adolescence, girls had higher perceived attractiveness ratings than boys. At adolescence, this situation was reversed; boys' perceived attractiveness ratings were higher than girls'. These developmental trends, coupled with the strong relationship between attractiveness and self-esteem for girls, suggest that possible selves related to attractiveness may be related to the decline in girls' self-esteem as they approach adolescence.

Closely related to the concept of perceived attractiveness is perceived body image. Researchers who have addressed this topic consistently have found that approximately fifty percent of pre-adolescent girls are unhappy with their bodies (Orenstein, 1994; Wolf, 1991). Further, perceived body image appears to be related to female self-esteem (Harter, 1990). In American culture, the feminine ideal is generally an image of a thin person. For example, for approximately one half of American women, the ideal self is several pounds thinner than the real self. Women's beauty role models, such as fashion and print models as well as beauty contest winners, tend to be significantly thinner than the average American female (Wolf, 1991). Wolf (1991) insists that the American culture has a "cultural fixation on female thinness" (p.187) that serves to undermine girls' and women's self-confidence.

Female self-views may be most closely related to their ability to avoid the feared possible selves related to physical appearance as opposed to their ability to achieve their hoped-for possible selves in this domain. In a recent study, physical appearance hoped-for selves were not related to girls' self-esteem, but physical appearance feared selves were (Knox et al., 1998). That is, the perceived likelihood of feared possible selves such as "being fat" was associated with self-esteem for girls; this was not true for males.

A focus on feared possible selves may be vital to the treatment of eating disorders. Researchers exploring the etiology of anorexia nervosa have found that this disorder is closely associated with "an intense fear of becoming obese" (Bruch, 1988; p. 304). Many of the girls in the Knox et al. (1998) study alluded to such fears, listing physical appearance feared selves of "being fat" or "being obese." These findings suggest that it may be a fear of being unattractive or overweight that most affects adolescent girls' self views. If this is the case, although it is highly speculative, a recalibration of feared selves may be one approach to treatment of eating disorders in adolescent girls.

POSSIBLE SELVES, GENDER, AND MOTIVATION

The second function of possible selves is to motivate behavior. Activated possible selves have a motivating function in that aspects of positive (or "hoped for") possible selves give an individual direction toward aspired goals, while aspects of negative (or "feared") possible selves specify what negative consequences can be avoided (Markus and Nurius, 1986). Thus, an understanding of an individual's possible selves will provide information about what that person strives to become or avoid becoming.

GENDER ROLES

The feminine gender role is traditionally characterized as incorporating qualities of expressiveness, including a strong emphasis on interpersonal relationships, expressiveness, sensitivity, and nurturing (Block, 1983; Gilligan, 1982; Josephs et al., 1992; Ruble and Martin, 1998; Wilson and Cairns, 1988). In contrast, masculinity has been said to include characteristics such as agency, instrumentality, individuation or independence, and competition (Block, 1983; Gilligan, 1982; Josephs et al., 1992; Nicholls, Licht, and Pearl, 1982; Ruble and Martin, 1998; Wilson and Cairns, 1988). The incorporation of traditional gender roles into the self-concept may have a significant impact on the array of possible selves conceived by an individual. Males who adhere strictly to a traditionally masculine gender role may have to give up or avoid altogether possible selves in more feminine domains. Likewise, females who incorporate a traditionally feminine gender role may limit the possible selves that may be considered. For example, Markus and Oyserman (1989) assert that girls who observe their mothers modeling a subordinate role in the family environment may experience a sense of limited possibilities for the future. For both genders, feared possible selves perceived to be characterized by qualities of the opposite gender may exist and serve to direct behavior away from nontraditional domains. For males, an emotionally sensitive or expressive feared self may exist which motivates behavior away from the overt expression of emotion. For females, an overly competitive feared self may motivate behavior away from involvement in competitive sports.

Results of studies addressing parenting (Hooker, Fiese, Jenkins, Morfei and Schwagler, 1996; Morfei, Hooker, Fiese and Cordeiro, 2001) also indicate gender differences in possible selves related to gender roles. In contrast to fathers, mothers demonstrated greater balance in parenting possible selves, with hoped-for possible selves balanced by countervailing feared possible selves. This balance may result in higher levels of motivation to guide parenting behaviors. These findings are consistent with research addressing men's and women's personal goals during the transition to parenthood. During this period, men's personal goals have been found to change less than those of women, the content of which move substantially in the direction of childbirth, child's health, and motherhood (Salmela-Aro, Nurmi, Saisto and Halmesmaeki, 2000). These findings suggest that gender role stereotypes that define child rearing as a primarily female duty may continue to guide parents' views of their parenting roles and responsibilities.

AGGRESSION AND DELINQUENCY

The level of incorporation of gender norms into self-concept and possible selves may influence motivation toward or away from aggressive or delinquent behavior. For example, recent research indicates that the incorporation of gender roles into the self-concept for males and females may reduce the likelihood of delinquency. Heimer (1996) found that incorporation of the traditional feminine gender role into the self-concept was related to a lower occurrence of delinquency for females. Ford, Stevenson, Wienir and Wait (2002) examined the impact of internalization of gender norms on college students' self-evaluations when imagining themselves involved in delinquency. Their findings suggest that gender norms may serve the adaptive function of decreasing the likelihood and motivation toward delinquent possible selves. Although results suggest this may be true for both genders, this may be particularly true for females, for whom "delinquent behaviors are higher in gender inconsistency" (Ford et al., 2002; p. 209).

In contrast, incorporation of some of the gender norms perpetuated by the media may be harmful. By way of video games, television, movies, music, and magazines, the media provides many aggressive and antisocial role models for children and young adults. A clear link has been established between media violence and aggressive behavior in youth (Anderson and Bushman, 2002). Exposure to violence in the home, school and neighborhood also increases the likelihood of future aggression in youth (Gorman-Smith and Tolan, 1998; Knox, Carey, Kim and Marciniak, in press). Modeling theory posits that observing violent models relates to increased likelihood of aggression, particularly when the model is similar to the observer. Possible selves are social in nature and determined in part by exposure to salient others' characteristics and behaviors (Markus and Nurius, 1986), and media may provide the "salient others," or models, that form the basis for some of youths' possible selves. That is, aggressive models in the media may provide fodder for the development of aggressive possible selves in youth. In turn, the development of aggressive possible selves may contribute to the development of aggressive behavior in youth who witness or experience aggression. Because most of the aggressive acts displayed in the media are committed by males (Smith, Nathanson and Wilson, 2002), males may be at highest risk for developing aggressive possible selves after viewing aggressive models.

Increasingly, however, females are being depicted in the media as aggressive (Ventura, 1998). In video games, movies, and television women and girls are portrayed as using violence more than ever before. This change likely places females at heightened risk for the development of aggressive hoped-for possible selves, increased motivation toward aggressive behavior, and involvement in aggressive acts. In fact, increased aggression has been noted in females over past decades (Campbell, Sapochnik and Muncer, 1997; Knox, King, Hanna, Logan and Ghaziuddin, 2000; Tardiff, Narzuk, Loen, Portera and Weinir, 1997), perhaps in part due to this phenomenon. More research is clearly needed to explore how possible selves, the media, and gender role socialization may interact to contribute to the development of aggressive and delinquent behavior, and how treatment addressing possible selves might prevent or decrease these problems in youths.

ACHIEVEMENT

The interaction between parents' and teachers' gender-role stereotypes and youths' possible selves may relate to gender differences in academic achievement. Eccles, Jacobs, and Harold (1990) found that parents' gender role stereotypes affect children's confidence in their math, English, and sports abilities and that parental expectations appear to exist independent of actual performance differences in these areas. Parents generally have low expectations for girls' performance in math and sports, and a self-fulfilling prophecy effect seems to exist in these domains. In other words, parents do not expect girls to perform well in math and sports, and ultimately, parents' perceptions come true; girls *do not* do well in these areas.

There may be a gradual developmental change in parental expectations of children's academic abilities. Eccles et al. (1990) found that the child's gender did not affect parents' judgments of younger (Kindergarten, first, and third grade) children's math ability. A gender effect, however, was apparent in the judgments of mothers of sixth grade children. If parents' expectations and perceptions of girls' abilities change at pre-adolescence, this may be followed by the development of possible selves in accordance with parents' expectations, and the ultimate fulfillment of such judgments by girls.

Differences in girls' and boys' tendency to internalize success in academics, and to use such success in the development of possible selves, may be related to gender role socialization by parents and teachers. Boys tend to attribute success to internal, stable causes while assigning external, unstable causes to their failures (Alpert-Gillis and Connell, 1989; Sadker and Sadker, 1994). Eccles, Adler and Meece (1984) found some support for a gender difference in attributional style; only females with low expectations for their performance on anagram and math tasks tended to rank ability as a more important cause of failure than success. Sadker and Sadker (1994) contend that girls attribute school accomplishments to effort rather than ability, but boys internalize their successes as due to ability. Eccles et al. (1990) found that parents attribute girls' successes in math and sports to effort rather than talent, while boys' successes are credited to talent. Such parental attributions were found to be followed by girls' decreased confidence and performance in those areas. Thus, girls, who may tend to integrate other's feedback into their possible selves, and who may not attribute academic success to ability, may be less likely to develop and maintain hoped-for possible selves in these domains. For example, following such socialization influences, a girl who once imagined herself as a scientist may no longer harbor a "scientist" hoped-for possible self. Therefore, motivation and subsequent success in science may be diminished.

CONFLICT IN GENDER ROLES

Markus and Kitayama (1991) suggested that the independent, achievement-oriented self, a highly masculine, as opposed to feminine orientation, is the ideal of American culture. Further, Block and Robins (1993) found that the qualities defined by adolescents as characteristic of high self-esteem become progressively more and more similar for boys and girls between the ages of 14 and 23. By age 23 years, the criterion for self-esteem converges on a masculine standard characterized by qualities such as assertiveness, being turned to for advice, and being quick to act.

The feminine ideal is clearly very different from the more masculine societal standard of the U.S. In fact, Linehan (1993) asserts that, "normative feminine behavior, at least that part having to do with interpersonal relationships, is in a collision with current Western cultural values" (p. 55). Girls from the American and European cultures may attempt to live up to a male-defined societal ideal that emphasizes unique achievements, individuality, competitiveness, and superiority while *simultaneously* attempting to meet the demands of gender-role socialization that insist that they be dependent, passive, and relationally-oriented. In fact, the feminine gender role itself may be broadening to include traditionally masculine characteristics. Recent research indicates the feminine stereotype may be changing to include such previously masculine characteristics as assertiveness and independence (Baum, Whitesell and Harter, 1999). However, the masculine gender role does not seem to be making a similar turn in the direction of the opposite gender.

A number of studies indicate that females' possible selves may be composed of features of both femininity and masculinity. In a study addressing African-American mothers' and daughters' academic and career possible selves, participants' responses indicated expectations of college education, employment, responsibility, and a balance between independence and social connection (Kerpelman et al., 2002). Future education and occupation are highly salient for both male and female adolescents, but in addition, females explore more family-related issues than males do (Kalakosli and Nurmi, 1998), and a greater number of life domains seem to be encompassed in girls' self-concepts and possible selves (Curry, Trew, Turner, and Hunter 1994; Knox et al., 2000).

The apparent broadening of the feminine gender role may lead to improved opportunities for females. That is, some females may experience greater freedom and more alternatives in formulating possible selves and choosing future goals. Females increasingly may consider entering either feminine or masculine careers. Girls may consider, for example, both "engineer" and "nurse" possible selves. Further, females' possible selves may be progressively more likely to include characteristics such as "assertive" and "self-sufficient."

On the other hand, in the attempt to integrate the possible roles or selves into a coherent sense of self, girls may find themselves in a double-bind situation. How can they be both passive and assertive? Both competitive and communally-oriented? Both independent and dependent? Internal conflict must be aroused for adolescent girls when they attempt to integrate two antithetical traits. Higgins (1987) contends that movement away from an internally-defined, parentally-defined, or societally-defined "ideal" will lead to an actual self/ideal self discrepancy, which in turn, leads to sadness and disappointment in the self. For an individual who simultaneously attempts to adapt qualities that exist on opposite ends of a continuum, movement in any direction may lead to discomfort. In a sense, such individuals will never be satisfied with themselves.

There is some evidence that conflict among contrasting possible selves may be problematic for females. High socioeconomic status, European-American, female adolescents have been found to report lower levels of global self-esteem than other race by socioeconomic status groups (Richman, Clark and Brown, 1985). Richman et al. (1985) proposed that this finding is related to high socioeconomic status, European-American girls' attempts to achieve two incompatible ideals. They contend that such girls are socialized to aspire toward aspects of both the traditional feminine gender role and, conversely, the traditional masculine gender role, which emphasizes high educational achievement, value competence, and skill mastery (Richman et al., 1985). Another study (Chalk, Meara and Day, 1994) found that college females tended to fear both masculine and feminine occupations, and imagined relatively few occupational possibilities. Thus, feared possible selves predominated and women's feared selves were not well balanced with more positive, or hoped-for occupational selves. In contrast, college males demonstrated more balance in possible selves; that is, males' feared occupational possible selves were balanced with hoped-for occupational possible selves. This is consistent with the conclusions of Knox et al. (2000), who suggested that males as a group demonstrated more balance in occupational possible selves than did females. As suggested by Markus and Ruvolo (1989), this "balance" may result in higher levels of motivation toward occupational selves for males, and limited motivation toward hoped-for occupational selves for women.

Conflict between possible selves also may be problematic for males. Findings of research addressing parenting possible selves indicated poor continuity of fathers' hoped-for and feared parenting possible selves (Hooker et al., 1996; Morfei et al., 2001). The authors suggested that this may indicate possible change or confusion in the fathering role, and concluded that conflict between the roles of caregiver and wage earner may result in relatively lower levels of consistency in parenting possible selves for fathers. Roles and expectations for American men may be changing. Over recent decades, men are becoming more involved in housework and caregiving roles in the home (Bianchi, Milkie, Sayer and Robinson, 2000). This is in addition to continued expectations for most men to work outside the home. As may be the case for females, conflicting expectations to be both a nurturing caregiver and a breadwinner may be difficult for males to resolve.

The problem of conflicting gender role expectations may be particularly severe for African American males. "Afrocentric values" have been described as being in collision with European American values, and particularly with the traditional European American masculine gender role. Afrocentric values stress collectivism over individualism, spirituality over materialism, and oneness with nature, and are at odds with traditional European American male gender norms (Harris, 1995). Further, most African American men have internalized some aspects of the traditional European American masculine gender role (Harris, 1995). However, inequities in earning potential and discrimination in academic and employment settings hinder African American males' efforts toward success in these domains, often making possible selves that were established based on societal standards very difficult to achieve.

Whether broadening gender roles and expectations are problematic or beneficial for males and females remains unclear. An understanding of gender issues in development suggests that conflict in the self may lead to more difficulties for females than for males. Harter and Monsour (1992) suggested that mid-adolescence is a period when conflict among aspects of the self may be particularly problematic. During this stage, self-concept is becoming increasingly differentiated. At the same time, the adolescent experiences increasing pressure to integrate these attributes into a meaningful self-concept. Harter and Monsour (1992) assert that the conflict among aspects of the selves may be more troublesome for girls. This is because girls' self-concepts are more relationally-bound and include aspects of functioning in multiple interpersonal roles that are considered important to them. On the other hand, boys may be more able to see their roles as independent of one another, and are therefore less distressed by conflict among them. Further research addressing the compatibility of possible selves will improve our understanding of the impact of changing gender roles on self-conceptions, achievement, and well-being.

THE APPLICABILITY OF POSSIBLE SELVES FOR MALES AND FEMALES

It is likely that there is a significant degree of individual variation in the level of development of possible selves, both hoped-for and feared, and this difference may be related in part to an individual's tendency toward self-reflection. Considered as a group, however, females may be more prone than males to reflect on and elaborate possible selves. In order to develop possible selves and to rate the real self in comparison to such selves, one must engage in a significant amount of inward focus. The intense self-reflection necessary for such tasks appears to be especially characteristic of adolescent girls (Allgood-Merten, Lewinsohn and Hops, 1990). Research indicates that adolescent girls rate their possible selves, both hoped-for and feared, as more important or affectively salient than boys do. In addition, the possible selves variables appear to be more highly correlated with girls' than with boys' self-esteem (Knox et al., 1998). Thus, possible selves may be more elaborated for females, particularly during adolescence. Support for this comes from the fact that girls at this developmental stage tend to be somewhat more psychologically mature (Harter, 1990). With psychological maturity comes the ability to think about and consider hypothetical self-views (Harter, 1988). It may be that adolescent males are less future-oriented and unlikely to place importance on hypothetical self-views. This is supported by research by Honora (2002) indicating that adolescent females (especially higher achieving females) reported more future goals and expectations compared to males.

Findings from recent research indicate that the importance or salience of feared possible selves may differ by gender. Feared possible selves appear to be highly salient to females, and gender differences may exist in the elaboration and perceived likelihood of feared selves. For example, mothers of infants and preschoolers have been found to be more likely than fathers to have feared parenting possible selves, including fears relating to negative outcomes in children's futures, fears regarding single parenthood, and fears regarding being "stretched too thin in terms of time commitments" (Hooker et al., 1996; p. 548). This finding was also evident at 2 to 3 years after the initial parenting possible selves assessment (Morfei et al., 2001). In research with a college-age sample, Ogilvie (1987) found that undesired self ratings, assessed as "How I hope to never be," were more specific and concretely described than were ideal self descriptions, which were significantly more abstract in nature. Ogilvie asserted that it is because the undesired self-ratings are so concrete, often rooted in very specific memories of past negative experiences, that they are so closely related to life satisfaction. Their findings suggest that females tend to identify past interpersonal conflicts as times when they were at their worst. Thus, females seem to have the ability to form very specific conceptions of their undesired selves.

In addition to having more elaboration in feared possible selves, females' possible selves may be more closely related to key domains of well-being and mental illness. Depressive symptomatology has been found to be more closely related to aspects of negative, as compared to positive possible selves (Allen, Woodfolk, Gara and Apter, 1996). Furthermore, the discrepancy between real and undesired selves is associated with depression and life satisfaction (Ogilvie and Clark, 1992); this was found to be especially true for females. Research with adolescents (Knox et al., 2000) indicated that female adolescents rated their feared possible selves as significantly more likely than boys did. In addition, females feared their feared possible selves more than boys do. No domains of feared selves were related to male global self-esteem. Results suggested that it may be girls' feared possible selves, for example regarding interpersonal functioning (which was mentioned most frequently by girls) or physical appearance (which was highly, negatively correlated with self-esteem scores) that produce disturbances in self-esteem and mood that some adolescent girls have been observed to experience during this developmental stage.

Together, these findings may indicate that feared possible selves are less salient for males. Alternatively, males may be less likely to report feared possible selves. This hypothesis is supported by past research indicating that men are less willing to disclose negative emotions including fear (Snell, Miller, Belk, Garcia-Falconi and Hernandez-Sanchez, 1989). This may be a result of gender-role socialization; that is, socialization by parents, the media and important others may prohibit males from disclosing feelings or self-views that might be construed as suggestive of weakness or limited power. Whether males have less elaborated possible selves, whether possible selves, and in particular feared possible selves, are less germane to males' well-being, whether aspects of feared selves might explain gender differences in self-esteem and depression, and whether gender differences exist in the likelihood of disclosure of possible selves are all important questions for future research.

SUMMARY

The concept of possible selves was introduced fairly recently and research addressing gender-related aspects of possible selves is emerging but scarce. However, improved understanding of males' and females' possible selves has the potential to explain the influence of gender on self-views, self-esteem, life satisfaction, achievement, occupation, mood, health, delinquency, aggression and perhaps an array of other domains of functioning. Males and females appear to develop and maintain self-esteem and perhaps other related aspects of well-being in somewhat disparate ways. Females may be more likely than males to incorporate the views of others or representations of others in forming possible selves, and in determining self-worth. Males' possible selves may serve to define them as unique and separate them from others. This difference may be in part developmentally determined and less pronounced during adolescence, however. Gender roles may limit the possible selves that females and males develop, and this may result in a constricted range of behaviors and aspirations, and attenuated achievement and occupational functioning in areas traditionally characteristic of the opposite gender. Contrasting possible selves may be problematic for both genders, and particularly for females who may be more distressed when perceiving opposing self-attributes. In some cases, the incorporation of gender norms into possible selves may be protective, for example, in decreasing the likelihood of involvement in aggression and delinquency. Possible selves related to perceived attractiveness may be particularly problematic for females, particularly those in cultures that emphasize excessive standards for female beauty. Lastly, possible selves, and particularly feared possible selves may be more closely related to the self-views of females.

Each of these conclusions is admittedly speculative, and much more research is needed to better understand the influence of gender on the development, characteristics, influence, and applicability of possible selves. Nevertheless, improved understanding of possible selves will provide insight into an multiple domains of human functioning. Kknowledge of how gender-related norms, expectations and socialization influence the development of possible selves, and in turn how those possible selves influence mood, motivation, behavior, and cognition, may prove to be extremely useful in treatment settings.

REFERENCES

Allen, L., Woolfold, R. L., Gara, M., and Apter, J. (1996). Possible selves in major depression. *Journal of Nervous and Mental Disease, 184*, 739-745.

Allgood-Merten, B., Lewinsohn, P. M. and Hops, H. (1990). Sex differences and adolescent depression. *Journal of Abnormal Psychology, 99*. 55-63.

Alpert-Gillis, L. and Connell, J. P. (1989). Gender and sex role influences on children's self-esteem. *Journal of Personality, 57*, 97-114.

American Association of University Women Educational Foundation. *The AAUW Report: How Schools Shortchange Girls*. Washington, DC: The AAUW Educational Foundation and National Educational Association, 1992.

Anderson, C. A., and Bushman, B. J. (2002). Psychology: The effects of media violence on society. *Science, 295*, 2468-2471.

Baum, K., Whitsell, N. R., and Harter, S. (1999, April). Young adolescents' current views about sex-role stereotypes. Poster presentation at the Society for Research in Child Development meeting, Albuquerque, NM.

Bianchi, S. M., Milkie, M. A., Sayer, L. C., and Robinson, J. P. (2000). Is anyone doing the housework? Trends in the gender division of household labor. *Social Forces, 79*(1), 191-229.

Block, J. (1983). Differential premises arising from differential socialization of the sexes: Some conjectures. *Child Development, 54*, 1335-1354.

Block, J., and Robins, R. W. (1993). A longitudinal study of consistency and change in self-esteem from early adolescence to early adulthood. *Child Development, 64*, 909-923.

Bruch, H. (1988). Treatment in anorexia nervosa. *International Journal of Psychotherapy, 9*, 303-312.

Byrne, B., and Shavelson, R. (1987). Adolescent self-concept: Testing the assumption of equivalent structure across gender. *American Educational Research Journal, 24*, 365-385.

Campbell, A., Sapochnik, M., and Muncer, S. (1997). Sex differences in aggression: Does social representation mediate form aggression? *British Journal of Social Psychology, 36*, 161-171.

Carver, C., Reynolds, S. and Scheier, M. (1994). The possible selves of optimists and pessimists. *Journal of Research on Personality, 28*, 133-141.

Chalk, L. M., Meara, N. M., and Day, J. D. (1994 Fall). Possible selves and occupational choices. *Journal of Career Assessment, 2*(4), 364-383.

Cross, S. E., and Madson, L. (1997). Models of the self: Self-construals and gender. *Psychological Bulletin, 122*(1), 5-37.

Cross, S. and Markus, H. (1991). Possible selves across the lifespan. *Human Development, 34*, 230-255.

Curry, C., Trew, K., Turner, I., and Hunter, J. (1994). The effect of life domains on girls' possible selves. *Adolescence, 29*(113), 133-150.

Demo, D. H., Small, S. A. and Savin-Williams, R. C. (1987). Family relations and the self-esteem of adolescents and their parents. *Journal of Marriage and the Family, 49*, 705-715.

Dusek, J. B., and Flaherty, J. F. (1981). The development of self-concept during the adolescent years. *Monographs of the society for research in child development, 46*, 45-62.

Eccles, J. S. , Adler, T, and Meece, J. L. (1984). Sex differences in achievement: A test of alternate theories. *Journal of Personality and Social Psychology, 46*, 26-43.

Eccles, J. S., Jacobs, J. E., and Harold, R. (1990). Gender role stereotypes, expectancy effects, and parents' socialization of gender differences. *Journal of Social Issues, 46*, 183-201.

Ford, T. E., Stevenson, P. R., Wienir, P. L., and Wait, R. F. (2002 June). The role of internalization of gender norms in regulating self-evaluation in response to anticipated delinquency. *Social Psychology Quarterly, 65*(2), 202-212.

Gilligan, C. (1982). *In a different voice: Psychological theory and women's development.* Cambridge, MA: Harvard University Press.

Goethals, G., Messick, D. M., and Allison, S. T. (1991). *The uniqueness bias: Studies of constructive social comparison.* In J. Suls and TA Wills (Eds.), Social comparison: Contemporary theory and research (pp. 149-176). Hillsddale, NJ: Erlbaum.

Gorman-Smith, D., and Tolan, P. (1998). The role of exposure to community violence and developmental problems among inner-city youth. *Development and Psychopathology, 10*, 101-116.

Hagborg, W. J. (1993). Gender differences in Harter's Self-Perception Profile for Adolescents. *Journal of Social Behavior and Personality, 8*, 141-148.

Harris, S. M. (1995). Psychological development and black male masculinity: Implications for counseling economically disadvantaged African American male adolescents. *Journal of Counseling and Development, 73*(3), 279-287.

Harter, S. (1985). Processes in the formation, maintenance, and enhancement of the self-concept. In J. Suls and A. Greenwald (Eds.), *Psychological perspectives on the self* (Vol. 3, pp. 137-181). Hillsdale, NJ: Lawrence Erlbaum.

Harter, S. (1988). Developmental and dynamic changes in the nature of the self-concept: Implications for child psychotherapy. In S. Shirk (Ed.), *Cognitive development and child psychotherapy* (pp. 119-160). New York: Plenum Press.

Harter, S. (1990). Self and identity development. In S. S. Feldman, and G. R. Elliott (Eds.), *At the threshold: The developing adolescent* (pp. 352-387). Cambridge, MA: Harvard University Press.

Harter, S., and Monsour, A. (1992). Developmental analysis of conflict caused by opposing attributes in the adolescent self-portrait. *Developmental Psychology, 28*, 1-10.

Heimer, K. (1996). Gender, interaction, and delinquency: Testing a theory of differential social control. *Social Psychology Quarterly, 59*, 39-61.

Higgins, E. T. (1987). Self-discrepancy: A theory relating self and affect. *Psychological Review, 94*, 319-340.

Honora, D. T. (2002). The relationship of gender and achievement to future outlook among African American adolescents. *Adolescence, 37*(146), 301-316.

Hooker, K., Fiese, B. H., Jenkins, L., Morfie, M. Z., and Schwagler, J. (1996). Possible selves among parents of infants and preschoolers. *Developmental Psychology, 32*, 542-550.

Jordan, J. V., Kaplan, A. G., Miller, J. B., Stiver, I. P., and Surrey, J. L. (1991). *Women's growth in connection*. New York: Guilford Press.

Josephs, R., Markus, H., and Tafarodi, R. (1992). Gender and self-esteem. *Journal of Personality and Social Psychology, 63*, 391-402.

Kalakoski, V., and Nurmi, J-E. (1998). Identity and educational transitions: Age differences in adolescent exploration and commitment related to education, occupation, and family. *Journal of Research on Adolescent, 8*(1), 29-47.

Katz, P., and Boswell, S. (1986). Flexibility and traditionality in children's gender roles. *Genetic, Social, and General Psychology Monographs, 112*, 105-147.

Kemmelmeier, M., and Oyserman, D. (2001). Gender influence of downward social comparisons on current and possible selves. *Journal of Social Issues, 57*(1), 129-148.

Kerpelman, J. L., Shoffner, M. F., and Ross-Griffin, S. (2002). African American mothers' and daughters' beliefs about possible selves and their strategies for reaching the adolescents' future academic and career goals. *Journal of Youth and Adolescence, 31*(4), 289-302.

Knox, M., Carey, M., Kim, W and Marciniak, T. (in press). Exposure to violence and aggressive behavior in youth with psychiatric disturbances. *New Research in Mental Health, 15.*

Knox, M., Funk, J., Elliott, R., and Greene Bush, E. (1998). Adolescents' possible selves and their relationship to global self-esteem. *Sex Roles, 39*, 61-80.

Knox, M., Funk, J., Elliott, R., and Greene Bush, E. (2000). Gender differences in adolescents' possible selves. *Youth and Society, 31*(3), 287-309.

Knox, M., King, C., Hanna, G. L., Logan, D., and Ghaziuddin, N. (2000). Aggressive behavior in clinically depressed adolescents. *Journal of the American Academy of Child and Adolescent Psychiatry, 39*, 611-618.

Lavitt, M. R. (1992). The influence of gender on the self-perception of disturbed children. *Child and Adolescent Social Work Journal, 9*, 221-237.

Linehan, M. (1993). *Cognitive-behavioral treatment of borderline personality disorder*. New York: Guilford Publications, Inc.

Markus, H. R., and Kitayama, S. (1991). Culture and the self: Implications for cognition, emotion, and motivation. *Psychological Review, 98*, 224-253.

Markus, H., and Nurius, P. (1986). Possible selves. *American Psychologist, 41*(9), 954-969.

Markus, H., and Oyserman, D. (1989). Gender and thought: The role of the self-concept. In M. Crawford, and M. Gentry (Eds.), *Gender and thought: Psychological perspectives*. New York: Springer-Verlag.

Markus, H., and Ruvolo, A. (1989). Possible selves: Personalized representations of goals. In L. A. Pervin (Ed.), *Goal concepts in personality and social psychology* (pp. 211-241). Hillsdale, NJ: Lawrence Erlbaum.

Marsh, H. W., Byrne, B. M., and Shavelson, R .J. (1992). A multidimensional, hierarchical self-concept. *The self: Definitional and methodological issues*. Albany, New York: State University of New York Press.

Morfei, M. Z., Hooker, K., Fiese, B. H., and Cordeiro, A. M. (2001). Continuity and change in parenting possible selves: A longitudinal follow-up. *Basic and Applied Social Psychology, 23*, 217-223.

Nicholls, J. G., Licht, B. G., and Pearls, R. A. (1982). Some dangers of using personality questionnaires to study personality. *Psychological Bulletin, 92*, 572-580.

Ogilvie, D. M. (1987). The undesired self: A neglected variable in personality research. *Journal of Personality and Social Psychology, 52*, 379-385.

Ogilvie, D. M., and Clark, M. D. (1992). The best and worst of it: Age and sex differences in self-discrepancy research. In R. P. Lipka, and T. M. Brinthaupt (Eds.), *Self-perspectives across the lifespan*. Albany, New York: State University of New York Press

Orenstein, P. (1994). *School girls*. New York: Doubleday.

Oyserman, D., and Markus, H.R. (1990). Possible selves and delinquency. *Journal of Personality and Social Psychology, 59*, 112-135.

Richman, C., Clark, M., and Brown, K. (1985). General and specific self-esteem in late adolescent students: Race X gender X SES effects. *Adolescence, 79*, 555-566.

Ruble, D., and Martin, C. L. (1998). Gender Development. In: W. Damon, and N. Eisenberg (Eds.), *Handbook of Child Psychology: Volume 3, Social Emotional and Personality Development*. (pp. 933-1016); New York: Wiley.

Sadker, M., and Sadker, D. (1994). *Failing at fairness: How America's schools cheat girls*. New York: Macmillan Publishing Company.

Salmela-Aro, K., Nurmi, J-E, Saisto, T., and Halmesmaeki, E. (2000). Women's and men's personal goals during the transition to parenthood. *Journal of Family Psychology, 14*, 171-186.

Segal, H. G., DeMeis, D. K., Wood, G. A., and Smith, H. L. (2001). Assessing future possible selves by gender and socioeconomic status using the anticipated life history measure. *Journal of Personality, 61*(1), 57-87.

Simmons, R. G., and Rosenberg, F. (1975). Sex, sex roles, and self-image. *Journal of Youth and Adolescence, 4*, 229-258.

Smith, S. L, Nathanson, A. I., and Wilson, B. J. (2002. Prime-time television: Assessing violence during the most popular viewing hours. *Journal of Communication, 52*(1), 84-111.

Snell, W. E., Miller, R. S., Belk, S. S., Garcia-Falconi, R., and Hernandez-Sanchez, J. E. (1989). Men's and women's emotional disclosures: The impact of disclosure recipients, culture, and the masculine role. *Sex Roles, 21*, 467-486.

Thornton, B., and Ryckman, R. M. (1991). Relationship between physical attractiveness, physical effectiveness, and self-esteem: A cross sectional analysis among adolescents. *Journal of Adolescence, 14*, 85-98.

Tardiff, K., Narzuk, P. M., Leon, A. C., Portera, L., and Weiner, C. (1997). Violence in patients admitted to a private psychiatric hospital. *American Journal of Psychiatry, 154*, 88-93.

Ventura, M. (1998, December). Warrior women. *Psychology Today*

Walker, L. S., and Greene, J. W. (1986). The social context of adolescent self-esteem. *Journal of Youth and Adolescence, 15*, 315-322.

Wilson, R., and Cairns, E. (1988). Sex-role attributes, perceived competence and the development of depression in adolescence. *Journal of Child Psychiatry and Psychology, 29*, 635-650.

Wolf, N. (1991). *The beauty myth: How images of beauty are used against women.* New York: Doubleday.

Wylie, R. C. (1974). *The self-concept.* Lincoln, Nebraska: University of Nebraska Press.

In: Possible Selves: Theory, Research and Application
Editors: C. Dunkel and J. Kerpelman, pp. 79-96

ISBN 1-59454-431-X
© 2006 Nova Science Publishers, Inc.

Chapter 5

POSSIBLE SELVES, FANTASY DISTORTION, AND THE ANTICIPATED LIFE HISTORY: EXPLORING THE ROLE OF THE IMAGINATION IN SOCIAL COGNITION

Harry G. Segal
Cornell University

ABSTRACT

An alternative approach to assessing possible selves is introduced, the Anticipated Life History (ALH), which prompts 18 year old participants to describe in realistic, plausible terms, the course of their future lives from their 21st birthday to their death. The ALH narratives are coded for social cognitive qualities (*psychological complexity, life role complexity, mutuality of relationships, resolution of conflicts,* and *altruism*) as well as projective qualities (*narrative integrity, depression, fantasy distortion, impulsivity,* and *malevolence*). A sample of 409 participants completed the ALH as well as an extensive battery of convergent instruments assessing mood, quality of life satisfaction, life event history and early memories. This database has produced series of studies examining the impact of early experience, gender, social class and current mood on the imagining of future possible selves (Segal, DeMeis, Wood, and Smith, 2001; Segal, Wood, DeMeis, and Smith, 2003). In this chapter, the ALH database is used to explore the reliance on fantasy in the construction of future possible selves. Those participants who wrote future life narratives filled with fantasy elements tended to be more depressed, less satisfied with the qualities of their lives, yet reported "earliest" memories with lower negative scores than those whose ALH narratives were more realistic. The chapter ends with a discussion of the implications of these findings for possible selves as well as for research into the imagination and the creative process.

The contents of an individual's possible selves are frequently hidden and protected from the scrutiny of others, if not from their influence and they represent the creative productive efforts of the self-system. … For this reason, positive possible selves can be exceedingly liberating because they foster hope that the present self is not immutable. At the same time, negative possible selves can be powerfully imprisoning because their associated affect and expectations may stifle attempts to change or develop. Positive and negative possible selves are alike, however, in that they often make it difficult for an observer to fully understand another person's behavior.

                                                    -- Markus and Nurius explaining possible selves to us (1986)

        Get thee to a nunnery. Why, wouldst thou be a breeder of sinners? I am myself indifferent honest, but yet I could accuse me of such things that it were better my mother had not borne me. I am very proud, revengeful, ambitious, with more offences at my beck than I have thoughts to put them in, imagination to give them shape, or time to act them in. What should such fellows as I do crawling between heaven and earth?

                                    -- Hamlet explaining his possible selves to Ophelia (Act 3, scene I)

TWO REVOLUTIONS IN THE ASSESSMENT OF THE SELF

When Hazel Markus and Paula Nurius published their seminal article on possible selves in the *American Psychologist* (Markus and Nurius, 1986), they pointed out an important contradiction between the theory and measurement of the self-concept. After citing various theorists who describe the self-concept as a dynamic and complex construct, they argue that "most self-concept inventories ask, in effect, who you are *now*, but they do not inquire who you want to be, or who you are afraid of becoming." For them, the self-concept "is a more expansive phenomenon" than the self-attributions measured by questionnaires because it "extends its reach deeper in time ... [and] reflects the potential for growth and change" (957). They went on to match their insight with an ingeniously straightforward method to measure the impact of future possible selves on current self-esteem, mood, and hopefulness, and by doing so made good their claim to demonstrate empirically both the presence and impact of future possible selves on participants' self-esteem, mood, and degree of hopefulness.

What they were careful *not* to emphasize was that they were, essentially, adding fantasy to the self-concept; they preferred, throughout the article, to refer to *hopes, wishes, future planning* and their links to current self-esteem and motivations. And yet it is the integrating of fantasy with the self-concept construct which marks their work as truly innovative. Why minimize the use of the word *fantasy*? (Indeed, they only use it once in their entire article.) When they were conducting their research, fantasy was essentially "owned" by the psychodynamic theorists. At that time, adding fantasy explicitly to a psychological instrument would, by implication, mean trespassing on the forbidden region of projective tests, the bastion of psychodynamic clinical psychologists, who for many years had simply claimed the validity of the TAT and the Rorschach by asserting their clinical insight and characterizing the projective material as "derivatives" of erotic or aggressive drives. Personality and social psychologists, having rejected psychodynamic models as unverifiable myths, had turned to the experimental work of cognitive psychologists who had been identifying mental processes in the laboratory, such as schema development, memory retrieval, and cognitive priming. It was the cognitive research proving that children develop schemas for categories – *collies*, for example, as a belonging to the larger schema of *dogs* (Gelman, 1986) – which led to the notion of a self-concept or, more specifically, a self-schema, which contains the attributes and traits of the self. By the rejecting the psychodynamic model, particularly the notion of unconscious processes, researchers were content to test and observe the way their participants *consciously* described themselves with trait measures or other self-report instruments. Although this was an important foundation, the self-concept was doomed to simplicity when its theorists left out the workings and effects of fantasizing – something all human beings do every single day of their lives.

Like the proverbial saying that only someone with Nixon's cold warrior pedigree could have opened the door to China, so Hazel Markus was one of a handful of researchers with the credentials to bring the imagination to the self-concept. Having established herself in the early 1980s as an expert on self-knowledge and gender roles, her subsequent work on self-schemas, in particular her assertion that the self-schema has unconscious effects on judgment and perfection, were not only bold challenges to the prevailing intellectual climate but also ten years prescient. Her work easily anticipated and lay the groundwork for the current research on "implicit" and "nonconscious" processes developed by Bargh and others, who have shown how the mind uses shortcuts, is primed by perception and subliminal processes, and is determined by early experience and significant others (Bargh and Chartrand, 1999; Bargh, Gollwitzer, Lee Chai, and Barndollar, 2001; Berk and Andersen, 2000)

I began graduate training in clinical psychology at the University of Michigan in 1986, the year Hazel Markus published her possible selves paper. She was then a member of the Michigan psychology department, but the clinical track remained quite separate from the other subfields because it was then primarily psychoanalytic – when I arrived a two-year Rorschach sequence had just been dropped from the curriculum – and there was little empirical or experimental literature to be found on our syllabi. But despite the emphasis on object relations theory, long-term therapy, and qualitative research, our training using projective techniques was judicious and measured. Unlike clinicians who claimed a kind of clairvoyance from their reading of Rorschach protocols, our supervisors insisted that we let the projective material shape our clinical hypotheses, rather than impose a theoretical or fanciful narrative coming from our own associations. In other words, we were taught not to *project* onto the *projections* of our patients. Nonetheless, the use of projective material -- such as the Rorschach, TAT, sentence completions or early memories -- was under attack by experimentalists for being subjectively interpreted without any standards for reliability or validity. (Indeed, projective measures were being dropped from the curriculum of mainstream clinical programs.)

As a response to these attacks, a second revolution started, a mirror image of the one Hazel Markus began. At the same time and, as it turns out, at the same University, Drew Westen was developing an empirical method for scoring and analyzing projective material, primarily the TAT. He defined specific psychological qualities to be measured, developed scoring rules for assessing them, and achieved rigorous inter-rater reliability for well-trained coders. The result was the Social Cognition and Object Relations scoring system which proved to be sensitive to diagnostic categories – TAT narratives scored by coders unaware of diagnostic groups distinguished patients with borderline personality disorder from depressive patients and normal comparisons (Westen, 1990). Of course, researchers at other universities were working on their own approaches to empirical validation of projective techniques (McAdams, Hoffman, Mansfield, and Day, 1996; McClelland, Koestner, and Weinberger, 1989; Woike, 1994), nevertheless it is a remarkable coincidence that in 1986 at the University of Michigan two complementary projects were restoring breadth to their respective disciplines. Markus was ushering fantasy and projections into the empirical measuring of social cognition, while Westen was bringing the empirical methods of social cognition to the practice and study of projective material.

This was an exciting time. As a graduate student with a background in literary theory, I was developing with Westen a scoring system for stories told to the Picture Arrangement subtest of the WAIS-R, while going to lectures by Hazel Markus on possible selves or Nancy Cantor on defensive pessimism. It seemed that social psychology was taking on the subtlety of psychodynamic process, while clinical psychology was taking on the rigor of social psychology. While neither side overtly recognized the other, a genuine integration was taking place. For their contribution to our understanding of the self, Markus and Nurius essentially married a social-cognitive instrument with a projective. Future possible selves are fantasy tempered by expectation (or expectations leavened by fantasy) and so, conceptually, eliciting them invokes two central actions of mental life: The social cognitive act of future planning with the equally human act of generating fantasy.

THE INVISIBLE PROCESS OF FANTASY AND ITS ROLE IN DEVELOPMENT

Future planning is not too difficult to understand, but what *is* the act of creating a fantasy? How does it work cognitively? Leaving out drive theory, psychodynamic clinicians would argue that people's fantasies express wishes and fears -- some masked, others overt -- but all created by a process similar to, but not identical with, dreaming. [1] Although this may be true, it is statement more about the content of fantasy rather than about the process of generating it.

To begin afresh, let us compare two different requests. If someone were to ask you to describe the house of your childhood, you could easily describe the mental steps you took to oblige them: first you visualized the house from the sidewalk, then the first floor – the kitchen, living room and back porch, before moving upstairs to your room. If asked to describe the neighborhood, you could easily recall the houses on either side as well as the cultural ethos of the block. However, if someone were to ask you to make up a story about a 35 year old lawyer, man or woman, you might follow your first associations and say that *the lawyer is a man, unmarried, who is carrying a bottle of scotch in a paper bag up to his apartment door, an apartment in Chelsea that he pays too much for but which has, until recently, made him feel quite happy.* Here's the point: you would have no idea how or why this particular association came to mind. To use current theoretical terms, by agreeing to make up the story you initiated an implicit process, that is a set of "non-conscious" mental acts, that resulted in a fictional character, his motivation, an imagined world, none of which you consciously chose or designed. Although you can take that material and then shape it into a short story, it nevertheless emerged outside of your conscious control. Most of the instances of implicit processes – primed perceptions or reliance on heuristics – occur without our being aware of them. Fantasy, by contrast, is one of the few implicit process that we can consciously initiate; we direct our minds to create a fantasy, but once that direction has been

---

[1] One theorist, Rothenberg (1982) took this one step further, arguing that the creative process lies in taking dream material and decoding it – his data consisted of one-on-one sessions with poets as they brought in dream or dreamlike material and refined it into a poem. He termed his model "dreamwork in reverse."

given, we're out of the loop until it arrives full-blown, like Athena from the head of Zeus (a myth that may represent the implicit process I've described).

Not only is the act of generating fantasy one that is universal yet mysterious, but in our early childhood we learn to do it in every way possible, from transitional objects and imaginary friends to action figures, dolls, and fantasies about characters from books and television. I've argued elsewhere that what was once called "pre-latency," ages 2-7, is the *projective phase* of development – it is a time when fantasy is the dominant cognitive mode (Segal, 2003). As developmentalists note, the hallmark of these years is the primacy of play (Corrigan, 1982; Fenson, 1986). This richness of the child's inner world is universally recognized, but what is less obvious to most is that children use play to express feelings, to take symbolic risks, and to resolve conflicts. Child therapists' term for this is *projection* -- children project onto stuffed animals and action figures their feelings, thoughts, wishes and fears – and in doing so, reveal their inner experience which they cannot directly put into words, primarily because they don't yet have the cognitive capacity to do so (Bromfield, 1997).

The projective phase ends because children achieve a greater cognitive complexity which allows them to assemble self-schemata strongly influenced by their family's cultural, social, and moral values. The earlier "projective" mode of consciousness is gradually superseded by self-attribution, objective judgment, and the capacity for abstract thought. I call this the *social-cognitive phase*, and it coincides with important changes in neurological and cognitive functioning. Researchers across disciplines note the sudden leap in abilities at this age: Psychoanalysts call it "latency," Piagetians call it "concrete operations," sociologists note that children begin to exclude others for the social reasons by the time they are in second grade – a dramatic change from kindergarten where peer rejection is virtually absent. But because social-cognitive judgment is powerfully influenced by social and cultural expectations, it necessarily involves censoring some of the wishes, fears, feelings, and thoughts that were so spontaneously projected when the child was young. It may leave people believing things about themselves that are socially acceptable, but which are not true. This accounts for the kinds of biases and distortions found in self-judgment by social psychologists (for a recent example, see Kruger and Dunning, 1999) or in the difficulties gay teenagers have recognizing their desires on the way to coming out (Savin-Williams, 1996).

Of course, the projective way of thinking is not replaced by social cognition. We are always ready to project. When you "suspend" your disbelief while watching a movie or reading a novel you are, in essence, returning to the projective mode (Singer, 1998; Harris and Beggan, 1994). Similarly, intense emotional states, such as falling in love or feeling intense rage, often compel a return to the projective mode through unavoidable daydreams or fantasies. Finally, severe personality disturbance – such as borderline personality disorder – is often marked by a person's inability to refrain from falling into the projective mode and ascribing implausible and idiosyncratic interpretations to interpersonal events (e.g., Gunderson, 1984). Indeed, psychotherapy may be reconceived as helping patients to regain an adaptive *balance* between these two modes of consciousness, avoiding the flood of projecting on the one hand and over-intellectualizing on the other.

Since both modes of consciousness are available to adults, it might be useful to consider self-report and norm-based psychological instruments as designed to measure social-cognitive awareness. Conversely, projective instruments measure spontaneously generated associations – that is, they measure fantasy, the most common expression of the projective phase. If you accept this idea, then what Markus and Nurius accomplished can be seen in a different light: They found a way to measure the role of fantasy *within* the self-concept. In other words, they created a method to measure quantitatively the projective aspects of the self, the social-cognitive aspects of the self, as well as the impact of their interaction. For example, they found that their participants' self-esteem was significantly lower if they believed that their feared possible selves would come true; that is, an anxious fantasy about the future changed the way these young adults objectively valued their traits and qualities.

THE ANTICIPATED LIFE HISTORY: AN ALTERNATIVE APPROACH TO POSSIBLE SELVES

Although the possible selves method had accomplished the feat of integrating projective and self-report techniques in one measure, the one element it lacked was narrative. Their approach did not ask participants to describe the development of the possible selves as they unfold in time. Partly as a response to this, I developed a hybrid measure that explicitly draws from projective technique and social-cognitive research and provides an alternate way to assess possible selves. Eighteen-year old respondents are asked to write a narrative describing the course of their future life, from their 21st birthday until their death, and they are told specifically *not* to imagine an idealized life but one they plausibly expect to live. This instrument, the Anticipated Life History (ALH), challenges young adults to integrate fantasy and reality in their future life stories. Consider it: They must objectively assess their strengths, their economic resources, the likelihood of reaching their goals – all of which requires social cognitive reasoning -- while allowing themselves to dream up their future with all of the excitement and anxiety such fantasies evoke. The ALH narratives are scored for social cognitive qualities *and* projective qualities, as well as for future life events such as marriage, children, and professional accomplishments. Finally, to study the cognitive-affective processes influencing the writing of the ALH, participants complete a battery of instruments and structured interviews measuring early life events, early parental memories, socio-economic status, family demographics, psychiatric history, current depression levels, quality of life satisfaction, and an estimate of I.Q. Currently our research team has recruited and tested more than 400 subjects drawn from several sites including a private liberal arts college, a rural community college, a rural high school senior class, and several university and college counseling centers.[2] Aside from the validation studies listed below, the ALH has also been used to look at the way familial and adolescent substance abuse affect future life expectations (Segal, Frantz, and Mapstone, 2003), as well as at the relationships between adult children and their parents (Segal, 2003).

My colleagues and I devised a detailed scoring manual for coding ALH narratives for projective and social cognitive qualities (Segal, DeMeis, and Wood, 1997) which includes training procedures for establishing scorer reliability and provides coders with detailed rules for scoring on a 4-point scale, from little or no presence of the quality to pervasive presence of the quality. The clinical scales, which measure *projective* qualities, were designed to gauge the integrity and coherence of the participants' thinking (*Narrative Integrity*), their mood and

---

[2] NIMH R0355498 made possible the recruitment and testing of 275 participants.

self-esteem *(Depression)*, the degree to which they impose fantasies on their future even when asked to write a realistic one *(Fantasy Distortion)*, deficits in self-regulation which leads to risky behaviors *(Impulsivity)*, and the quality of their interpersonal expectations *(Malevolence)*. For validation data, see (Segal, Wood, DeMeis, and Smith, 2003). The *social cognitive - possible selves* scales were designed to gauge participants' awareness of their self-concept as well as the qualities of others *(Psychological Complexity)*, their sense of the social demands of adult developmental stages *(Life Role Complexity)*, the quality of their imagined future interpersonal relations *(Resolution of Conflicts* and *Mutuality of Relationships)*, and their projected commitment to family and community (Altruism) For validation data, see (Segal, DeMeis, Wood, and Smith, 2001). Figure 1 presents a brief synopsis of each scale.

Scales	Principles
	Social Cognitive
Psychological Complexity	The degree to which the subject understands him or herself and others, including tolerance of positive and negative qualities; self-awareness and psychological functioning improve over time.
Life Role Complexity	The degree to which the subject understands him or herself and others, including tolerance of positive and negative qualities; self-awareness and psychological functioning improve over time
Mutuality of Relationships	The degree to which relationships are depicted as mutual, where individuals make compromises and where family relations involve reciprocity
Resolution of Conflicts	The degree to which the subject anticipates conflicts and imagines their resolutions.
Altruism	The degree to which subjects intend to perform selfless acts for their family or for society at large. The degree to which subjects intend to perform selfless acts for their family or for society at large. General intentions andspecific plans are scored.
	Clinical Features
Narrative Integrity	The degree to which the narrative is coherent, progresses logically, and is easily understood, regardless of content.
Depression	The degree to which depression colors the ALH. Sadness, low-self-esteem, hopelessness and early deaths are scored
Fantasy Distortion	The degree to which the ALH resembles fiction, dreams, or movies, rather than a plausible account of one's future
Impulsivity	The degree to which impulsive acts are found in the ALH. These include substance abuse, rage attacks, and reckless behavior
Malevolence	The degree to which the narrator intends, enacts, or expects physical or psychological malevolent actions

Figure 1 ALH Scoring Categories

Here are two sample ALH narratives, with scores and their justification

s for *clinical* and *social cognitive - possible selves* features.

ALH 1 – Clinical Scores

After graduating from [college] I plan to go on to graduate school, where I will major in biology and minor in psychology. The university of B------ is the school I will choose to further my education at, and it is where I will meet my future husband by the name of Rob. (my favorite name) He and I will first see each other in our biology class and coincidently become lab partners. From there we become close friends and that in turn develops into a very romantic relationship. We both graduate from B_____ after two years - with our masters. Rob gets a job in G------, working as a Biology teacher at G------ High School. I, myself go on in my education and receive an MD from the University of R------. I then get a job at G------General Hospital, where I am an Emergency Room doctor. I am 26 years old, and so is Rob. My (27th) birthday, March 25, 2002, Rob proposes to me and we get married on Valentines Day the following year. (Feb 14, 2003) We are both very happy and believe that we have a lot to offer, so we decide to have children. On Jan. 4, 2004 our first son is born by the name of Zachary and only a year after on Jan. 31, 2005 our daughter Allie is born. Everything goes well for the first 5 years - Rob gets tenure, I get a raise, the kids are growing up well, we have a nice house on the lake, two nice cars - even a great St. Bernard dog, named Bo - who the kids adore.

Then suddenly one day - another woman called the house for Rob. I didn't get paranoid, she was probably just a friend. Her name was Reneé. I gave him the message when he got home from working out at the YMCA. It was a Thursday night. He blew it off, saying he had no idea who she was. I had forgotten about it after awhile, until my best friend Karen told me she thought that she saw Rob and some young girl eating dinner at an exquisite restaurant in R_____. Karen lives there. When I confronted Rob with this -I knew it was true. I can always tell when a man [is] lying. So I kicked him out at the age of 33. (My salary was enough for me to provide for the children and myself) and filed for a divorce. 6 months later Rob remarried - to Reneé, the high school English teacher. He got nothing from the divorce except weekend visitation rights to see our kids.

At the age of 37, I finally meet the right guy. His name is Chris, and he is the neurologist at our local hospital. My kids love him - he has wit, a great sense of humor, compassion, and I believe he is trustworthy. We get married in July of 2013. This marriage will last.

Ten years down the road, Chris and I are still happily married, the kids are in college on full scholarships. We are very proud of both of them. Zach is a sophomore and Allie is a first year student. We are all happy until one day Chris has a heart attack at the age of 51. Unfortunately it was too bad to save him. He died in the ambulance on the way to the hospital. I was devastated. I had to see a psychiatrist for two years and even after that I was never truly myself again.

Then my day came. After fighting ovarian cancer for 5 years, I died at the age of 56. The date was November 23, 2031. I donated my body to science.

Luckily - for me, I died before my mother, father and siblings. I didn't have to experience that type of grief in my life - except for the death of my grandmother and grandfather in 2010. My grandmother died of cancer less than 6 months before my grandfather died of the same thing. I guess I know who I inherited the gene from.

Narrative Integrity: This ALH scores a "4" because it well structured, develops clearly, and holds together well as a story.

Depression: This ALH scores a "4" because of the husband's betrayal, her second husband's early death, her own depression after his death (and was "never truly herself again"), as well as her own premature death to cancer.

Fantasy Distortion: This ALH scores a "4" because of the participant's extreme use of fantasy, even though the task required that she only write a plausible life, not an idealized or fantasied one.

Impulsivity: This scores a "1" because of a lack of impulse behavior.

Malevolence: This scores a "2" because of the first husband's betrayal of the narrator.

When I graduate I will go on to graduate school. Possibly Harvard or somewhere in England. Where ever it is it will be a prestigious law school. Having majored in Environmental Studies, I will get my law degree and begin to practice law. (At around age 27) Note: It may have taken me more than once to pass the bar. Either I would stay single because I couldn't find someone that would please my dad or I would find a "nice jewish boy" and be a workaholic. I would be good at practicing law. But knowing myself the way I do, I would eventually get bored and want to do something different with my life. So at this point, say age 30-32 I would have 3-4 kids. After that 37-40 I would work on getting back into the fast lane so that I could run for Senate no later than age 45. (To me this is not just an ideal life, but a realistic view of what will occur if I continue doing what I've been doing.) Through the years I will have grown closer to my dad, but we would still fight from time to time. I would live in some little town outside of a major city, such as N.Y. or L.A. I would be a good, firm parent with a tendency to raise my voice a little too much. The friends I'd had since elementary school, I would still be close with. The friends from [college] I doubt it. Craig . . . a present boyfriend would have eventually realized that I was never going to be able to marry him and we would part and go our separate ways. Though I truly think we will still be friends 20 or 30 years from now. Crew -- I got good my junior year . . . But never got way serious about it. Throughout life I continue to have 10-25 pounds to lose depending on the year. I got more responsible about my sexual behavior. And I learned to control my emotions and not react about every little thing.

My temper (unfortunately) stayed with me right until the end. I finally learned to fly and got my pilot's license. My husband would love me intensely with a tendency to be a bit too overprotective. His career would be more successful than mine. I would feel that we were in competition. It would be a constant on going fight.

Though, by the time I'm 45 and running for Senate I will gave grown up a lot. I will still have a certain immaturity (young at heart) that I got from my mother. My kids would be very attractive, though possible I may have had trouble like my mom, in getting pregnant.

I will have stuck to my "no" against drugs motto and my kids will respect me because of it. I will make plenty of money, but I will never be able to hold on to it for very long, because of my generous nature. (Its always getting me into trouble) I will remain extremely close with my sister, S------, but there will be a certain distance between my other sister, my brother and I.

After my running for Senate . . . I would win I think. I would do that until I was appoint[ed] to be a judge. (if ever) I think if stress doesn't kill me first I would die of old age.

I would never take many vacations, sleep would be something quite foreign to me. However, overall, I think I would feel like I'd led a pretty fulfilling life.

Psychological Complexity: This scores a "3" because of the participant's awareness of her psychological qualities, her goals in life, her conflicts with family members, and her sense of how she wants to improve and mature.

Life Role Complexity: This scores a "1" because she doesn't consider how to manage the conflicting responsibilities of parent, spouse, adult child and professional.

Mutuality of Relationships: This scores a "1" because there is minimal mention of reciprocal relationships.

Resolution of Conflicts: This scores a "2" because she enumerates conflicts – with her current boyfriend, her father, her husband – without presenting ways to resolve them.

Altruism: This scores a "2" because of the vague mention of her being generous with money.

ALH PRINCIPAL FINDINGS

Before presenting the principal findings from the ALH Project, here is a description of the participants, the protocol, and how it was administered.

Sample Demographics: Participants were 234 women and 175 men recruited from a private liberal arts college (n=150), a rural community college (n=100), a rural high school senior class (n=60) and first- and second-year students seeking psychotherapy at one of three college counseling centers (n=99). Male and female participants did not differ significantly on the WAIS-R subtests, SES, ethnicity, or quality of life satisfaction. As predicted, they differed on depressive symptoms as determined by the CES-D summary score (see Table 1).

PROCEDURE

Participants from the private college (n=130) responded to the self-report battery in groups of 20 or less. Participants then scheduled an individual session to undergo structured interviews and cognitive tests within 10 days. Fourteen participants who failed to appear for scheduled interviews were excluded from the study. The rest of the sample (n=259) participants completed both the self-report battery and the individual session in one session. The mean age for both men and women, with equal numbers of each recruited from each site, was 18 years old. Participants signed an informed consent, written in accordance with APA guidelines, giving permission for researchers to contact them in four years.

Table 1 Sample Characteristics and Word Count by Gender

	Women	Men
N	232	175
Mean Age	18.3(2.4)	18.6(.8)
SES		
Upper Middle/Upper	58.1%	58.9%
Middle	25.2%	19.9%
Lower Middle/Lower	16.7%	21.2%
CES-D Summary Score*	37.9 (9.9)	35.8 (10.0)
QOLI Summary Score	2.42 (1.5)	2.35 (1.5)
ALH Total Word Count**	453 (169)	412 (155)
ALH Narrative Integrity	3.63 (.54)	3.65 (.54)
ALH Depression	1.46 (.82)	1.53 (.80)
ALH Fantasy Distortion	2.21 (1.12)	2.30 (1.10)
ALH Impulsivity[+]	1.21 (.53)	1.60 (.92)
ALH Malevolence	1.11 (.41)	1.15 (.57)
ALH Psychological Complexity	1.64 (.83)	1.53 (.73)
ALH LifeRole Complexity[++]	1.74 (.78)	1.39 (.62)
ALH Mutuality of Relationships	1.56 (.69)	1.55 (.70)
ALH Resolution of Conflicts[&]	1.50 (.70)	1.36 (.56)
ALH Altruism[&&]	1.49 (.80)	1.29 (.64)

Note. * $t=2.03$ $p=.04$ (2-tailed) **$t=2.06$ $p=.04$ (2-tailed) [+]$t=-5.04$ $p=.0001$ (2-tailed) [++]$t=-4.81$ $p=.0001$ (2-tailed) [&]$t=-2.2$ $p=.03$ (2-tailed) [&&]$t=-2.7$ $p=.008$ (2-tailed)

MEASURES

For the self-report battery, participants began with the ALH which asks them to imagine their entire future life, beginning with their 21st year and ending with their death. Participants are asked to give a *realistic* account of their entire future life as it is *most likely* to occur, and to spend approximately 25 minutes composing it. They also completed a measure developed for this study: a 45-item Life Events Checklist eliciting significant life events and their impact (LEC;(Segal, 1996b)). From the LEC, a composite variable, *negative early life events* (NEGLIFE), was created by summing the presence of negative events from the LEC: parental strife and divorce; parental job loss, substance use or criminal activity; deaths of parents, family members, or close friends; participant serious injury or illness; participant trouble with school or police; participant substance abuse; and participant being shot, wounded, or raped. To assess participants' current mood and satisfaction with their current lives, they completed the Center for Epidemiological Studies Depression Scale (CES-D; (Radloff, 1977)) and the Quality of Life Inventory (QOLI; (Frisch and Retzalaff, 1992)). The CES-D is a 20-item instrument measuring depressive symptoms in the past week in non-clinical populations; higher scores indicate higher levels of depression. The QOLI is a 34-item instrument which measures the participant's satisfaction with, and the importance of, four life domains: self, personal fulfillment, relationships and environment. The QOLI yields individual scores for issues within each domain, such as satisfaction with friends or family, as well as a summary score adding across all items. For the QOLI, higher scores indicate greater satisfaction with life domains.

During the interview session, participants were first administered the Family Demographics and Medical History (FDMH; (Segal, 1996a)), a structured interview developed for this project which collects data on family demographics, composition of family of origin, ethnicity, religious preference, individual medical history, and SES (Hollingshead and Redlich, 1958). Participants were then administered two subtests of the Wechsler Adult Intelligence Scale - Revised (WAIS-R; (Wechsler, 1981)): Vocabulary and Picture Arrangement. Vocabulary subtest scores have been found to correlate with full scale IQ and thus may be used to control statistically ALH scores for intelligence; Picture Arrangement subtest scores measure the degree to which the subject can place narrative elements in a logical order and were used for discriminant validity, since this capacity should be unrelated to mood and interpersonal expectations. They also were administered a modified version of the Early Memory Test (Mayman, 1968) which prompted them for their earliest memory, earliest memory of mother, and earliest memory of father.

Early Memory Coding: Participants provided recollections of their earliest memory, earliest memory of mother, and earliest memory of father. Using the Adelphi Early Memories Index (AEMI; (Karliner and Mayman, 1996)), each memory was double coded on a 5-point scale (with 1=not applicable, 3=somewhat applicable and 5=highly applicable) along the following dimensions with reliability calculated by using Pearson's *r* with Rosenthal correction: Affect tone is positive .82, affect tone is negative .86, others are benevolent .86, others are malevolent .84, subject is confident .85, subject is insecure .87, the memory's outcome is positive .86, the memory's outcome is negative .84, caregivers are abandoning .81.

Once this extensive database was scored and analyzed, the results supported the developmental model of the projective and social-cognitive phases. After coding the ALH narratives for social cognitive qualities, we found that the 18-year-old women were more astute than men about the social aspects of their future lives: They scored higher on Psychological Complexity, Life Role Complexity, and Resolution of Conflicts (Segal et al., 2001). In keeping with this theory that the social cognitive mode supersedes the projective, none of the variables from early childhood – early life events, early memories of father or mother – had any impact on these scores. Even the current mood and quality of life satisfaction scores was divorced from the ways our participants imagined the social and psychological quality of their future lives.

Findings with the clinical scales were nearly the reverse of these. There were no gender differences on any of these measures except for Impulsivity; current mood and quality of life satisfaction correlated with high scores on ALH Depression, Fantasy Distortion, and Malevolence. Most intriguing, though, was the impact of the maternal memories. The participants were asked to describe their earliest memory, earliest of mother, and earliest of father. These memories were then scored for positive and negative qualities on two separate scales using the Adelphi Early Memory Index (Karliner and Mayman, 1996). Positive qualities include joy, excitement, happiness or "coziness"; the memory has a happy ending; the participant remembers feeling well cared for or soothed. Negative qualities include fear, anger, loneliness or physical injury; the memory ends in fear, loss, harm or rage; the participant recalls a sense of being abandoned or abused by the primary caregivers. Each of the three memories is given a positive and negative score, since memories can have good and bad elements. Here is the most striking finding: If the participants had an elevated negative early memory of mother, they were likely to write a narrative high on ALH Depression and Malevolence (Segal, Wood et al., 2003). This was not true for the earliest memory or earliest memory of father, which suggests that the projective coding of the ALH was tapping into the participants' earliest experiences -- in particular, their memories of their mothers.

This finding may hold a key to unraveling the mystery of fantasy production. Since negative memories of mother predicts ALH Depression and Malevolence, it is possible that the act of using one's imagination implicitly evokes early memories which then contribute to the emotional tone, and the content, of the fantasy. Our research team tested this thesis with another measure, the Narrative Completion Test, an assessment instrument prompting participants to add key elements to seven story stems. Using a similar coding system, negative early memories of mother predicted depressive and malevolent features, while positive early memories of mother predicted affiliation. Other researchers have noted the link between projective material and early childhood (Loevinger and Wessler, 1970; Main, Kaplan, and Cassidy, 1985; Nigg and Silk, 1992) though none have specifically proposed that early memories contribute covertly to the use of the imagination.

FANTASY DISTORTION AND THE EARLIEST MEMORY RESULTS

This link between early memories and the act of imagining returns us to research in possible selves. It is well established that the degree to which participants expect their feared or wished for possible selves to come true affects their self-esteem, current mood, and optimism. However, researchers have not tried to quantify the reliance on fantasy that their participants bring to the task. If the model presented in this chapter is correct – that adult functioning depends on a delicate balance between projective and social-cognitive thinking – then those participants who depend too much on fantasy should be functioning at a lower level than those do not. Moreover, it would be useful to see if early memory activation predicts degree of fantasy.

The ALH longitudinal dataset provides an opportunity to test these hypotheses. According to the protocol, each participant is told– while maintaining eye contact with the examiner – not to write an idealized life, but to write a plausible, realistic version of the future. One of the projective scales, Fantasy Distortion, measures the degree to which participants disregard these directions and include specific details, implausible outcomes, and unlikely coincidences (see Figure 1). It was designed to identify those participants who seem to rely on projective phase thinking and, like the other scales, provides a score from a four-point scale, with 1 = no elements of Fantasy Distortion, to 4= the ALH is characterized by Fantasy Distortion. (It is important to note that Fantasy Distortion can lead to both positive and negative fantasies in the future, and that the analyses which follow have covaried for negative future events as coded in each ALH.)

Table 2 Correlations Among Fantasy Distortion and Convergent Measures

Variables	1	2	3	4	5	6	7
ALH Fantasy Distortion		10	15**	08	15*	15**	11*
CES-D Summary Score			-.53***	-.53***	-.33***	-.40***	15*
QOLI Summary Score				.65***	51***	48***	-.10*
QOLI Self-Regard					30***	33***	-.05
QOLI Love Relationships						18**	06
QOLI Friendships							.04
Early Negative Life Events							

Note. *p< .05 ** p< .01 ***p< .001 ****p< .0001

Table 2 shows that FD correlates with self-report depression as measured by the CES-D, and negatively correlates with quality of life satisfaction (Quality of Life Inventory Summary Score), satisfaction with one's self (QOLI Self-Regard), romantic relationships, and friendships. It is also negatively correlated with negative early life events.

Table 3 shows the results of taking a median split of Fantasy Distortion (FD), comparing those whose scored 1 or 2 compared with those scoring 3 or 4. Men and women did not differ on their average FD score (see Table 1). However, those with High FD are less satisfied with their lives generally, with their romantic relationships, with their friendships and with their families.

Given the correlations, a hierarchical regression was generated, with FD as the dependent variable and a series of predictor variables forced out of the model: ALH Word Count, IQ estimate (Vocabulary subtest of the WAIS-R), SES, sex, self-report depression, negative life events, as well as negative and positive early memories.

Table 3 Comparison of Participants Low and High on Fantasy Distortion*

	Low FD	High FD	t	Probability
N	249	148		
Female	149	80		
Male	105	68		
QOLI Summary Score	2.49 (1.5)	2.15 (1.4)	-2.30	.028
QOLI Love	71 (4.2)	1.62 (3.9)	-2.10	.040
QOLI Friendships	3.99 (2.6)	3.42 (3.1)	-1.77	.078
QOLI Family	3.12 (2.9)	3.59 (2.8)	-1.69	.092

Note. Low FD= score of 1 or 2; High FD=score of 3 or 4; all tests are 2-tailed

The results are intriguing. ALH narrative length positively predicts FD – which simply means that longer ALH narratives are likley to contain more details, some of which may reflect the intrusion of fantasy. Estimated IQ negatively predicts FD, suggesting that participants with greater vocabulary, and thus arguably higher intelligence, are better at stemming projections when writing their ALH. But most interesting is the last predictor. After controlling for so many variables, the Negative Earliest Memory score still negatively predicts FD. As a reminder, each of the three memories – earliest memory, earliest memory of mother, earliest memory of father – receive one score for positive features and another score for negative features. And so participants scoring high on FD do *not* have more positive earliest memories; they simply have earliest memories that are less negative.

To check on the strength of this finding, the effective size was calculated as moderate according to Cohen's guidelines (f^2=.21) with a part correlation of -.214. But what if the sample's homogeneity has produced a statistically significant yet spurious findings? After all, our participants are primarily white college students. To counter this possibility, we ran a second hierarchical regression with data our research team has been collecting and analyzing from a population of young male convicts, aged 18-24, serving time in a Pennsylvania penitentiary. Although only 60 participants are entered into the model, with fewer predictor variables, the same result emerges with a lower significance but a higher R^2 and a comparable part correlation (see Table 4).

Table 4 Hierarchical Regression of Fantasy Distortion on Negative Earliest Memory

Predictor Variables	β Std Error	β	R	R^2	Part R	Partial R	Probability
College Sample N=402							
ALH Word Count	.001	.272	.256	.066	.258	.273	.004
Estimated I.Q.	.008	-.219	.321	.103	-.211	-.226	.017
SES	.086	-.010	.321	.103	-.009	-.010	ns
SEX	.205	-.113	.324	.105	-.106	-.116	ns
CES-D Summary Score	.010	-.027	.327	.107	-.025	-.028	ns
Early Negative Life Events	.039	-.116	.344	.118	-.104	-.113	ns
Negative Maternal Memory	.165	.068	.347	.121	.050	.055	ns
Negative Paternal Memory	.154	.006	.347	.121	.005	.005	ns
Positive Maternal Memory	.098	.068	.348	.121	.049	.054	ns
Positive Paternal Memory	.092	-.020	.355	.126	-.014	-.016	ns
Positive Earliest Memory	.116	-.209	.356	.127	-.137	-.149	ns
Negative Earliest Memory	.161	-.324	.415	.173	-.214	-.229	.016
Prison Sample N=60							
ALH Word Count	.001	.343	.334	.111	.333	.349	.009
SES	.004	.005	.334	.112	.005	.005	ns
CES-D Summary Score	.007	-.031	.334	.112	-.029	-.032	ns
Early Negative Life Events	.039	-.191	.390	.152	-.187	-.205	ns
Negative Maternal Memory	.014	-.017	.390	.152	-.016	-.018	ns
Negative Paternal Memory	.010	.056	.393	.155	.054	.060	ns
Negative Earliest Memory	.026	-.221	.449	.202	-.217	-.236	.083

Note. Dependent Variable: Fantasy Distortion
Beta refers to the final-step beta weights; r values are additive

FANTASY DISTORTION AND THE EARLIEST MEMORY DISCUSSION

We may have stumbled upon one of the universal mechanisms of fantasy production, since two populations as diverse as college students and convicted felons show the same effect. Still, using narrative scores to shine light on the workings of an implicit process is an inherently noisy business, statistically and otherwise. With this in mind, a precise summary of these results may reduce some of the ambiguity. What, exactly, do we know?

1. Participants with elevated FD scores are currently more depressed and less satisfied with the quality of their lives than those with lower FD scores.
2. Participants with elevated FD scores do not have higher rates of negative early life experience. Negative early life events was not a predictor of FD.
3. Participants with elevated FD scores do not have higher rates of positive qualities in their earliest memory; they only have lower rates of negative qualities.

The first explanation one could give is that this is simply a defensive style. Some participants use fantasy to defend against painful ideas, anxiety, expected loss, and so they construct their futures by turning them into fiction while, conversely, they turn their early memories into fiction as well by leaving out the negative qualities. The major problem with this hypothesis: why aren't the other memories affected? The positive scores on the three memories do not predict FD, nor does the negative scores of the maternal and paternal memories. Why is only the earliest memory affected? And finally, if this simply reflects a distortion to reduce anxiety or sadness, why wasn't the earliest memory more positive?

One place to start is with the nature of the earliest memory. It may be the most direct route to the "self" of childhood, even though family members often people the memory as supporting characters, because it is the first remembered experience of one's own consciousness.[3] And so the tendency to soften the earliest memory, to block out the negative features, may reflect a wish to control the fundamental experience of the self. This would explain why they bring excessive fantasy to their ALH: They mean to control their future selves just as they are attempting to control the experience of their earliest self. However, as good clinicians know, facing reality is always better than avoiding or distorting it. The participants are not feeling as satisfied with the quality of their lives as those who score lower on FD, and they are feeling more depressed.

To put all this in another way: High FD participants are relying heavily on the cognitive functions of the projective phase when it comes to describing their futures. They may well represent a subset of the young adults Markus and Nurius unknowingly studied almost 20 years ago – a group of participants whose dream of a future self not only affects their self-esteem, but also reflects an over-reliance on fantasy dating from early childhood that continues to interfere with their necessary human struggle to perceive themselves and others as accurately as they can. For them, the feared and wished for possible selves may seem too real, too possible, lowering their mood and possibility of hope. For when we depend too much on fantasy to structure our experience and to shape our judgment, it *becomes* reality,

---

[3] Here it is important to note that the verification of these memories is unnecessary: They are the participants' mental associations to an early event, however distorted or even untrue, and so they are still relevant to an exploration of their mental functioning.

banishing, it seems, the hard facts of our first memory while dressing up with certainty a future we have yet to meet and so cannot begin to know.

REFERENCES

Bargh, J. A., and Chartrand, T. L. (1999). The unbearable automaticity of being. *American Psychologist, 54*(7), 462-479.

Bargh, J. A., Gollwitzer, P. M., Lee Chai, A., and Barndollar. (2001). The automated will: Nonconscious activation and pursuit of behavioral goals. *Journal of Personality and Social Psychology, 81*(6), 1014-1027.

Berk, M. S., and Andersen, S. M. (2000). The impact of past relationships on interpersonal behavior: Behavioral confirmation in the social-cognitive process of transference. *Journal of Personality and Social Psychology, 79*(4), 546-562.

Bromfield, R. (1997). *Playing for real: Exploring the world of child therapy and the inner worlds of children*. Northvale, NJ: Aronson.

Corrigan, R. (1982). The control of animate and inanimate components in pretend play and language. *Child Development, 53*, 1342-1353.

Fenson, L. (1986). The developmental progression of play. In A. W. Gottfried and C. C. Brown (Eds.), *Play Interactions: The contribution of play materials and parental involvement to children's development* (pp. 53-66). Lexington: Heath.

Frisch, M. B., Cornell, J.,Villaneueva, M., and Retzalaff, P. J. (1992). Clinical validation of the Quality of Life Inventory: A measure of life satisfaction for use in treatment planning and outcome assessment. *Psychological Assessment, 4*, 92-101.

Gelman, S. A. M., Ellen M. (1986). Categories and induction in young children. *Cognition, 23*(3), 183-209.

Gunderson, J. (1984). *Borderline personality disorder*. Washington, D.C.: American Psychiatric Press.

Harris, M. J., and Beggan, J. K. (1994). Making believe: A descriptive study of fantasies in middle childhood. *Imagination, Cognition and Personality, 13*, 125-145.

Hollingshead, A. B., and Redlich, F. (1958). *Social class and mental illness*. New York: Wiley.

Karliner, R., Westrich, E. K.,Shedler, J., and Mayman, M. (1996). Bridging the gap between psychodynamic and scientific psychology: The Adelphi Early Memory Index. In J. M. Masling and R. F. Bornstein (Eds.), *Psychoanalytic perspectives on developmental psychology*. Washington, D.C.: American Psychological Association.

Kruger, J., and Dunning, D. (1999). Unskilled and unaware of it: How difficulties in recognizing one's own incompetence lead to inflated self-assessments. *Journal of Personality and Social Psychology, 77*, 1121-1134.

Loevinger, J., and Wessler, R. (1970). *Measuring ego development* (Vol. 1). San Francisco: Jossey-Bass.

Main, M., Kaplan, N., and Cassidy, J. (1985). Security in infancy, childhood, and adulthood: A move to the level of representation. In I. Bretherton and E. Walters (Eds.), Growing points of attachment, theory and resarch., *Monographs of the Society for Research in Child Development* (Vol. 50, pp. 67-104).

Markus, H., and Nurius, P. (1986). Possible Selves. *American Psychologist, 41*, 954-969.

Mayman, M. (1968). Early memories and character structure. *Journal of Projective Techniques and Personality Assessment, 32*, 303-316.

McAdams, D. P., Hoffman, B. J., Mansfield, E. D., and Day, R. (1996). Themes of agency and communion in significant autobiographical scenes. *Journal of Personality, 64*, 339-377.

McClelland, D. C., Koestner, R., and Weinberger, J. (1989). How do self-attributed and implicit motives differ? *Psychological Review, 96*(4), 690-702.

Nigg, J. T., Lohr, N. E., Westen, D., Gold, L., and Silk, K. R. (1992). Malevolent object representations in borderline personality disorder and major depression. *Journal of Abnormal Psychology, 101*, 61-67.

Radloff, L. S. (1977). The CES-D scale: A self-report depression scale for research in the general population. *Applied Psychological Measurement, 1*, 385-401.

Savin-Williams, R., Cohen, K.M. (Ed.). (1996). *The lives of lesbians, gays and bisexuals: Children to adults.* Forth Worth: Harcourt Brace.

Segal, H. G. (1996a). Family Demographics and Medical History, Self-Report Version. Unpublished instrument.

Segal, H. G. (1996b). Life Events Checklist. Unpublished instrument.

Segal, H. G. (2003). The once and future parents: Exploring the impact of early parental memories on the anticipated life histories of young adults. In K. Pillemer and K. Lüscher (Eds.), *Intergenerational ambivalences: New perspectives on parent-child relations in later life.* (Vol. in press). New York: Elsevier.

Segal, H. G., DeMeis, D. K., and Wood, G. (1997). *Anticipated life history qualitative scoring manual. Unpublished manuscript.*Unpublished manuscript.

Segal, H. G., DeMeis, D. K., Wood, G. A., and Smith, H. L. (2001). Assessing future possible selves by gender and socioeconomic status using the Anticipated Life History measure. *Journal of Personality, 69*(1), 57-87.

Segal, H. G., Frantz, M., and Mapstone, T. (2003). The impact of parental and adolescent substance abuse on adolescent future life expectations: Findings using the anticipated life history measure. *Adolescent and Family Health, 3*(2), 71-80.

Segal, H. G., Wood, G. A., DeMeis, D. K., and Smith, H. L. (2003). Future events, early experience and mental health: Clinical assessment using the Anticipated Life History measure. *Assessment, 10*(1), 1-12.

Singer, J. L. (1998). Imaginative play in early childhood: A foundation for adaptive emotional and cognitive development. *International Medical Journal, 5*, 93-100.

Wechsler, D. (1981). *WAIS-R manual.* New York: Harcourt Brace Janovich.

Westen, D., Lohr, N. E., Silk, K., Gold, L., Kerber, K. (1990). Object relations and social cognition in borderlines, major depressives, and normals: A thematic apperception test analysis. *Psychological Assessment: A Journal of Consulting and Clinical Psychology, 2*, 355-364.

Woike, B. A. (1994). The use of differentiation and integration processes: Empirical studies of "separate" and "connected" ways of thinking. *Journal of Personality and Social Psychology, 67*, 142-150.

In: Possible Selves: Theory, Research and Application   ISBN 1-59454-431-X
Editors: C. Dunkel and J. Kerpelman, pp. 97-121   © 2006 Nova Science Publishers, Inc.

Chapter 6

IDENTITY HEALTH, STRESS, AND SUPPORT: PROFILES OF TRANSITION TO MOTHERHOOD AMONG HIGH RISK ADOLESCENT GIRLS

Paula S. Nurius[1], Erin Casey and Taryn P. Lindhorst
University of Washington
Rebecca J. Macy
University of North Carolina—Chapel Hill

Since its introduction nearly 20 years ago, the conceptualization and application of possible selves as a vital and complex component of identity has mushroomed across domains of basic and applied research. Although this research has added significantly to knowledge of identity, more work is needed to foster the translation of self-concept research into relevant aspects of human functioning, particularly psychosocial functioning. Toward addressing this gap, we take advantage of person-oriented analytic tools that allow us to identity subgroups on the basis of patterned relationships among current and possible selves and indicators of psychosocial functioning; specifically self-esteem and global mental health. By integrating information on current and possible selves with concurrent self-esteem and global mental health, we provide a picture of *how* these self-concept components meaningfully combine to characterize a state we term identity health. Thus, we can examine the descriptive characteristics of current and possible selves in salient life domains such as the prominence of positivity or negativity, balance, and change as one set of indicators of a healthy identity. Yet we add the innovation of embedding self-concept with clinical indicators of psychosocial well-being to anchor evaluations of identity health in functioning.

This investigation examines possible selves and identity during a transition to parenthood within the life stage of adolescence among teenage women. Becoming a parent holds

---

[1] This article is based on work supported by Grant DA05208, Diane Morrison (P.I.) from the National Institute on Drug Abuse and grant 5 T32 MH20010, Paula Nurius (P.I.) from the National Institute of Mental Health. We would like to express appreciation to investigators of the parent project, to Steven Lewis for assistance in accessing the data, and to Linda Thurman for graphics support.

substantial implications for identity development at any life stage. One's self-concept must be altered to incorporate this new role as well as one's anticipated future identity (Cowan, Cowan, Heming, and Miller, 1991; Morfei, Hooker, Fiese, and Cordeiro, 2001). However, the life task of identity formation critical for young adults is complicated by the parenting role and demands and for parenting adolescents. Cross and Markus (1991) illustrate the salience of independent identity formation and relationship building in later adolescence in addition to the identity questions that accompany this critical and oftentimes precarious juncture of personal growth. However, little is known about clinically and theoretically relevant differences in how adolescent mothers experience this transition relative to young women who are not mothers. In this chapter, we show the importance of understanding a person's representation of their possible selves for contributing to our understanding of psychological well-being (cf., Ryff and Heincke, 1983; Ryff and Migdal, 1984).

Teen pregnancy and parenting have largely been regarded by applied researchers and the general public as a significant social problem. And there is certainly compelling evidence to fuel a concerned view of teen pregnancy. Osofsky and Thompson (2000) summarize research on parenting with the conclusion that children born to and raised by adolescent mothers are at higher risk of experiencing maladaptive parenting than children born to older parents. Specifically, children of teen mothers often have increased exposure to environmental, family, and lifestyle risk factors that impair physical and mental health These factors can reflect social and economic disparities (poverty, limited education, marginalization) as well as patterns or conditions of risky behavior; e.g., substance use, truancy, delinquency, violence, estrangement from stable support networks (Furstenberg and Hughes, 1995; Osofsky and Thompson, 2000).

In short, evidence to date urges attention to the stresses and needs of adolescent mothers toward fostering healthy adult development and adaptive parenting. However, as Oxford and colleagues (2003) point out, recent findings illustrate heterogeneity among adolescent mothers—countering a view of them as a relatively homogeneous, problem-prone group. Differing etiological pathways into teenage childbearing shifts focus to understanding differences among subgroups of adolescent mothers which, if found, hold implications for differences needed in preventive and supportive interventions (cf. Hamburg, 1988; Miller Johnson et al., 1999 cited in Oxford et al., 2003).

Consistent with calls for using a developmental context when examining adolescent childbearing (Coley and Chase-Lansdale, 1998), we focus on self-concept variation and change inherent within the developmental struggle typical during adolescence and early adulthood to determine "Who am I?"; a normative struggle that gets compounded with the addition of parenting. The cognitive consequences of current and possible selves in guiding selective information processing (attention, expectancies, perception) as well as decision-making and action have been well-established over the lifespan. As visions of hoped for and feared future selves, possible selves may be particularly important during a significant period of transition such as parenting (Antonucci and Mikus, 1988). In studying the impact of parenting on adult self-development, Hooker, Fiese, Jenkins, Morfei, and Schwagler (1996) found important variation. Although most new parents had parenting among their possible selves, a significant minority did not and mothers were significantly more likely than fathers to have feared selves in the parenting realm.

To date, we are unaware of research that has applied similar analysis regarding the transition to parenting in a younger, unmarried, low income sample such as that in our analysis. Possible selves research on adolescents has focused on other topics such as delinquency, school achievement, and negative health behaviors (see Aloise-Young, Hennigan, and Leong, 2001). There has been insufficient research exploring important variation within this population that holds implications for developmentally targeted intervention. Given the role of self-concept— both positive and negative--as a mediator of biological, social, and cultural antecedents of risky behavior (Stein et al., 1998), we consider ways that the self-concept operates to create both risk and protective potential for individuals' functioning in the context of adolescent parenting. In this pursuit, we take a functional approach to the self-concept, integrating the descriptive characteristics of current and possible selves with key indicators of these young women's psychological health—self-esteem and global mental health. This clinically-oriented approach to gauging identity differences and implications is consistent with research summarized by Osofsky and Thompson (2000). We aim to provide new insights to foster optimal identity health among at-risk mothers in order to better position them to provide adaptive parenting to their children and to increase their social competence in the interpersonal adult world. Given the developmental stage of the girls in this study, we include developmentally salient dimensions of social competence in addition to parenting as we construct and test identity profiles.

In examining the role of current and possible selves relative to both identity health and psychosocial outcomes for adolescent mothers, we need analytic tools that help identify differences in self-concepts, and *how* these differences combine to create distinctive multivariate risk and protective profiles relative to subsequent psychosocial functioning. Recent developmental research has provided guidance in capturing individual variation, especially when there is evidence that aggregated variable-centered data may misrepresent important diversity (Coley and Chase-Lansdale, 1998; Magnusson, 1998; Oxford et al., 2003).

The negative to positive composition of current and possible selves has constituted an ongoing theme of descriptive analysis. Research of possible selves related to issues such as adolescent health behaviors, delinquency, and academic achievement have found important differences associated with the degree of positivity and negativity (Aloise-Young, Hennigan, and Leong, 2001; Oyserman, Gant, and Anger, 1995; Oyserman and Saltz, 1993). Moreover, the configuration of positive to negative selves within the active working self-concept affects perception, emotional responding, and decision-making (Nurius and Berlin, 1994; Nurius and Markus, 1990). For example, reducing the number of negative selves will be unlikely to support desired behavioral changes if the presence of relevant positive selves is not elaborated to provide guidance toward actualizing desired outcomes. This concern about the relative composition of salient selves is also evident in the study of balance. That is, when negative selves complement or are balanced by positive selves, there should be stronger motivation (for example, desires to be a good mother is augmented by feared representations of being a bad mother) as well as scripted guidance about what good parenting and bad parenting look like, and strategies for achieving or avoiding these respective outcomes (Markus and Ruvulo, 1989; Oyserman and Markus, 1990). Findings hae been mixed with respect to support of balance theory (Aloise-Young et al., 2001).

Identification of distinct subgroups as a function of identity health may help illuminate differences relative to balance tht have previously been obscured. A final dimension of self-concept characteristics that we will examine is change. In addition to changes in current and possible selves from pregnancy to a year later in parenting, we add the dimension of self-actualization. That is, to what extent are self-changes, envisioned through possible selves actually seen by the individual to be achieved a year later; to then be part of their current selves? Our view is that charting self0-actualization can help sort our variability in balance that would otherwise be difficult to interpret.

In sum, the goal of our research is to identify the role that current and possible self-concept plays in the transition to parenting among adolescent girls. To accomplish this goal, we undertake the following aims in this chapter:

1. To identify multivariate profiles of identity health that integrate descriptive perceptions of one's current and possible selves with key indicators mental health among adolescent mothers;
2. To examine differences as a function of these identity health profiles relative to demographic characteristics and respondents' postnatal psychosocial, risky behavior, and social engagement outcomes; and
3. To analyze dynamic changes in self-concept among subgroups of adolescent mothers during the critical developmental transition from pregnancy to parenthood.

We postulate heterogeneity in the identity profiles of adolescent mothers. In this we build on prior findings with this sample (Oxford et al., 2003) that challenge a view of adolescent mothers as relatively homogeneous with respect to alcohol use patterns. We argue for the importance of recognizing differing etiological pathways in adolescent parenting, represented by different subsets of adolescent mothers. We anticipate that diversity as a function of identity health profiles based on possible selves will be predictive of clinically meaningful differences in subsequent, postpartum psychosocial functioning. By understanding differential assets and vulnerabilities which characterize subgroups of adolescent mothers, we can refine interventions to best equip these mothers for developmental and role changes.

METHOD

Procedures

The data for these analyses are part of a longitudinal study assessing the natural history and correlates of drug and alcohol use among a community sample of pregnant and parenting adolescents. This study has been tracking a sample of females who were aged 17 years or younger, unmarried, pregnant, planning to carry their babies to term, and living in a large metropolitan area in the Northwest. Participants were recruited from urban prenatal clinics, alternative school programs for pregnant and parenting adolescents, and social service agencies serving inner-city adolescents. Because recruitment procedures included use of advertising to encourage eligible adolescents to contact study staff, a conventional overall response rate could not be calculated. In the only agency (a large county hospital prenatal clinic) where recruitment procedures allowed collection of complete approach and consent data, 76 percent of eligible informed adolescents consented to participate. Parent or guardian consent was obtained for participants who were not emancipated minors. Two time points within the longitudinal study were utilized for this analysis, the initial interview during participants' pregnancies, and an interview occurring twelve months post-partum. Retention over this period was high, with 236 of the original 240 respondents participating in the second interview (98 percent of the original sample).

The sample is multi-ethnic and relatively low-income. The ethnic make-up of the sample, fully described below, is representative of the ethnic mix of adolescent mothers for the years and geographic location in which the sample was recruited. Respondents were paid for their participation, ranging from $15 to $50 based on the wave of data collection. Respondents were assured of the confidentiality of their responses as spelled out in the consent form, and as reiterated by the interviewers at the beginning of the interview as well as during the more sensitive sections. In addition, respondents were aware that the project had obtained a Certificate of Confidentiality from the federal government to avoid subpoena regarding confidential information from study participants. The only exceptions to the pledge of confidentiality were if the respondent reported incidents of child abuse, or risk of immediate harm to herself or others; such cases would be referred to appropriate agencies.

RESPONDENT CHARACTERISTICS

Respondents ranged in age from 12 to 17 ($M = 16$ years) at the initial data collection time point. Of the 236 women participating in both the initial and 12-month follow up interviews, 49.4 percent were non-Hispanic Caucasian, 27.2 percent African American, and the remainder were from other racial and ethnic groups, including American Indian, Asian American, Latina, and those reporting mixed ethnicity. At the time of the initial interview, participants had finished on average 9.4 years of school, and 36 percent had dropped out before obtaining a high school diploma. Most (92.5 percent) of these young women planned to return to school. In the 12-month follow-up interview, 88.3 percent were caring for their children, while roughly 4 percent had given their babies up for adoption and an additional 8 percent were relying on relatives or others to care for their children. At the second interview, nearly 9 percent of the women supported themselves through a job, 57 percent relied on welfare or other social services and nearly 34 percent were financially supported by partners or relatives.

MEASURES

Self-concept. Two underlying dimensions of current and possible self-concept were assessed utilizing items specifically selected to be developmentally meaningful for this sample. Respondents' perception of their own *social competence* (SC) was measured via a semantic differential scale assessing emotional stability, general competence and specific competencies related to employment, financial security and social and intimate relationships. *Parenting* (PAR) self-concept was assessed through the same semantic differential scale measuring respondents' perceptions of their level of ease in being mothers and their abilities to meet the physical, emotional and safety needs of their children. A five point scale was used in which "1" represented a very negative self-perception, "2" somewhat negative, "3" neutral, "4" somewhat positive and "5" a very positive self-perception. Participants responded to the self-concept items first based on their perceptions of their *current* self-concept, and next on their *possible* self-concept (how they expected to feel about themselves in one year). Reliability analyses demonstrated acceptable alpha levels for current and possible social competence during pregnancy of .68 and .70 respectively, and an alpha level for current and possible parenting of .63 and .58, respectively. The post-partum interview alpha levels for current and possible social competence were .71 and .77; and current and possible parenting alphas were .58 and .68.

For the purpose of these analyses, several dynamic self-concept values were calculated to capture change in self-concept over time. *Post-natal self-concept* was computed as the mean of the social competence and parenting sub-scales for both the current and possible self-concept scales. *Change in self-concept* was calculated by subtracting mean SC and PAR self-concept scores during pregnancy from mean post-natal scores for current and possible selves. This resulted in a positive value for respondents who experienced a growth in self-concept, and a negative value for participants whose self-concept became poorer over the time period. *Actualized self-concept* represents the extent to which a respondent's possible self-concept at the initial interview coincided with her current-self-concept at the post-natal interview. This value was calculated by subtracting current post-natal self-concept SC and PAR means from the possible self-concept scores reported by respondents during pregnancy. Scores near zero represent actualized development of self-concept, with positive and negative scores reflecting more or less growth respectively, from possible selves representations during pregnancy. Finally, *self-concept balance* signifies the extent to which respondents report a balance of positive to negative perceptions of their social competence and parenting abilities. Patterned after Oyserman and Saltz (1993), a balanced response to self-concept questions was calculated as the number of negative to positive responses within each of the self-concept domains (SC and PAR). Higher values reflect greater balance between positive and negative current and possible selves, whereas scores of zero reflect a positive-only or negative-only self-concept in that domain.

Psychological well-being. Self-esteem was gauged via Rosenburg's Self-Esteem Scale (1965). The scale's 10 items are scored on a 4-point scale; strongly agree ("1") to strongly disagree ("4") with higher scores indicating greater levels of self-esteem. Respondents' global *mental health* was assessed utilizing the depression, anxiety, hostility and interpersonal sensitivity subscales of the SCL-90 (Derogatis, 1994). These items are based on a 5-point scale ranging from Not At All ("0") to Extremely ("4") indicating the degree to which negative feelings or symptoms have bothered the respondent in the past week. Self-esteem and SCL-90 scores at pregnancy were used in identifying profile groups. Post-natal scores were used as dependent variables in tests of differences across the groups. The remaining psychological well-being variables were measured solely as post-natal outcomes.

Life events were measured utilizing 23 items from Coddington's Life Events scale (1972), relevant to the lives of young women, assessing whether respondents had faced events ranging from death of a family member to relocating or accomplishing an outstanding personal achievement in the past six months. A twenty-fourth item allowed respondents to include an additional ("other") important incident. Total scores were based on a sum of checked items. *Violent victimization* was measured in terms of lifetime exposure to parental or sexual violence. Parental violence was assessed via seven yes/no items from the Conflict Tactics Scale (Straus, 1979), asking whether the respondents had been subjected to behaviors ranging from threats to use of a weapon at the hands of their parents. Sexual violence consisted of a single item in the prenatal interview asking respondents to indicate whether they had ever been forced to have sexual intercourse against their will. Parental and sexual violence was collapsed into an aggregate violent victimization variable, dichotomized to distinguish participants who had experienced low parental violence only ("0") or whether they had experienced severe parental violence (punching, kicking, etc.) and/or sexual assault ("1"). We used low parental violence as our base value as no respondents reported being completely free of past parental violence.

Parenting stress was assessed utilizing an 18-item scale with questions adapted from three sources (Abidin, 1983; Barth, 1982; Jonston & Mash, 1989). Based on a four-point scale ranging from strongly agree ("1) to strongly disagree ("4"), these items measured respondents' perceptions about issued including the ease od dealing with their children's problems, the extent to which they possessed needed parenting skills, and the extent to which the workload of parenting felt manageable. Higher scores reflect greater levels of parenting stress.

Locus of control was assessed utilizing Nowicki and Strickland's Locus of Control Scale (1973), a seven-item measure summed so that higher scores indicate a more externalized control orientation. Finally, *mental health and alcohol/drug treatment services* were each measured as dichotomous variables indicating respondents' yes/no responses to whether they had sought these forms of formal assistance in the past six months.

Risky behaviors. Post-natal *drug use frequency* was calculated as the maximum of frequency levels of past month use reported for 11 substances excluding alcohol (including smokeless tobacco, cocaine/crack, amphetamines, barbiturates, psychedelics, stimulants, inhalants, heroin or other narcotics). Responses were measured on a six-point scale (1 = never, 2 = once, 3 = 2-3 times, 4 = once per week, 5 = several times per week and 6 = every day). *Consequences of substance use* was calculated as the mean of 11 items assessing potential outcomes of substance use, including missing school, behaving in ways the respondent later regretted, or whether the respondent had been injured or in trouble with the police as a result of substance use. These items were measured on a 5-point scale ranging from never ("1") to very often ("5").

Frequency of alcohol use with sex before pregnancy (assessed at the initial interview) and *frequency of drug use with sex* (assessed post-natally) were both measured on a 5-point scale ranging from never ("1") to always ("5"). *Delinquent behavior* was measured as a sum of affirmative responses to 12 items asking whether the respondent had engaged in specific illegal behaviors or had been in contact with the criminal justice system. These items included behaviors such as selling drugs, theft, arson and spending time in jail. Delinquency scores therefore had a possible range of 0 – 12. Finally, *number of sexual partners* in the past 6 months was assessed via a single item asking respondents to recall the number of male partners in the previous six months

Social engagement. Engagements were conceptualized as the extent to which respondents were connected with and adequately supported by various aspects of their lives, including family, partners, friends and school. All of these constructs were assessed post-natally with the exception of educational attainment plans. *Social support* was calculated as the sum of responses to 9 items assessing the degree to which respondents felt they could "count on" friends and family members when they needed help. These items were measured on a 5-point scale ranging from not at all ("1") to a great deal ("5"), for a total possible range of scores of 5 - 45. *Family support* was calculated as the sum of 14 items measuring the extent to which respondents felt bonded to and respected by their immediate family members. Family support items were calculated on a 4 -point scale ranging from strongly agree ("1") to strongly disagree ("4"), resulting in a score range of 14-56 in which higher scores indicate greater family support. Six of the family support items were adapted from pre-existing measures (Kaplan, Martin and Robbins, 1984) and the remainder was developed for the purposes of this research.

Frequency of arguments with others was computed as the mean of two items assessing the regularity with which respondents verbally fight with parents or others. Argument items were measured on a 5-point scale ranging from never ("1") to very often ("5"). *Frequency of sharing feelings with friends* was calculated as the mean of two items asking respondents to indicate the extent to which they disclose their feelings to their close friends. These two items were measured on a five point scale ranging from never ("1") to always or almost always ("5"). *Needing help* was a summed variable aggregating five dichotomous items. These questions assessed whether respondents felt they needed more emotional or tangible help than they were currently receiving, such as financial assistance, help with transportation or support around personal problems. Higher scores represent a greater perceived need for support. *Enough help with child care to pursue goals* was measured dichotomously as a yes/no question. Scores for each group on this variable reflect the percentage of respondents in that group who felt they were receiving enough assistance with child care to pursue their own goals. Finally, *importance of doing well in school* was assessed through a single 5- point item ranging from extremely important ("1") to not at all important ("5").

RESULTS

Identifying Profiles of Self-Concept

The person-centered analysis technique of latent profile analysis was used to investigate the differences in self-concept among adolescent mothers, together with descriptions of current and possible selves during pregnancy, concurrent psychosocial indicators of self-esteem and mental health were used in the analysis. Latent profile analysis, through maximum likelihood procedures, makes use of the heterogeneity within a sample to determine distinct sub-samples or groups (Everitt, Landau, and Morven, 2001; Gibson, 1959; Muthen, 2002). This analytic technique determines a latent categorical variable that describes the different sub-group membership of the participants in the sample by explaining the relationships among the variables used in the analysis. Each sub-group within the overall sample is assumed to come from a population with a distinct probability distribution (Everitt Landau, and Morven, 2001). Unlike traditional variable-centered analysis which relies on measures of central tendency within the sample, a person-centered approach illuminates the heterogeneity among the participants and determines distinct profiles based on intercorrelations in the sample among the variables of interest. This analytic approach provides a multivariate, holistic understanding of the participants that is more nuanced than a determination based on sample means (Magnusson, 1998).

Mplus 2.0 was used to perform the latent profile analysis (Muthen and Muthen, 1998). Sub-classes in the sample were identified using six variables representing facets of self-concept during pregnancy: current SC and PAR self-concepts, possible SC and PAR self-concepts, overall mental health, and self-esteem (See Table 1). Fourteen of the 235 participants had missing data on at least one of the variables of interest. Mplus estimates missing data using maximum-likelihood estimation based on the assumptions that the data are missing at random (Little and Rubin, 1987), are continuous, and are normally distributed. The missing data in the study were determined to meet these requirements.

Table 1. Pre-Natal Latent Profile Four-Class Model Solution: Descriptive Statistics

	Group 1 Strong Id Hlth		Group 2 Average Id Hlth		Group 3 Impaired Parenting		Group 4 Vulnerable Id Hlth	
Sample size	63		100		27		50	
Means and Standard Deviations								
	M	SD	M	SD	M	SD	M	SD
Current Parenting	4.65	.32	4.32	.35	2.99	.44	3.99	.41
Current Social Competence	4.39	.33	3.62	.37	2.97	.48	2.75	.46
Possible Selves Parenting	4.67	.27	4.35	.35	3.37	.40	4.15	.35
Possible Selves Social Competence	4.58	.28	4.10	.43	3.62	.51	3.49	.49
Mental Health	.69	.42	1.05	.59	1.42	.64	1.84	.53
Self-Esteem	37.26	2.30	33.41	3.24	30.35	4.75	26.86	4.17

The optimal number of groups for this analysis was identified systematically through comparison of multiple models, which identified varying numbers of groups (one, two, three, four and five group models). To identify the best fit model, model fit statistics were evaluated (Everitt et al., 2001; Muthen and Muthen, 1998). The Bayesian Information Criterion (BIC) was used to examine the fit of the different models--the lower the BIC value, the more parsimonious and better fitting the model is. The BIC statistic of 2124.91 indicates that the four class model was most the parsimonious. The BIC values of the one, two, three and five class models were 2629.31, 2239.80, 2173.77, and 2137.28 respectively. Once the optimal solution was determined, the model was run using various sets of start values to determine the stability of the model. An additional evaluation of model fit is the posterior probabilities for each class within the model. These probabilities indicate the model's likelihood of accurate participant classification and the model's capacity to distinguish subgroups within the sample. In the four-class model, the probabilities of classification are .91 for class one, .90 for class two, .94 for class three, and .90 for class four, indicating the model's strong ability to distinguish distinct sub-groups within the sample. The final model was tested using multiple start values to determine its stability (Muthen and Muthen, 1998) and consistent solutions were found.

Based on findings reported in Table 1, Group 1 (Strong Identity Health) is distinguished by substantially more favorable means on every variable; higher on self-esteem and all self-concept variables and lower levels of the global index of mental health problems. At considerable contrast is Group 4 (Vulnerable Identity Health), characterized by the least favorable means on all but parenting self-concept measures. Group 3 (Impaired Parenting) is also characterized by less favorable means in comparison to Groups 1 and 2, and what particularly distinguishes these respondents are substantially lower current and possible parenting selves. Group 2 (Average Identity Health) is midrange on all variables relative to strong identity health respondents on the one hand and those with vulnerable or impaired parenting identity profiles on the other.

TESTS OF DIFFERENCES ACROSS LATENT PROFILE GROUPS

MANOVA tests were used for each of the following sets of group comparisons. This technique allows for the testing of multiple outcomes simultaneously and diminishes the risk of an inflated type I error caused by the use of multiple univariate tests (Stevens, 1996). Wilk's Lambda was used to test the multivariate null hypothesis that there would be no difference among the classes on these relevant variables. F tests were then examined to determine significant differences among the classes on individual measures. Tukey post hoc tests were used following significant results to examine pairwise group differences while holding the error rate constant (Stevens, 1996).

Significance tests for each of the groups of variables shows that although there are no overall significant differences among the classes on demographic characteristics, the groups differ significantly on psychological well-being, risky behaviors, and social engagement (see tables 2 through 5

Table 2. Demographic Differences by Group

Variables:	Group				Pearson X^2
	Strong Id Hlth	Average Id Hlth	Impaired Parenting	Vulnerable Id Hlth	
Percentage respondents living with partner during pregnancy	25.4	21.0	37.0	26.0	2.97
Percent living with partner post-partum	27.6	34.0	26.9	35.6	1.27
Baby lives with respondent (%)	88.3	88.5	80.0	90.0	1.72
Percentage relying on welfare for financial support during pregnancy	36.5	26.0	14.8	26.0	4.91
Percentage relying on welfare post-partum	50.0	59.8	46.2	64.0	3.77
Plans to access higher education (%)	74.5	70.7	81.5	72.0	1.36
Percentage women of color	55.5	51.0	44.4	50.0	1.00
					Univariate ANOVA F
Mean years school completed at pregnancy	9.63	9.44	9.19	9.32	.920

DEMOGRAPHIC CONTRASTS AMONG GROUPS

Because all variables except one were measured nominally, a MANOVA test was not prudent. Therefore, chi-square tests were undertaken for the eight variables measured dichotomously and a univariate ANOVA was used to test the one continuous variable in this set (see Table 2). Differences did not achieve significance, but some trends are notable. Those adolescents who had impaired parenting identity profiles were less likely to have used welfare during pregnancy or post-natally than the other, less likely to live with their parents during pregnancy, and more likely to live with their partners during and after pregnancy. The strong and average identity health girls reported more use of welfare during pregnancy than the other two groups, but their change in welfare use from pre- to post-natally was notably smaller than the other two groups. The strong and average identity health groups were more similar to each others in terms of whether they lived with their partners.

Table 3. Analysis of Differences in Psychological Well-Being Across Groups

Psychological Well-Being[1]	Group Membership				F
	Strong Id Hlth	Average Id Hlth	Imp'd Parent.	Vulnerable Id Hlth	
	Wilk's Lambda (24, 560.36) = .65, F = 3.80***				
Life Events	4.50	4.40	4.40	4.62	.14
Family/sexual violence [b,d]	.46	.45	.85	.53	3.86**
Parenting Stress [c]	1.69	1.87	1.93	2.06	6.48***
Locus of Control	12.55	12.82	13.45	13.62	1.78
Global Symptom Index [c,e]	0.64	0.74	.86	1.23	10.26***
Self – Esteem [b,c,e]	35.33	33.48	32.00	29.47	14.10***
Received mental health svcs.	.09	.11	.30	.27	3.64*
Received drug/alc. services [c,e]	.00	.00	.00	.09	5.07**

Note. * $p<.05$, ** $p<.01$, *** $p<.001$.

[1]MANOVAs of psychological well-being variables, followed by Tukey tests of group difference.

[a] Significant difference between Strong Id. and Avg. Id.

[b] Significant difference between Strong Id. and Imp. Par.

[c] Significant difference between Strong Id. and Vulnerable Id.

[d] Significant difference between Avg. Id. and Imp. Par.

[e] Significant difference between Avg. Id. and Vulnerable Id.

[f] Significant difference between Imp. Par. and Vulnerable Id.

GROUP CONTRASTS ON PSYCHOSOCIAL
AND PARENTING NEED OUTCOMES

All of the psychological well-being variables were significantly different among the groups except for life events (see Table 3). The groups also differed on three risky behaviors: frequency of drug use, consequences of drug use and frequency of drug use accompanying sexual activity (see Table 4). Within risky behaviors, the groups did not differ in level of delinquency, number of sexual partners within the past month or sex with alcohol before pregnancy. Within the construct of engagement, the four groups were significantly different on social support, family support, needing additional help and viewing school performance as important (see Table 5). Groups did not differ significantly on frequency of arguments or of sharing feelings with others, and reported similar needs around child care. It should be noted that the impaired parenting group is relatively small, potentially impacting our ability to detect statistical differences between this group and the others.

Across these four domains, the group of strong and average identity health adolescents was remarkably similar and consistently scored more positively than the impaired parenting or vulnerable identity health groups. Strong identity girls' higher perceptions of the importance of school performance were the only significant difference from the young women in the average group. Together, these two groups also differed in similar ways from the impaired parenting group. Both the strong and average identity health groups were less likely than the impaired parenting group to use drugs in conjunction with sexual activity and were less likely to have experienced severe violence. Additionally, strong identity adolescents reported higher self-esteem and greater family support than the impaired parenting identity adolescents.

Table 4. Analysis of Differences in Risky Behavior Variables Across Groups

| Risky Behavior Variables[1] | Group Membership | | | | F |
	Strong Id Hlth	Average Id Hlth	Imp'd Parent.	Vulnerable Id Hlth	
	Wilk's Lambda (18, 574.66) = .80, F = 2.59***				
Frequency of drug use [d]	1.28	1.17	1.77	1.35	3.15*
Consequences of drug use [c,f]	1.05	1.13	1.05	1.22	4.18**
Frequency alcohol with sex	1.47	1.51	1.91	1.78	2.43
Frequency drugs with sex [b,d]	1.16	1.18	1.68	1.22	3.34*
Delinquency	0.23	0.26	0.64	0.59	2.45
No. sex partners in past 6 mo.	1.75	1.45	1.73	1.59	0.52

Note. * $p<.05$, ** $p<.01$, *** $p<.001$.
[1]MANOVAs of risky behavior variables, followed by Tukey tests of group difference.
[a] Significant difference between Strong Id. and Avg. Id.
[b] Significant difference between Strong Id. and Imp. Par.
[c] Significant difference between Strong Id. and Vulnerable Id.
[d] Significant difference between Avg. Id. and Imp. Par.
[e] Significant difference between Avg. Id. and Vulnerable Id.
[f] Significant difference between Imp. Par. and Vulnerable Id

Perhaps the most dramatic differences can be seen between those with strong and vulnerable identity health profiles. Strong identity health girls scored more positively on family support, needing additional help, importance of school performance, parenting stress, mental health and self-esteem. Additionally, those with strong identity health were less likely to have experienced consequences due to drug use or to have received drug and alcohol treatment. Not surprisingly, those with average identity health significantly differed from those with vulnerable identity health on many of the same variables, including family support, needing additional help, mental health and self-esteem. Finally, those characterized by impaired parenting identity and vulnerable identity health did not differ significantly on any of the engagement, psychological well-being, or risky behavior variables.

Table 5. Analysis of Differences in Social Engagement Variables Across Groups

Engagement Variables[1]	Group Membership				F
	Strong Id Hlth	Average Id Hlth	Imp'd. Parent.	Vulnerable Id Hlth	
Wilk's Lambda (21,494.44) = .70 F = 3.06***					
Total social support	21.28	18.99	18.53	18.72	2.77*
Total family support [b,c,e]	44.72	43.55	37.05	39.00	4.81**
# arguments with family/friends	2.15	2.01	2.13	2.37	1.61
Freq. share feelings with friends	4.09	3.88	3.74	3.77	1.32
Need additional help [c,e]	0.96	1.24	1.84	2.44	7.35***
Enough child care to pursue goals	.85	.79	.89	.66	1.95
Imp. to perform well in school [a,c]	4.48	3.96	3.89	3.67	5.86***

Note. * $p<.05$, ** $p<.01$, ***$p<.001$.
[1]MANOVAs of engagement variables, followed by Tukey tests of group difference.
[a] Significant difference between Strong Id. and Avg. Id.
[b] Significant difference between Strong Id. and Imp. Par.
[c] Significant difference between Strong Id. and Vulnerable Id.
[d] Significant difference between Avg. Id. and Imp. Par.
[e] Significant difference between Avg. Id. and Vulnerable Id.
[f] Significant difference between Imp. Par. and Vulnerable Id.

DYNAMIC CHANGES IN SELF-CONCEPT AMONG ADOLESCENT MOTHERS

Again a MANOVA was first run to test for overall significant group differences among the different aspects of self-concept, including self-concept measured post-partum, change in self-concept, actualized self-concept, and balance. The omnibus F test was significant, followed by post-hoc Tukey tests, all of which were also significant except for balance in parenting possible selves (Table 6). Figures 1-5 further illuminate these findings. Line graphs in figures 1 and 2 visually show change in current and possible selves for parenting and social competence. The magnitude of differences among groups is less pronounced post-partum relative to pregnancy due to positive increases, particularly for those with impaired parenting and vulnerable identity health. Although the magnitude of change was equivalent for these two groups relative to social competence, the impaired parenting group achieved striking gains in both parenting current and possible selves post-partum.

Table 6. Analysis of Differences in Self-Concept Across Groups

Self-Concept Variables[1]	Group Membership				F
	Strong Id Hlth	Average Id Hlth	Imp'd Parenting	Vulnerable Id Hlth	
	Wilk's Lambda (48, 539.13) = .08 F = 15.63***				
Post-natal Self-Concept					
Possible Soc. Comp. [a,b,c]	4.68	4.31	4.20	4.15	11.36***
Possible Parenting [a,c]	4.80	4.63	4.61	4.53	4.56**
Current Soc. Comp. [a,b,c,e]	4.28	3.82	3.65	3.48	20.35***
Current Parenting [a,b,c]	4.62	4.43	4.26	4.31	5.71**
Change in Self-Concept:					
Possible Soc. Com. [b,c,d,e]	0.10	0.27	0.72	0.66	11.37***
Possible Parenting [b,c,d,f]	0.10	0.28	1.27	0.37	26.46***
Current Soc. Comp. [a,b,c,d,e]	-0.12	0.20	0.75	0.78	21.05***
Current Parenting [b,c,d,e,f]	-0.09	0.07	1.24	0.36	40.48***
Actualized Self-Concept:					
Social Competence [b]	0.31	0.23	-0.17	0.02	3.87**
Parenting [b,d,f]	0.08	-0.08	-0.91	-0.15	17.30***
Prenatal Balance:					
Possible Soc. Comp [b,c,d,e]	0.13	0.40	0.88	0.86	11.83***
Possible Parenting [a,b,c,d,f]	0.02	0.25	0.59	0.23	9.84***
Current Soc. Comp. [a,b,c]	0.36	1.27	1.53	1.43	21.13***
Current Parenting [b,c,d,e]	0.09	0.30	0.94	0.61	17.72***
Post-natal Balance:					
Possible Soc. Comp. [a]	0.00	0.26	0.18	0.18	4.26**
Possible Parenting	0.04	0.06	0.06	0.09	0.42
Current Soc Comp. [a,c]	0.24	0.81	0.71	1.07	9.65***
Current Parenting [a]	0.02	0.19	0.12	0.11	3.21*

Note. * $p<.05$, ** $p<.01$, *** $p<.001$.

[1]MANOVAs of self-concept variables, followed by Tukey tests of group difference.

[a] Significant difference between Strong Id. and Avg. Id.

[b] Significant difference between Strong Id. and Imp. Par.

[c] Significant difference between Strong Id. and Vulnerable Id.

[d] Significant difference between Avg. Id. and Imp. Par.

[e] Significant difference between Avg. Id. and Vulnerable Id.

[f] Significant difference between Imp. Par. and Vulnerable Id.

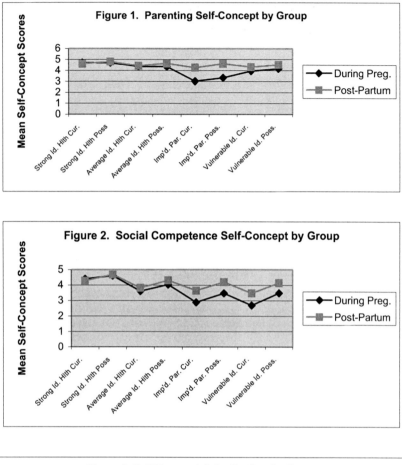

Figure 1. Parenting Self-Concept by Group

Figure 2. Social Competence Self-Concept by Group

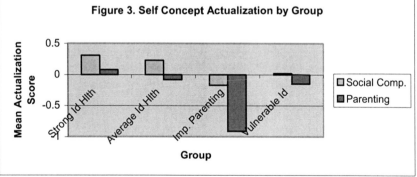

Figure 3. Self Concept Actualization by Group

Figures 3-5 visually reflect tests reported in Table 6 to facilitate interpretation. Figure 3 illustrates self-concept actualization--the extent to which possible selves reported during pregnancy are indeed achieved a year later postpartum. The negative values, most notable for those with prenatal impaired parenting identities, indicate positive change above and beyond that envisioned during pregnancy. Figures 4 and 5 elucidate trends in the balance findings: generally, higher balance (a greater ratio of positive to negative beliefs) is reported among current relative to possible selves, within social competence relative to parenting self-conceptions, and pre-natally relative to post-natal balance scores. Overall those with impaired parenting identities reported highest balance followed by those with vulnerable identity health. Balance was higher in the social competence domain for those with average identity health; those with strong identity health showed comparatively low balance across both domains.

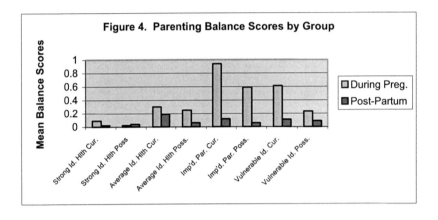

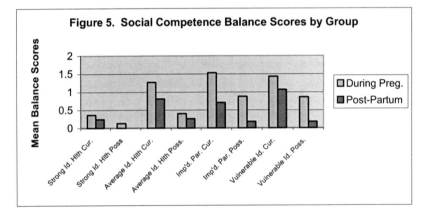

DISCUSSION

A growing body of literature documents the clinical and theoretical relevance of understanding both the here and now conceptualization of self, and the sense of one's future self in relationship to other desired outcomes (Markus and Nurius, 1986; Morfei, Hooker, Fiese and Cordeiro, 2001; Stein, Roeser and Markus, 1998). This investigation extends previous work by examining how identity health as a function of both current and possible self concepts plays a critical role in a young woman's capacity to effectively manage the developmental tasks of adolescence while also managing the roles and responsibilities of parenthood.

This analysis further supports work suggesting that teenage mothers are varied and diverse (Hamburg, 1988; Miller-Johnson et al., 1999; Oxford et al, 2003). The latent profile analysis shows that the young women in this study (who become mothers as adolescents) have distinct identity health profiles that have important implications for psychosocial functioning, interpersonal relationships, social support, engagement in risk behaviors, and parenting. A particularly compelling finding is the level and nature of change in self-concept during a difficult year of transition; particularly evident for the vulnerable and impaired parenting identity groups. The recognition of distinct identity health groups within this study population holds important implications for conceptualizations of identity, as well as for understanding the psychosocial needs of adolescent mothers. The findings show that self-concept valence and identity health matter for adolescent mothers since it explains risk and protective factors, which respectively enhance or diminish young women's well-being and capacity for positive interpersonal relationships. To the extent that identity is not static, it suggests a target for supportive interventions to adolescent mothers.

Adolescents in this study were engaged in a critical transition in which parenting became incorporated into typical developmental life tasks such as independent identity formation and relationship building activities. The research presented here underscores the importance of understanding how self-concept is differentially related to risk for as well as protective buffering of impairment in psychosocial functioning. In this discussion, we return to our original aims of investigating diversity among adolescent mothers in relation to their self-concepts, review how knowledge of possible selves enriches our understanding of psychosocial functioning , consider the effects of change in self-concept over time, and reflect on interventions that are suggested from this study.

DIVERSITY AMONG ADOLESCENT MOTHERS

Our findings support efforts to develop a more nuanced approach to understanding adolescent mothers who are often treated as a homogeneous and stigmatized population. The negative societal views of adolescent parenting might be expected to significantly hamper the development of a positive self-concept among teen mothers. However, a key finding from this study is that girls who are transitioning from adolescence to adulthood as parents do not have uniformly negative self-concepts. A significant minority (26 percent) had strong identity health--highly positive current and future conceptions of self combined with high self-esteem and mental health. A slightly higher number (32 percent) evidenced weaker identity health, through impairment in their parenting self-concept (11 percent) or their overall vulnerability to mental health problems (21 percent). The majority of respondents (43 percent) fell in the mid-range in terms of their current and future self-concepts and mental health scores. Differences among these groups' identity health profiles suggest the need for prenatal interventions that can first distinguish these girls through assessment, and then tailor support strategies attentive to their needs. This research supports the notion that self-concept and identity health may well be important to disaggregating "problem behavior" (Oyserman and Saltz, 1993) as well as etiological pathways to strength versus vulnerability within high risk populations.

This study did not find significant differences in demographic characteristics among the four groups. Identity health does not appear to be associated with traditional socio-demographic categories such as race, education, economic need reflected through welfare use, and living arrangements. Overall, it is notable that identity health profiles are not significantly associated with sociodemographic factors that might otherwise indicate structural antecedents for evolution of these differences. However, this study was not explicitly designed for this purpose and cannot address in depth the role of social structural issues on identity development. This low income, urban youth sample may share more comparability than variability in regard to their socio-economic status. The absence of demographic differences may also reflect that cell sizes on some variables were smaller than is optimal for observing relevant variance. In addition, data on the use of welfare during pregnancy and after birth, and whether the respondents were living with a parent or partner during pregnancy may well be insufficient to adequately portray respondents' social and economic resources under current poverty and welfare policy. These limitations in the data warrant some caution in interpreting the findings.

POSSIBLE SELVES IN RELATION TO PSYCHOSOCIAL FUNCTIONING

Despite the fact that mothers in the four identity health profiles had no significant differences in terms of their socio-economic statuses and their experience of stressful life events, psychosocial functioning among the groups varied significantly. Relative to psychosocial outcomes, the group with strong identity health pre-natally consistently demonstrated better psychological outcomes and benefited from significantly higher levels of social engagement and lower parenting stresses one year post-partum. Those with vulnerable identity health profiles were generally more distressed and had greater use of mental health and substance use services post-partum than any of the other groups. Those with impaired parenting identities and vulnerable identity health also reported the lowest levels of family and total social support and the highest levels of additional help needed. They were somewhat more involved in risky behaviors post-partum, but the overall levels do not reflect high levels of substance abuse or delinquency. Greater use of services reflects higher need, but may also indicate a strength in help-seeking behaviors or help-seeking assistance. The finding that more help is needed than being received indicates that self-generated help-seeking or use of natural networks is insufficient to the level of need of many adolescent mothers.

The majority of the mothers in this sample have considerable need for economic assistance as suggested by the mean years of school completed and percentage relying on welfare post-partum. When we consider identity health within the contexts of respondents' socio-economic resources, different interventions are suggested. For example, those with vulnerable identity health profiles may identify a possible self that plans to access continued education, but they may lack sufficient resources to follow through on this desired self. In addition, they have higher need for additional help in their new parenting role and place less importance on performing well in school, factors that are likely to impede elaboration of this possible self and the attendant logistical strategies needed to accomplish this goal.

These findings point to identity health as an important clinical marker for predicting diversity in post-partum psychosocial functioning and, by implication, risk level for maladaptive behaviors. The current and possible self-concepts of girls across the four groups contribute to our understanding of how their cognitive framing is different relative to their psychosocial functioning. For example, the mean level of social competence predicted in a year by the vulnerable and impaired parenting identity groups--their prenatal possible self scores—matched the level that average identity health girls currently saw themselves as already achieving. Possible self-conceptions of parenting were more positive for those with vulnerable identity health relative to those with impaired parenting identities, but the former were struggling with more serious mental health risk factors. Left untreated, these mental health issues hold serious risk for parenting adaptiveness (Osofsky and Thompson, 2000). Thus, although both the vulnerable and impaired parenting groups would benefit from supportive prenatal interventions, differences in the qualitative nature of their identity health profiles would suggest that effective interventions for each group would stress different foci. For example, the vulnerable group may benefit from services with a mental health focus and the impaired group may benefit from services that help develop effective parenting skills.

The effects of violence exposure on self-concept is particularly germane for this population, as all respondents reported at least one instance of prior physical and/or sexual violence or threat of violence from a parent or other person. Kellogg, Hoffman, and Taylor (1999) review findings among teenage mothers with histories of victimization that link adolescent pregnancy with sexual abuse and concomitantly higher levels of psychosocial problems (e.g., higher depression, substance use, lower social support, self-esteem, and younger age at first drinking and consensual sex). Over half of vulnerable identity respondents and 85 percent of those with impaired parenting identity reported high levels of prior victimization. Those with impaired parenting identities had evidence of diminished psychological well-being post-partum, perhaps related to their comparatively higher levels of previous family and sexual violence victimization. In a prior examination of this sample, Lanz (1995) reports psychosocial correlates comparable to our findings associated with early forced sexual intercourse, noting the lack of established direct links from violence exposure to increased risk for maladaptive psychosocial functioning. Our findings suggest the value of adding identity health in assessing risks related to adaptive parenting and resilient social competence development among this high-risk population.

EFFECTS OF CHANGE IN SELF-CONCEPT OVER TIME

Studies of changes in self-concept over time have raised the question of the role of the ratio, or balance, between positive and negative possible selves as motivators for behavior. Some have found balance associated with positive change (Alois-Young, Hennigan and Leong, 2001), while others find no evidence for this (Oyserman and Saltz, 1993). In this study, balance appears to be more relevant for some identity health groups than others. Across all four groups, we see higher levels of balance during pregnancy than post-natally, and higher for current selves relative to possible selves. But, those with impaired parenting and vulnerable mental health seem to have benefited the most from higher ratios of positive to negative possible self-concepts. Their higher balance scores were associated with greater degrees of positive gain, although we cannot assume a causal relationship. Balance in these two groups functions in a way that is consistent with balance theory.

However, we see a lower ratio of positive to negative self-concepts among the highest functioning group; they are biased toward positivity rather than balance. This makes sense in light of research that people with stronger mental health, self-esteem, and social support view themselves and their futures in highly, even exaggerated positive terms, and that this positive interplay between person and environment becomes mutually reinforcing and stable (e.g.,

Nurius, 1991; Taylor 1989). In the current study we cannot disentangle temporality between positivity in self-conceptions and positivity in social resources and psychosocial functioning. This generates questions regarding the conditions under which internal tension of balance-- the juxtaposition of currently salient feared and hoped-for selves—is necessary or at least beneficial to guide and motivate adaptive action.

Our findings related to balance may provide clinically relevant information about how possible selves galvanize change and protect against challenges. For those with high levels of identity health, measuring balance per se may be less informative than measuring strategies used to attain possible selves and tracking developmental pathways that spawned pronounced positivity in self-views. For example, although groups did not significantly vary as a function of socio-economic characteristics, they did differ by clinical risk markers such as substance use, prior violence exposure, and social support. For those showing higher degrees of vulnerability and impairment, greater prenatal balance is associated with positive self-concept change one year later as well as greater self-concept actualization; that is, the extent to which prenatal possible selves were actually achieved. However, their balance scores at this one year point were dramatically lower and indistinguishable across groups within parenting selves.

One interpretation is that those with lower identity health needed the counterbalance provided by concurrent positive and negative selves to fuel and guide the stressful transition to parenting and that this year of "doing" parenting provided the social, cognitive, and affective input to change their self-concept set-points. This identity tension may be an asset to the more deliberative information processing necessary to making significant changes in cognitive and behavioral patterns. However, the work of significant goal pursuit involving identity change is taxing and difficult to sustain. Fear has a powerful but disorganizing effect on behavior and may be less likely to promote a specific, reasoned course of action indefinitely even when paired with positive envisioned selves (cf.,Aloise-Young, Hennigan and Leong, 2001; Orlandi, 1996). Ultimately, it may be beneficial to encourage the evolution or sequencing from a high ratio of positive to negative possible selves, towards a more uniformly positive sense of future self that can provide an opportunity for consolidating gains and buffering against stress.

IMPLICATIONS FOR INTERVENTION

The possible selves construct provides a useful tool for understanding how individuals develop behavioral goals to direct their efforts at change and growth. As with other schemas, possible selves become more detailed, vivid and anchored in experience with development, containing greater information about the means to achieve them and having an impact on self-regulation (Day et al., 1992; Higgins, 1998). People come to see themselves in ways consistent with their behaviors even when the new self-conceptions are contradictory to an existing self-view, and the behaviors of "doing" a possible self elicit reactions and expectations from the social environment that further stabilize related self-conceptions and behavioral patterns (Stein et al, 1998). This is one theorized basis for the gains achieved by the adolescents in this study, most pronounced for the impaired parenting identity group.

Consistent with other research on the role of possible selves in coping with stressful circumstances (e.g., Aloise-Young and Hennigan, 2001; Nurius, Lovell, and Edgar, 1988), parenting adolescents with negative current and future possible selves, such as those in the impaired parenting or vulnerable identity health groups, may need help to focus on increasing the production and elaboration of adaptive parenting and socially competent possible selves. Within a coping framework, higher numbers of negative current and possible selves are associated with use of less effective coping strategies such as avoidance. The presence of positive current and possible selves increases a sense of control and self-efficacy that fuels active coping and perseverance, leading to better success in overcoming adversity (Nurius, 1991; Penland et al., 2000). Cooper et al. (2003) found that dysfunctional styles of regulating emotions and emotionally driven behaviors are core features of risky or problem behaviors during adolescence. This large body of research has not typically included self-concept analysis, focusing instead on issues of personality. Yet our findings suggest that one mechanism for how dysfunctional emotional coping is translated into risky behavior is through its effect on self-concept. Future research in this area would benefit from including the notion of identity health.

By enhancing, promoting, and defending certain selves over others, the individual can optimize the use of certain knowledge and skills in the elected selves (Baltes and Cartensen, 1991). Possible selves can thus motivate and direct change both by initiating activities to reach positively valued future states (such as being a good mother or returning to school), and by encouraging action to avoid negative or threatening future possibilities (such as being a neglectful parent or unable to make it economically). When positive possible selves are deficient, the adolescent has fewer internal cognitive, emotional, or motivational guides for identifying and fulfilling a valued outcome and may be more susceptible to confusion and self-doubt as well as negative external influences (cf., Dunkel, 2003; Nurius, 1993a). For instance, interventions focused on adaptive parenting for adolescents would want to include as a component of skills training the process of identifying and elaborating valued possible selves as a motivational aid, in addition to the skills involved in goal attainment. One intervention strategy may include experiential exercises that aid young women to envision positive futures and future selves through art or journaling.

As has often been found in cognitive therapy, a dual focus on promoting positive possible selves as well as challenging or constraining negative possible selves is essential. Exposure to new ideas operationalized through roles, attributes, and skills can lead to generation of new possible selves. But to effectively compete for influence within the working self-concept active in any given moment, interventions also need to limit exposure to, enactment, or reinforcement of problematic behaviors to impede elaboration and accessibility of problematic possible selves (Nurius, 1993b; Stein et al., 1998). Our findings argue for the need to assess and support adolescent mothers with identity health vulnerabilities through traditional services, including mental health counseling, work with families and peer networks to strengthen social and instrumental supports, educational and employment assistance, and education about child development and parenting. These support services would need to be augmented with cognitive strategies that bolster more positive and adaptive visions of a future self, in conjunction with work to increase supportive external resources.

An important implication of this research for interventions targeting teenage mothers is that current and future possible selves are dynamic and are determined in the context of interactions with others. For example, having more information-rich experiences—whether these be formal services, social support from others, being engaged in contexts where we will interact with relevant others—helps us accumulate knowledge about parenting, work, relationships, and independent living. This knowledge is the foundation for actual and perceived adult competence. Strengthening the resources available for adolescent parents to access appropriate social networks can assist them in feeling less overwhelmed, facilitate access to additional tangible and intangible resources, and, ideally, ensure availability of a strong relationship with one or more competent, caring, positive adult who can provide the modeling, guidance and affirmation key to adaptive development and resilience (Osofsky and Thompson, 2000). Contextual influences are key factors to consider when examining social networks. For poor and uneducated parents, personal social networks are often determined by access to those individuals in the immediate geographical environment. A large body of research documents the powerful effects of social capital in network analyses (see Wilson, 1996). Although beyond the limits of this analysis, issues of social capital may limit the pool of available resources, lessening access to its benefits.

CONCLUSION

In conclusion, by anchoring descriptive characteristics of current and possible self dimensions of self-concept with concomitant indicators of psychological well-being, we capture a functional depiction of the self that we term identity health. The approach in this study was not intended to provide a definitive blueprint in this regard but rather to stimulate further research in this vein and to assess the value of identity health for a high risk population undergoing challenging identify transitions. This conceptual innovation paired with use of person-centered analytic techniques holds promise to discern meaningfully distinct groups within populations that heretofore may have remained underidentified. Applied here to a high risk sample of unwed, adolescent mothers, the method should have broad-based generalizability. This study has limitations related to sample size, generalizability of outcomes, measurement, and lack of controls that limit causal interpretation. However, the findings provide fresh insights regarding identity health diversity, implications for subsequent well-being, and targets for intervention as well as further research.

REFERENCES

Abidin, R.R. (1983). *Parenting Stress Index (PSI) administration booklet.* Charlottesville, V.A.: Pediatric Psychology Press.

Aloise-Young, P. A., Hennigan, K. M., Leong, C. W. (2001). Possible selves and negative health behaviors during early adolescence. *The Journal of Early Adolescence, 21*, 158-181.

Antonucci, T. C. and Mikus, K. (1988). The power of parenthood: Personality and ttitudinal changes during the transition to parenthood. In G. Y. Michaels and W. A. Goldberg (Eds.), The transition to parenthood: Current theory and research (pp. 62-84). Cambridge, England: Cambridge University Press.

Baltes, M. M and Carstensen, L. L. (1991). Commentary [on Possible selves across the lifespan]. Human Development, 34, 256-260.

Barth, R.P. (1982). *Coping skills training for school-age mothers.* Unpublished doctoraldissertation, University of California, Berkeley.

Coddington, R.D. (1972). The significance of life events as etiologic factors in the diseases of children: II. A study of a normal population. *Journal of Psychosomatic Research.*16, 205-213.++

Coley, R. L. and Chase-Lansdale, P. L. (1998). Adolescent pregnancy and parenthood: Recent evidence and future directions. *American Psychologist, 53,* 152-166

Cooper, M. L., Wood, P. K., Orcutt, H. K., and Albino, A. (2003). Personality and the predisposition to engage in risky or problem behaviors during adolescence. *Journal of Personality and Social Psychology, 2,* 390-410.

Cowan, C. P., Cowan, P. A., Heming, G., and Miller, N. B. (1991). Becoming a family: Marriage, parenting, and child development. In P. A. Cowan and M. Hetherington (Eds.), *Family transitions* (pp. 79-109). Hillsdale, NJ: Erlbaum.

Cross, S. and Markus, H. (1991) Possible selves across the life span. *Human Development, 34,* 230-255.

Day, J. D., Borkowski, J. G., Dietmeyer, D. L., Howsepian, B. A., and Saenz, D. S. (1992). Possible selves and academic achievement. In L. T. Winegar and J. Valsiner (Eds.). *Children's development within social context, Vol. 2: Research and methodology* (pp. 181-201). Hillsdale, NJ: Lawrence Erlbaum.

Derogatis, L.R. (1994). *SCL-90 Administration, Scoring and Procedures Manual - Third Edition.*Minneapolis, MN: National Computer Systems, Inc.

Dunkel, C. S. (2000). Possible selves as a mechanism for identity exploration. *Journal of Adolescence, 23,* 519-529.

Everitt, B. S., Landau, S., and Morven, L. (2001). *Cluster Analysis* (Fourth Edition ed.). New York: Oxford University Press.

Furstenberg, F. F. and Hughes, M. E. (1995). Social capital and successful development among at-risk youth. *Journal of Marriage and the Family, 57,* 580--592.

Gibson, W. A. (1959). Three multivariate models: Factor analysis, latent structure analysis, and latent profile analysis. *Psychometrika, 24*(3), 229-252.

Gold, M. (1966). Undetected delinquent behavior. *The Journal of Research in Crime and Delinquency, 3,* 27-46.

Higgins, E., T. (1998). Promotion and prevention: Regulatory focus as a motivational principle. *Advances in Experimental Social Psychology, 3*0, 1-45.

Hooker, K., Fiese, B. H., Jenkins, L., Morfei, M. Z., and Schwagler, J. (1996). Possible selves among parents of infants and preschoolers. *Developmental Psychology, 32,* 542-550.

Johnston, C. and Marsh, E.J. (1989). A measure of parenting satisfaction and efficacy. *Journal of Clinical Child Psychology*, 18, 167-175.

Kaplan, H., Martin, S., and Robbins, C. (1984). Pathways to adolescent drug use: Self-derogation, peer influence, weakening of social controls, and early substance use. *Journal of Health and Behavior.* (25) 270-289.

Kellogg, N. D., Hoffman, T. J., and Taylor, E. R. (1999). Early sexual experiences among pregnant and parenting adolescents. *Adolescence, 34,* 293-303.

Little, R. J. A., and Rubin, D. B. (1987). *Statistical analysis with missing data.* New York: Wiley and Sons.

Lanz, J. B. (1995). Psychological, behavioral, and social characteristics associated with early forced sexual intercourse among pregnant adolescents. *Journal of Interpersonal Violence*, 10, 188-200.

Magnusson, D. (1998). The logical and implications of a person-oriented approach. In R. B. Carins, l. R. Bergman and J. Kagan (Eds.), *Methods and models for studying the individual* (pp. 33-64). Thousand Oaks: Sage.

Markus, H. and Nurius, P.S. (1986). Possible selves. American Psychologist, 41, 954-969.

Markus, H. and Ruvulo, A. (1989). Possible selves: Personalized representations of goals. In L. A. Pervin (Ed.), Goal concepts in personality and social psychology. Hillsdale, NJ: Erlbaum.

Miller-Johnson, S., Winn, D. M., Coie, J., Hyman, C., Terry, R., and Lochman, J. (1999). Motherhood during the teen years: A developmental perspective on risk factors for childbearing. *Development and Psychopathology, 11*, 85-100.

Morfei,M. Z., Hooker, K., Fiese, B. H., and Cordeiro, A. M. (2001). Continuity and change in parenting possible selves: A longitudinal follow-up. *Basic and Applied Social Psychology, 23*, 217-223.

Muthen, B. O. (2002). Beyond SEM: General latent variable modeling. *Behaviormetrika, 29*(1), 81-117.

Muthen, L. K., and Muthen, B. O. (1998). *Mplus user's guide*. Los Angeles, CA: Muthen and Muthen.

Nowicki, S. and Strickland, B. (1973). A locus of control scale for children. *Journal of Consulting and Clinical Psychology*. 40(1), 148-154.

Nurius, P. S. (1993a). Human memory: A basis for better understanding the elusive self-concept. *Social Service Review, 67*, 261-278.

Nurius, P. S. (1993b). Assessing and changing the self-concept: Guidelines from the memory system. *Social Work, 39*, 221-229.

Nurius, P. S. (1991). Possible selves and social support: Social cognitive resources for coping and striving. In J. Howard and P. Callero, *The self-society dynamic: Cognition, emotion, and action*. London: Cambridge Press.

Nurius, P. S. and Berlin, S. B. (1994). Negative self-concept and depression. In D. Granvold (Ed.), *Cognitive and behavioral treatment: Methods and applications*. Pacific Groves, CA: Brooks/Cole.

Nurius, P. S., Lovell, M., and Edgar, M. (1988). Self-appraisals of abusive parents: A contextual approach to study and treatment. *Journal of Interpersonal Violence, 3*, 458-467.

Nurius, P. S. and Markus, H. (1990). Situational variability in the self-concept: Appraisals, expectancies, and asymmetries. *Journal of Social and Clinical Psychology, 9*(3), 316-333.

Orlandi, M. A. (1996). Prevention technologies for drug-involved youth. In C. B. McCoy, L. R. Metsch, and J. A. Inciardi (Eds.), *Intervening with drug-involved youth* (pp. 81-100). Thousand Oaks, CA, Sage.

Osofsky, J. D. and Thompson, M. D. (2000). Adaptive and maladaptive parenting: Perspectives on risk and protective factors (pp. 54-75). In J. P. Shondoff and S. J. Meisels (Eds.), *Handbook of early childhood intervention (2nd ed.),* Cambridge: University Press.

Oxford, M. L., Gilchrist, L. D., Morrison, D.M., Gillmore, M. R., Lohr, M. J., and Lewis, S. M. (2003). Alcohol use among adolescent mothers: Heterogeneity in growth curves, predictors, and outcomes of alcohol use over time. *Prevention Science, 4*, 15-26.

Oyserman, D., Gant, L., & Ager, J. (1995). A socially contextualized model of African American identity: Possible selves and school persistence. *Journal of Personality and Social Psychology, 69,* 1216-1232.

Oyserman, D. and Saltz, E. (1993). Competence, delinquency, and attempts to attain possible selves. *Journal of Personality and Social Psychology*, 65, 360-374.

Oyserman, D. and Markus, H. R. (1990). Possible selves and delinquency. Journal of Personality and Social Psychology, 59, 112-125.

Oyserman, D. and Markus, H. (1990). Possible selves in balance: Implications for delinquency. *Journal of Social Issues*, 46, 141-157.

Penland, E. A., Masten, W. G., Zelhart, P., Fournet, G. P., and Callahan, T. A. (2000). Possible selves, depression, and coping skills in university students. *Personality and Individual Differences*, 29, 963-969.

Rosenburg, M. (1965). *Society and the adolescent self-image.* New Jersey: Princeton University Press.

Ryff, C. D., and Heincke, S. G. (1983). Subjective organization of personality in adulthood and aging. *Journal of Personality and Social Psychology, 44*, 807-816.

Ryff, C. D. and Migdal, S. (1984). Intimacy and generativity: Self-perceived transitions. *Signs, 9*, 470-481.

Stein, K. F., Roeser, R., and Markus, H. R. (1998). Self-schemas and possible selves as predictors and outcomes of risky behaviors in adolescents. *Nursing Research, 47*, 96-106

Stevens, J. (1996). *Applied multivariate statistics for the social science* (Third Edition ed.). Mahaw, NJ: Lawrence Erlbaum Associates.

Straus, M. (1979). Measuring intrafamily conflict and violence: The conflict tactics (CT) scales. *Journal of Marriage and the Family*, 41, 75-88.

Taylor, S. E. (1989).*Positive illusions: Creative self-deception and the healthy mind.* New York: Basic Books.

Wilson, W. J. (1996). *When work disappears: The world of the new urban poor.* New York: Knopf.

In: Possible Selves: Theory, Research and Application   ISBN 1-59454-431-X
Editors: C. Dunkel and J. Kerpelman, pp. 123-140   © 2006 Nova Science Publishers, Inc.

Chapter 7

POSSIBLE SELVES IN THE LIVES OF ADULT WOMEN: A SHORT-TERM LONGITUDINAL STUDY

Kristine Anthis
Southern Connecticut State University

ABSTRACT

The current study examined the number and content of possible selves in the lives of adult women over the course of a five-month interval. Based on previous empirical studies of possible selves, a variety of hypotheses were proposed that addressed cohort differences in possible selves, continuity and change in possible selves, and predicting changes in possible selves over time with ego-identity. The results indicated mixed support for the hypotheses, but basically replicated previous research findings on possible selves. The findings are discussed in terms of how they extend both descriptive and predictive knowledge of possible selves.

I hope to become a middle-aged jock. I fear becoming a cancer patient. Should an individual endorse statements such as these -- his or her future athletic prowess, as well as chronic disease status, embody his or her possible selves. Possible selves are representations of the self in the future (Markus & Nurius, 1986), and concern both our hopes and our fears.

As Markus and Nurius have pointed out, the choices one has regarding the content of possible selves are endless, yet those possible selves most salient to an individual are frequently a function of one's socio-historical context. Although the content of possible selves is partly a function of one's current situation, possible selves symbolize 'prospective intentions', which provide an individual with the hope (and the fear) of possibilities beyond his or her present and immediate circumstances as well as the larger context. Therefore, the construct of possible selves itself implies both determinism and free will. As Giesen (1996) purports, "Thus, life circumstances may restrict an individual's structural progression but prospective intentions may provide views and goals beyond present circumstances..." (p. 214).

SOCIO-HISTORICAL CONTEXTS

Numerous psychological investigators have urged the field to acknowledge the importance of the role of socio-historical context in empirical studies of development. For example, as early as 1981, Anastasi recommended that in order to truly understand the causes of sex differences in psychological variables (such as personality), researchers need to better explain how the socio-historical contexts within which these individuals develop play a role in such differences -- rather than merely describing the pattern of differences between the sexes. A description of sex differences, isolated from the context in which they occur is inadequate, because different age cohorts represent changing social contexts. Contexts embody norms and values that impact the culture as a whole, as well as dictate what is acceptable and not acceptable behavior for the sexes. Contexts therefore have implications for the study of human development.

More recent investigators (e.g., Grotevant, 1987; Elder & Caspi, 1990; Markova, 1990; Kroger, 1993a) have made similar suggestions (i.e., that a more thorough understanding of development would result if the ways in which individuals interact with and are shaped by the cultural and historical contexts in which they are embedded in are systematically investigated). For example, as Duncan and Agronick (1995) have found, social events such as World War II and the second wave of the Women's Movement in the United States (Greenspan, 1994) have had a differential impact on individuals depending on their life stage (Stewart & Healy, 1989). Elder and Caspi (1990) refer to this assertion as the 'Life Stage Principle', which is the first component in their model of the mechanisms that link changing times and changing lives. That is, the life stage one is in (i.e., childhood, adolescence, early adulthood, mature adulthood, or late adulthood) when a social event is experienced will partially determine the effect that this social event has on an individual.

Stewart (1994) discusses how her longitudinal research with a cohort of women who graduated from Radcliffe College in 1964 simultaneously confirms and disconfirms Stewart and Healy's (1989) model of women's personality as a reflection of their particular life stage during a salient social event. For instance, over 90% of the women Stewart studied identified the second wave of the Women's Movement as the social event most meaningful to them (an event that took place during their late adolescence/early adulthood). But Stewart also found that individuals responded to this event differently (i.e., some welcomed the Women's Movement with open arms at that time, whereas others only felt the movement's influence later in life). Hence, Stewart (1994) has argued that determining the factors that contribute to variation within a cohort is just as important to understanding personality, as identifying those factors that contribute to variation between cohorts.

Consistent with this suggestion, Agronick and Duncan (1998) reported that women who experienced the second wave of the Women's Movement during early adulthood -- and who attributed a great deal of importance to it in determining their life goals -- reported significantly higher levels of achievement, independence, dominance, self-acceptance, empathy, and psychological mindedness during middle adulthood than those women in the same cohort who attributed little or no importance to the Women's Movement in influencing their selves. This finding was present even when controlling for individual differences in these variables at age 21. Consequently, although the cohort an individual belongs to may be a factor in the extent to which a social event influences one's personality, the individual's unique interpretation of the event itself also greatly contributes to the impact it will have on the individual.

EGO-IDENTITY

Although personality has often been defined as the characteristic and unique ways an individual behaves, thinks, and feels consistently over time (Engler, 1999) identity is, according to Kroger (2000), "a subjective feeling of self-sameness and continuity over time" (p. 8). Personality may have its origins in temperment, but the emphasis of its correlate, ego-identity, is conscious self-awareness. Most of the current research on ego-identity is based upon the work of Erikson (1959) and Marcia (1966). For Erikson, ego-identity was a concern with finding out who one is, a process that is usually begun in adolescence, and that is either resolved (i.e., ego-identity resolution) or not resolved (i.e., ego-identity confusion).

Elaborating on Erikson's (1959) theory that the crisis of adolescence was that of ego-identity resolution versus ego-identity confusion, Marcia (1966) proposed that ego-identity development consisted of four distinctly different ego-identity statuses in which an individual could be assigned, including Diffusion, Foreclosure, Moratorium, and Achievement. Diffusion involves a lack of exploring alternatives for one's identity (e.g., failing to experiment with different potential careers while in college, not questioning societal norms regarding sex roles, etc.), and a lack of commitment to any alternatives. Foreclosure involves a commitment to an identity, but does not involve exploration of alternatives. On the other hand, Moratorium involves an exploration of alternatives, but a lack of commitment to any of them. Achievement involves both an exploration of alternatives and a commitment to one or more of them.

Studies examining the personality trait correlates of the four different statuses (see Marcia, 1980, for a review) indicate that individuals classified as Moratorium report the highest levels of anxiety of all the statuses, while those classified as Foreclosure report the lowest levels of anxiety. Moratoriums and Achievements report higher levels of self-esteem than individuals classified as Foreclosure or Diffuse. Individuals classified as Foreclosure report significantly higher levels of dogmatic thinking and authoritarianism than do the other three ego-identity statuses. Foreclosures score significantly higher on the need for social approval and lowest on autonomy, as compared to the other three statuses.

EGO-IDENTITY STATUS AND HISTORICAL CONTEXT

In an attempt to establish a relationship between historical contexts and ego-identity, Helson (1992) conducted a retrospective study with a cohort of women whose average age was 43 years, and who graduated from college in 1958 or 1960. Participants were asked to describe the most difficult (i.e., unstable, troubling, discouraging, etc.) time of their life since college, and those who were classified as either Moratorium or Achieved tended to report their most difficult times as occurring during the middle period (from ages 36 to 46). On the other hand, women who were Diffuse or Foreclosed during mid-life tended to report these troubling times as occurring early in their lives (from approximately 21 to 27 years), or late (from ages 47 to 53). Helson attributes this latter finding to "...the experience of dependence and restriction associated with marriage and motherhood, followed by a lessening of that dependence and restriction as children grow up and the resistance of partners to a change in the roles in which they lose power" (p. 344).

In addition, the nature of these difficult times also varied as reported by the different ego-identity statuses. Helson (1992) found that for this sample of women, those who were classified as Diffused reported difficult times characterized by a general unhappy self, whereas women who were classified as Foreclosed reported difficult times characterized by either a bad partner or overload, whereas Moratorium and Achieved women's stories were characterized by unpleasant consequences of independence and put-downs at work. Helson interprets these findings as evidence for behavior patterns consistent with characteristics associated with each of the statuses. That is, women who failed to engage in the exploration process reported difficulties early in adulthood, at time when one begins to solidify her identity commitments to unquestioned roles, and/or later in life, perhaps after a accumulation of events that demonstrate the lack of adaptability of Diffuse or Foreclosed's choices. In addition, the themes associated with these two statuses, as opposed to the other two statuses (who are currently or have previously engaged in active exploration), are consistent with the lack of introspection and initiative often found in individuals classified as Diffuse or Foreclosed.

In order to provide a base rate assessment of the proportions of women classified according to these four different identity statuses, Helson, Stewart, and Ostrove (1995) compared three different cohorts of women: those who reached early adulthood in the 1950s, the early 1960s, and the late 1960s. The results of their study showed that women who came of age during the late 1960s were more likely to be identity Achieved during mid-life than the other two cohorts. For both of the younger cohorts, the Achieved status at mid-life was associated with significantly greater current psychological adjustment and well-being than this same status was for the oldest cohort. Helson et al. (1995) interpreted their findings as reflecting the few gains incurred (and perhaps even costs) by those who had established an independent identity while coming of age before the second wave of the Women's Movement. One may conclude then, that the adaptability of both personality characteristics such as assertiveness, as well as one's identity status, depends on the socio-historical context in which one is embedded.

EGO-IDENTITY AND POSSIBLE SELVES

In terms of the relationship between ego-identity and possible selves, Dunkel (2000) found that traditional age university students within the Moratorium status generated significantly more (hoped-for and feared) possible selves than the other three identity statuses, and also endorsed a smaller percentage of hoped-for and larger percentage of feared possible selves than the other statuses. Dunkel concluded that this pattern of results was consistent with the identity Moratorium's characteristics of both active exploration and anxiety. In a study with a similar sample, Dunkel and Anthis (2001) again found identity exploration to be associated with the generation of possible selves, but also demonstrated that changes in identity exploration were associated with changes in both hoped-for and feared possible selves over a four-month interval.

Specifically, those who experienced low levels of change in exploration showed a decrease in hoped-for possible selves over time, and increases in hoped-for possible selves over time occurred for those experiencing high levels of change in exploration. In terms of feared possible selves, those individuals who had experienced high levels of change in exploration showed a decrease in feared possible selves over time, whereas increases in feared possible selves over time occurred for those who experienced low levels of change in exploration. Hence, Dunkel and Anthis (2001) found tentative evidence for a relationship between possible selves and ego-identity (exploration), yet it remains to be determined which variable acted as the precursor and which as the outcome.

AGE AND POSSIBLE SELVES

In a sample of 18 to 96 year-old men and women, Cross and Markus (1991) found that for 18 to 24-year-olds, most of the hoped-for possible selves reported were within the realms of family (e.g., 'marrying', 'being a mother') and occupation (e.g., 'to be successful', 'to have a job I enjoy'), whereas the most-hoped-for possible selves for the 25-39 age group were personal (e.g., 'to be a more loving and caring person') and occupation (e.g., 'to be a professor', 'to excel at my job'). In terms of the 40 to 59 year-olds, the most frequently mentioned hoped-for possible selves (in descending order) were within the realms of family, personal and physical (e.g., 'the be fifteen pounds lighter', 'to be healthy'). Those respondents representing the 60+ age groups were most likely to report hoped-for possible selves (in descending order) within the personal, physical and family domains.

In terms of feared possible selves, the domain of physical-related was most often mentioned by all groups. This was particularly true for the 60+ age group, and material loss was reported significantly more by the 40 to 59 year-old age group than the other groups. The authors also reported significant negative correlations between age and both the number of hoped-for and the number of feared possible selves, suggesting an age-related trend in possible selves over time. Markus and Herzog (1992) also reported a similar pattern of findings, i.e., that older adults report fewer possible selves than do younger adults.

Frazier, Hooker, Johnson, and Kaus (2000) conducted the first longitudinal study of possible selves. Their study occurred over the course of five years, with a sample predominantly composed of female European-Americans between the ages of 55 and 89. At both the beginning and the end of the study, the participants listed health-related (e.g., 'not getting cancer') hoped-for possible selves as most important, and family-related as next most important. In terms of feared possible selves, dependency-related (e.g., 'not being a burden to my family') feared possible selves were listed as most important at the beginning of the study, with health-related feared possible selves listed as next most important.

In terms of the degree of continuity or change of these possible selves, Frazier et al. (2000) reported that there was strong evidence for continuity in the dependency-related, family-related and physical-related possible selves, with change more prominent in the health-related possible selves. Specifically, there was greater frequency of emergent (i.e., mentioning a possible self at Time 2, but not at Time 1) change in hoped-for health-related (e.g., not getting Alzheimer's disease) possible selves than there was fading (i.e., mentioning a possible self at Time 1 but not at Time 2) change, and the same emergent pattern held for physical-related (e.g., becoming disabled) possible selves from Time 1 to Time 2. As a result, the authors concluded that although there was some evidence of intraindividual change in possible selves over a five year period, the overwhelming majority of patterns across all possible selves categories reflected continuity.

THE CURRENT STUDY

Prior empirical studies of possible selves have unearthed both a static and a dynamic relationship between possible selves and ego-identity, so the purpose of the current study was to replicate dynamic changes in possible selves over time with adults (rather than with adolescents), and to be able to predict these changes in possible selves. Because previous findings on ego-identity have pointed to contextual influences on development, this study also attempted to address how such factors influence possible selves.

Given past research findings by Cross and Markus (1991), Hypothesis 1 stated that there would be differences in both the content of and the number of possible selves by age. Hypothesis 2 stated that, based on research by Frazier, Hooker, Johnson, and Kaus (2000), both continuity and change in possible selves would be evident over a five month period, but that continuity would be the predominant pattern. Hypothesis 3 stated that because past research (Dunkel & Anthis, 2001) has identified a relationship between ego-identity and possible selves, ego-identity scores (i.e., exploration and commitment) would predict the above-mentioned changes in possible selves over a five-month period.

METHOD

Participants

A total of 120 women participated in the study. The participants ranged in age from 21 to 64 years (M = 41.98, SD = 13.65). In terms of frequencies and percentages for participant racial/ethnic identification, 99 (83%) identified themselves as European-American, 4 (3.3%) as African-American, 1 (<1%) as Latina, 2 (1.7%) as Asian, and 14 (11.7%) did not respond to the question. Participants' level of education ranged from 'Some High School' to 'Post-College Professional Degree'. When asked if they were involved in a long-term romantic relationship, 102 (85%) indicated they were, with 18 (15%) indicating they were not. In terms of employment, 17 (14%) were not employed outside the home, while 103 (86%) were. Of those employed, 22 (18%) were employed full-time, and 81 (68%) were employed part-time. See Table 1 for frequencies and percentages within each educational category, both across the entire sample, and by cohort. The participants in the current study also participated in Anthis (2002a, 2002b).

Table 1 Frequencies and Percentages for Education by Cohort

	Total	Average-Age 30		Average-Age 55	
Education	n	n	%	n	%
Some High School	04	01	<01	04	03
High School	06	01	<01	05	06
Some College	41	37	31	11	10
College Degree	28	21	17	13	11
Some Professional	06	01	<01	06	05
Professional Degree	15	01	<01	17	14
Total	120	62	51	58	49

With the hope of obtaining as heterogeneous sample as possible, participants were recruited from a university with a campus-wide electronic mail message, and from a women's magazine circulated free of charge in a Midwestern city in the United States. The magazine advertisement announced an opportunity to learn more about one's self by participating in a study of women's personality. Participants were also recruited by offering undergraduate university students extra credit in exchange for participation in the study, or in exchange for enlisting the participation of female friends and family members.

MATERIALS

The participants completed a demographics sheet, the Possible Selves Inventory (PSI), and the Ego-Identity Process Questionnaire (EIPQ), along with a number of other measures not relevant to this study. The PSI is an open-ended measure of possible selves developed by Cross and Markus (1991). Respondents are asked to list the possible selves (both hoped-for and feared), that are currently relevant to them after being provided with a definition and examples of possible selves. Responses can be analyzed either by number of possible selves mentioned, and/or by the types of possible selves mentioned using a content analysis (Krippendorf, 1980). In the current study, both the number and the content of possible selves were examined. The possible selves listed on the PSI were independently rated by two undergraduate psychology students, using the coding categories established by Cross and Markus (1991). A random selection of the coding for 25% (i.e., 30) of the participants' hoped-for possible selves revealed a Cohen's Kappa of .69 for the first listed hoped-for possible selves, and a Cohen's Kappa of .78 for the first listed feared possible selves.

Balistreri, Busch-Rossnagel, and Geisinger's (1995) Ego-Identity Process Questionnaire (EIPQ) is a 32-item (16 of the items measure identity exploration, and 16 items measure identity commitment) scale that measures the dimensions of exploration and commitment, separately, and across eight different areas: Occupation, Religion, Politics, Values, Family, Friendships, Dating, and Sex Roles. Balistreri et al. (1995) report adequate reliabilities, and those for the current study included internal consistencies of .74 and .79 for the commitment and exploration scores, respectively, as well as test-retest reliabilities of .65 for commitment and .74 for exploration. In addition, the mean Time 1 commitment scores was 69.53 (SD= 9.10), with a range of 39 - 88 and the mean Time 2 commitment score was 69.66 (SD = 9.58), with a range of 46 – 96. The mean Time 1 exploration score was 66.47 (SD 10.53), with a range of 36 – 89 and the Time 2 exploration score was 65.33 (SD = 10.49), with a range of 31 – 92.

PROCEDURE

The measures were completed by the participants at both the first data collection period (Time 1) and the second data collection period (Time 2). Data collection at Time 1 occurred during the spring of 1999, and the data collection period at Time 2 took place five months later. Kroger (1993b) recommends frequent data collection intervals be used in longitudinal research, in order to better understand the process of transitions, and previous research (Dunkel & Anthis, 2001) on possible selves has found five months to be adequate for capturing movement in possible selves. Consequently, the current study was conducted over the course of five months. Although 230 of the original 267 participants indicated at Time 1 that they would be willing to participate at Time 2, 120 (44%) of the participants actually participated at Time 2.

RESULTS

Descriptive Data

Actual participation as second time and possible selves. Analyses were conducted in order to determine whether or not those who actually participated a second time were in any way different from those who did not participate a second time. A one-way analysis of variance (ANOVA) failed to reveal a significant relationship between participation a second time and the number of hoped-for possible selves at Time 1, $F(1, 265) = .26$, *ns*, and a one-way ANOVA between participation a second time and number of feared possible selves at Time 1 also failed to reveal a significant relationship, $F(1, 265) = .37$, *ns*.

Correlations Among Variables.

Table 2 displays the zero-order correlations between all the variables.

The mean number of possible selves at Time 1 and at Time 2 are presented in Table 3. It should be noted that the mean number of possible selves reported is relatively low, given past research on possible selves, yet this pattern precludes a simple explanation at this time.

Possible selves content. The frequencies for the first listed (i.e. the category of possible selves a participant lists first) hoped-for possible selves are presented in Figure 1, and the frequencies for the first listed feared possible selves are presented in Figure 2. As indicated in Figure 1, family (followed by career) was the most frequently reported first listed domain of hoped-for possible selves at Time 1, as well as at Time 2 (occupation was again listed most often after family at Time 2).

Table 2 Correlations between all Variables

Variables	1	2	3	4	5
1. Age	--				
2. T2 NHPS[a]	.15*	--			
3. T2 NFPS[b]	.14*	.86**	--		
4. T1 NHPS[c]	-.09	.19**	22**	. --	
5. T1 NFPS[d]	-.13*	.13*	.22**	.57**	--

Note. ** $p < .01$, * $p < .05$.
a = Time 2 Number of Hoped-For Possible Selves
b = Time 2 Number of Feared Possible Selves
c = Time 1 Number of Hoped-For Possible Selves
d = Time 1 Number of Feared Possible Selves

Table 3 Pre-Test and Post-Test Scores for the Number of Hoped-for and Feared Possible Selves

Variable	N	Pre-Test		Post-Test		t	p
		M	SD	M	SD		
NHPS[a]	267	4.53	2.32	2.37	3.23	9.80	.01
NFPS[b]	267	3.17	1.67	1.62	2.18	10.38	.01

Note.
[a]NHPS = Number of Hoped-for Possible Selves
[b]NFPS = Number of Feared Possible Selves

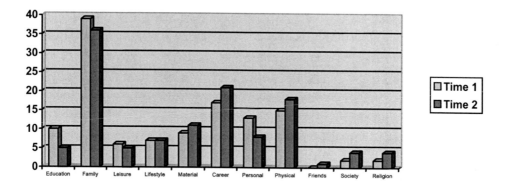

Figure 1 Frequencies of Hoped-for Possible Selves at Time 1 and at Time 2

In terms of feared possible selves, Figure 2 shows that physical was the most frequently reported first listed domain at both Time 1 and at Time 2, each time followed by family. Ten different categories of first listed hoped-for possible selves were mentioned at Time 1, and eleven were mentioned at Time 2. Eleven different categories of first listed feared possible selves were mentioned at Time 1, and ten were mentioned at Time 2.

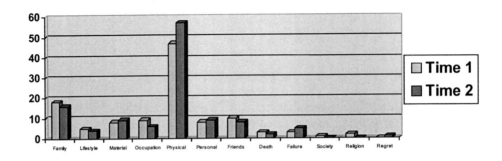

Figure 2 Frequencies of Feared Possible Selves at Time 1 and at Time 2

HYPOTHESIS 1A: CONTENT OF POSSIBLE SELVES BY AGE/COHORT

The 120 participants who remained in the study at Time 2 represented different cohorts, in that the ages ranged from 21-40, and from 50-64, with only one participant whose age (i.e., 49) fell between these two generational groups. Therefore, in order to take advantage of this representation, a variable of 'cohort' was created with two age categories. The '30 year-old cohort' had an age range of 21-40 and a mean age of 28.13 (SD = 4.91), and the '50 year-old cohort' had an age range of 49-64 with a mean age of 54.11 (SD = 3.31). In terms of the most important hoped-for possible selves for the 30 year-old cohort, family was mentioned most frequently and career next most often, at both Time 1 and Time 2. For the most important feared selves for the 30 year-old cohort, physical was mentioned most frequently and family next most often, at both Time 1 and Time 2. The hoped-for possible selves at Time 1 for the 50 year-old cohort were identical to those for the 30 year-old cohort, and at Time 2, family was mentioned most frequently and with physical next most often. The feared possible selves for the 50 year-old cohort were identical to those for the younger cohort, i.e., physical most frequently, with family next most often. Therefore, the results failed to support Hypothesis 1, as it appears that the differences between the two age groups in terms of the content of their most important possible selves were negligible.

HYPOTHESIS 1B: POSSIBLE SELVES NUMBER BY AGE/COHORT

One-way ANOVAs were then conducted to determine if there were significant differences in the number of possible selves generated by these two proxy cohorts. The first two ANOVAs used number of hoped-for possible selves (at Time 1 and at Time 2) as the dependent variable. When using Time 1 number of hoped-for possible selves, no significant differences between the two groups were found, $F(1, 116) = 1.24$, *ns*. When using Time 2 number of hoped-for possible selves, no significant differences between the two groups were found, $F(1,114) = .23$, *ns*. The second two ANOVAs used number of feared possible selves (at Time 1 and at Time 2) as the dependent variable. When using Time 1 number of feared possible selves, no significant differences between the two groups were found, $F(1,112) =$

.08, *ns*. When using Time 2 number of feared possible selves, no significant differences between the two groups were found, $F(1,110) = .12$, *ns*. These results also failed to support Hypothesis 1, as the differences between the two age groups (now in terms of the number of possible selves mentioned) were now non-existent.

HYPOTHESIS 2A: CONTINUITY AND CHANGE IN NUMBER OF POSSIBLE SELVES

As seen in Table 3, a paired sample t-test between the Time 1 and the Time 2 number of hoped-for possible selves indicated that there was a significant decrease in the mean number of hoped-for possible selves over the course of the study, $t(119) = -2.51$, $p < .01$. Similarly, a paired-samples t-test conducted between the Time 1 and the Time 2 number of feared possible selves indicated that there was also a significant decrease, over the course of the study, in the mean number of feared possible selves reported, $t(119) = -3.56$, $p < .001$. These results failed to support Hypothesis 2, as change, rather than continuity, was evident in both hoped-for and feared possible selves over the course of five months.

HYPOTHESIS 2B: CONTINUITY AND CHANGE IN CONTENT OF POSSIBLE SELVES

As mentioned above, the most frequently mentioned domains (across both cohorts) for hoped-for possible selves were, in respective order, family and career (then physical). At time 1, family was mentioned by 39 (or 33%) of the participants, career was mentioned by 17 (or 14%) of the participants, and physical hoped-for possible selves were mentioned by 15 (or 13%) of the participants. The most frequently occurring domains for the feared possible selves at time 1 were, in respective order, physical, family and friends. Physical possible selves were mentioned by 47 (or 39%) of the participants, family was mentioned by 18 (or 15%) of the participants, and the category of friends was mentioned by 10 (or 8%) of the participants. The domain of career was mentioned by 7% of the sample at Time 1 and 5% of the sample at Time 2. This domain was chosen for analysis over other categories though, because it would allow for comparisons to be made with the results from the hoped-for possible selves analyses.

The three above-mentioned (i.e., family, career and physical) categories were coded for continuity or change (either emergent or fading) from Time 1 to Time 2. Emergent change, according to Frazier, Hooker, Johnson and Kaus (2000), exists when a possible self is mentioned at Time 2, but not at Time 1. Should a possible self be mentioned at Time 1, but not Time 2, the change pattern is one of fading change. Similar to Frazier et al., McNemar's tests were conducted for each domain to determine if there was a significant difference between continuity and change in that domain from Time 1 to Time 2. McNemar's test is a nonparametric statistic that uses two dichotomous variables to test for changes in responses using the chi-square distribution. The results are presented in Table 4, with the frequencies (and corresponding percentages) representing the number (and percent) of times a pattern of continuity or a pattern of change occurred. As can be seen from the table, all but one of the analyses were significant, and of those that were significant, three out of five reflected continuity. The two significant findings for change were both in the domain of occupation, i.e., for hoped-for and feared possible selves regarding one's career.

Table 4 Frequencies, Percentages, and p Values for McNemar's Test of Change in Possible Selves

		Group				
		Continuity		Change		
Possible Selves	n	f	%	f	%	p value
Family						
Hoped for	84	52	62	38	45 .	05
Feared	65	29	45	36	55	ns
Career						
Hoped for	64	22	34	42	66	.05
Feared	29	07	24	22	76	.01
Physical						
Hoped for	55	41	74	14	26	.01
Feared	95	61	65	34	36	.01

Further McNemar's tests were then conducted for each domain to determine if there was a significant difference in the direction of change (i.e., between emergent and fading change) from Time 1 to Time 2. None of the analyses were significant, as both types of change occurred equally frequently. Yet overall, Hypothesis 2 was supported in this case, as the majority of possible selves patterns over the five-month interval reflected continuity rather than change.

HYPOTHESIS 3: PREDICTING CHANGES IN POSSIBLE SELVES OVER TIME WITH EGO-IDENTITY

In order to determine if ego-identity scores were able to predict changes in possible selves, hierarchical regression analyses were conducted. The analyses used EIPQ scores at Time 1 to predict possible selves scores at Time 2, beyond what possible selves scores at Time 1 were able to predict. Four analyses were conducted, two (one using EIPQ Exploration scores, the other using EIPQ Commitment scores) that examined changes in the number of hoped-for possible selves and two analyses (one using EIPQ Exploration scores, the other using EIPQ Commitment scores) that examined changes in the number of feared possible selves.

For the two hoped-for possible selves analyses, the number of Time 1 hoped-for possible selves scores were entered at step 1, and then either the EIPQ Exploration or EIPQ Commitment scores were added at step 2, with the number of Time 2 hoped-for possible selves scores as the outcome variable. For the two feared possible selves analyses, the number of Time 1 feared possible selves scores were entered at step 1, either the EIPQ Exploration or

EIPQ Commitment scores at step 2, with the number of Time 2 feared possible selves scores as the outcome variable.

Table 5 displays the F, R^2, R^2 Change, and standardized regression coefficients (β) after each step of predictor entry for hoped-for and for feared possible selves scores. As can be seen from the table, identity exploration was not a significant positive predictor of changes in hoped-for possible selves over time, but identity exploration was a significant predictor of changes in feared possible selves over time. In terms of identity commitment, it failed to serve as a significant predictor of changes in either hoped-for or feared possible selves over time.

Table 5 Hierarchical Multiple Regression of Number of Possible Selves at Time 1 and EIPQ Exploration and Commitment at Time 1 on Number of Possible Selves at Time 2

Variables	F	R^2	R^2 Change	β
		Time 2 Hoped-for Possible Selves		
Time 1 Number of HPS[a]	23.36**	.17	.17	.40**
Time 1 EIPQ Exploration	12.06**	.18	.01	.08
Time 1 Number of HPS	23.69**	.18	.18	.42**
Time 1 EIPQ Commitment	11.89**	.18	.00	.04
		Time 2 Feared Possible Selves		
Time 1 Number of FPS[b]	49.12**	.32	.32	.51**
Time 1 EIPQ Exploration	31.55**	.38	.06	.25**
Time 1 Number of FPS	50.35**	.32	.32	.56**
Time 1 EIPQ Commitment	25.39**	.32	.00	.06

Note. **$p < .001$
[a]Hoped-for Possible Selves
[b]Feared Possible Selves

DISCUSSION

The purpose of the current study was to identify and to provide potential explanations for patterns found within a sample of adult women's possible selves. A description of the pattern of findings for each tested hypothesis now follows, along with a potential explanation that corresponds to each pattern.

Hypothesis 1

It was proposed for Hypothesis 1, that based on past research, there would be differences in both the content of and the number of possible selves by cohort. In terms of the content of possible selves, the '30 year-old' and the '50 year-old' cohort groups in the current study reported almost identical first listed possible selves. That is, both age groups listed family (and then career) as the first listed hoped-for possible self at Time 1, while the younger cohort reported the same at Time 2 and the older group reported family (and then physical) as the first listed possible self. The two age groups reported identical possible selves when listing their feared possible selves, i.e., physical was mentioned most frequently and family next most often (categories which are identical to those reported for *hoped-for* possible selves by the 55 to 89 year-old women in Frazier, Hooker, Johnson, & Kaus' study in 2000 -- keeping in mind that they used both physical and health categories, unlike Cross and Markus and the current study, which collapsed both).

These patterns failed to support Hypothesis 1, which predicted age/cohort differences in possible selves. This hypothesis was primarily based on the work of Cross and Markus (1991), who found that with a sample of males and females, personal and occupation possible selves were the most important hoped-for selves in the 25-39 age groups; that family, personal and physical possible selves were the most important for 40 to 59 year-olds; and that personal, physical and family domains were for the 60+ age group. Although no major cohort differences were found in the current study (the within-cohort variability may have been artificially high though, given the wide range of ages represented in each cohort), the individual cohort patterns are somewhat similar to those found by Cross and Markus in 1990. The lack of male participants in the current study may partially explain the few remaining discrepancies with the original study, especially given that the most striking difference between the two studies is in the domain of career (i.e. it was the second-most important self for both age groups at Time 1). This suggests that the inclusion of career in both of the current cohorts' hoped-for possible selves is indicative of the increasing relevance of one's career to a woman's sense of self, even in mid-life.

Cross and Markus (1990) found significant negative correlations between age and both the number of hoped-for and the number of feared possible selves in their original study, yet the current study was only able to replicate this pattern when correlating age with the number of feared possible selves at Time 1. Cross and Markus' original findings seemed to therefore suggest an age-related trend in possible selves over time, in that the older individuals become, the fewer possibilities they foresee for themselves in the future. Now with the use of a longitudinal design in the current study, this very pattern was actually established, as both the number of hoped-for and number of feared possible selves significantly decreased over time, and only after a period of five months. Therefore, some support was established for Hypothesis 1 when examining the number of possible selves. An alternative explanation for the pattern found though, is that individuals may have listed fewer possible selves at Time 2 out of weariness over completing the materials a second time, rather than as evidence of stable change over time. This could very well be, given the short time interval of the study.

Assessment of the quantity of possible selves is just as potentially useful as the measurement of the content of quality of these selves, as Black, Stein, and Loveland-Cherry (2001) demonstrated using a sample of women 50-75 years of age. The authors administered a variety of health-related questionnaires to the participants, along with a measure of possible selves. They found that having one or more feared possible self regarding health, along with feeling one was capable of preventing this possible self coming to fruition, the more likely one was to obtain a mammography than those who also had health-related feared possible selves, but did not feel capable of preventing the occurrence of such.

Hypothesis 2

Hypothesis 2 stated that, based on past research by Frazier, Hooker, Johnson, and Kaus (2000), both continuity and change in possible selves would be found over a five month period, but that continuity would be the predominant pattern. The tests of this hypothesis produced mixed results, as change was apparent with the decrease in the number of both hoped-for and feared possible selves (across all domains) over the course of the study. This was remarkable, given the study was only conducted over five months. Yet when examining the content of possible selves, the results indicated that there was a significant difference between continuity and change in five of the six domains examined, and three of these five significant differences reflected continuity over time in possible selves. Unlike Frazier et al., the one domain in the current study that changed over time was not health-related, but career-related possible selves (the patterns of which were varied in that they were equally represented by both emergent and fading changes). As a result, these latter results supported Hypothesis 2 with the finding that continuity predominated over change in possible selves.

Hypothesis 3

Previous longitudinal research (Frazier, Hooker, Johnson, & Kaus, 2000) has demonstrated change in possible selves over time, as well as relationships between ego-identity and possible selves over time (Dunkel & Anthis, 2001), so the third hypothesis stated that identity scores would be predictive of changes in possible selves over a five month period. The results were limited, as they indicated that only identity exploration scores were able to predict changes in (feared) possible selves over time. Dunkel and Anthis (2001) reported that significant concurrent associations were found between changes in identity and changes in both hoped-for and feared possible selves, but the current study was only able to establish a predictive relationship between ego-identity (exploration) and feared possible selves. Consequently, Hypothesis 3 received only partial support, yet the pattern of exploration being associated with feared possible selves is consistent with previous research that has demonstrated the Moratorium status having the highest level of anxiety of all the statuses.

GENERAL DISCUSSION

The current study examined the relationship between possible selves and changes in ego-identity within two cohorts of women. Cohort differences are differences due to groups of people being born in different generations and as a result, subsequently exposed to radically different environments. Therefore, the variability between such groups are assumed to be greater than the variability within such groups, which Elder and Caspi (1990) support with their comment that "people are exposed to a range of experiences as they move through age-graded roles and accordingly share much of this world with other members of their cohort" (p. 201). Yet the findings from the current study did not support these presuppositions, as the content of each cohort's possible selves were almost identical. Stewart (1994) has argued that more studies are needed to explain why and how within-group differences are sometimes greater than between-group differences. It may be that the range of ages within each cohort (due to unequal samples in each age group) of the current study may have precluded any patterns from being identified though.

The current study was not cohort-sequential in design, only longitudinal. Because of this, a true test of cohort effects (versus age or period effects) in possible selves was not available in this study (see Glenn, 1977, for a discussion of true tests of cohort differences). Yet the changes found over five months are consistent with previous findings of decreases in possible selves with increasing age/the passage of time. The changes found in the current research may have been surprising given the relatively short time span of the study. Yet Caffarella and Olson (1993) found a primarily non-linear pattern that included discontinuities, along with periods of stability, in reviewing the literature regarding women's psychosocial development across the lifespan. The correlational method of this study prohibits causal inferences from being drawn about the relationship between possible selves and ego-identity, but regardless of whether possible selves serve as the chicken or the egg in their relationship with identity, the empirical literature is increasingly revealing that possible selves do appear to be intricately involved with process of ego-identity development during adulthood.

Cross and Markus' comment in 1991 perhaps foreshadowed this more recent body of work: "The underlying assumption is that in negotiating the changes and transitions of adulthood, individuals will use their possible selves as psychological resources to motivate and defend themselves" (p. 231). Shedding light on the process(es) of this mechanism is especially pressing, as researchers (e.g., Tomlinson-Keasey, 1993; Elder, 1995) in the field of human development are increasingly cognizant of the need to go beyond descriptions to that of explanations of their data, particularly in terms of heredity-environment interactions (Anastasi, 1958). It is recommended that future research heed to Holland's (1993) suggestion that in order to make causal inferences, an accumulation of known data from experimental research studies be available. Only then will the cause-effect of possible selves and ego-identity be untangled, along with greater clarity of the dynamics of possible selves.

Knowing how factors such as free will and determinism interplay with one another regarding possible selves is valuable in applied settings such as counseling, given Cross and Markus have noted motivational properties of possible selves, and subsequent research has found possible selves to be relevant in career planning with disadvantaged adolescents (Kerpelman, Shoffner, & Ross-Griffin, 2002; Robinson, Davis, & Meara, 2003). Therefore, understanding how prospective intentions provide hope for a life other than one's current, as Giesen (1996) suggests, would be especially useful.

AUTHOR NOTE

The author would like to thank Susan Goss and Lindsay Mason for their assistance with data coding and entry.

REFERENCES

Agronick, G. S., & Duncan, L. E. (1998). Personality and social change: Individual differences, life path, and importance attributed to the women's movement. *Journal of Personality and Social Psychology, 74(6),* 1545-1555.

Anastasi, A. (1958). Heredity, environment, and the question of "how?". *Psychological Review, 65,* 197-208.

Anastasi, A. (1981). Sex differences: Historical perspectives and methodological implications. *Developmental Review, 1,* 187-206.

Anthis, K. S. (2002a). On the calamity theory of growth: The relationship between stressful life events and changes in ego-identity over time. I*identity: An International Journal of Theory* and Research, 2(3), 229-240.

Anthis, K. S. (2002b). The role of sexist discrimination in adult women's ego-identity development. *Sex Roles: A Journal of Research*, 47(9-10), 477-484.

Balistreri, E., Busch-Rossnagel, N. A., & Geisinger, K. F. (1995). Development and preliminary validation of the ego ego-identity process questionnaire. *Journal of Adolescence, 18,* 172-192.

Black, M. E. A., Stein, K. F., Loveland-Cherry, C. J. (2001). Older women and mammography screening behavior: Do possible selves contribute? *Health Education & Behavior, 28(2),* 200-216.

Caffarella, R. S., & Olson, S. K. (1993). Psychosocial development of women: A critical review of the literature. *Adult Education Quarterly, 43(3),* 125-151.

Cross, S. & Markus, H. (1991). *Possible selves across the life span. Human Development, 34(4),* 230-255.

Duncan, L. E., & Agronick, G. S. (1995). The intersection of life stage and social events: Personality and life outcomes. *Journal of Personality and Social Psychology, 69(3),* 558-568.

Dunkel, C. S. (2000). Possible selves as a mechanism for ego-identity exploration. *Journal of Adolescence, 23(5),* 519-530.

Dunkel, C. S., & Anthis, K. S. (2001). The role of possible selves in ego-identity formation: short-term longitudinal study. *Journal of Adolescence, 24(6),* 765-776.

Elder, G. H., & Caspi, A. (1990). Studying lives in a changing society: Sociological and personological explorations. In A. I. Rabin, R. A. Zucker, R. A.

Elder, G. H., Jr. (1995). The importance of process. In P. Moen, G. H. Elder, Jr., & K. Luscher, with the assistance of H. E. Quick (Eds.), *Examining lives in context: Perspectives on the ecology of human development* (pp. 393-395). Washington, DC: American Psychological Association.

Engler, B. (1999). *Personality theories* (5th edition). Boston: Houghton Mifflin.

Erickson, E. (1959). *Ego-identity and the life cycle.* New York: W. W. Norton & Co.

Frazier, L. D., Hooker, K. Johnson, P. M., & Kaus, C. R. (2000). Continuity and change in possible selves in later life: A five-year longitudinal study. *Basic and Applied Social Psychology, 22(3),* 237-243.

Giesen, C. B. (1996). Self-initiated change: The dialectic of continuing development. In M. L. Commons, J. Demick, & C. Goldberg (Eds.), *Clinical approaches to adult development* (pp. 213-222).Norwood, NJ: Ablex Publishing Corporation.

Glenn, N. D. (1977). *Cohort analysis.* Newbury Park: Sage.

Greenspan, K. (1994). *The timetables of women's history.* New York, NY: Touchstone.

Grotevant, H. D. (1987). Toward a process model of ego-identity formation. *Journal of Adolescent Research, 2,* 203-222.

Helson, R. (1992). Women's difficult times and the rewriting of the life story. *Psychology of Women Quarterly, 16,* 331-347.

Helson, R., Stewart, A. J., & Ostrove, J. (1995). Ego-identity in three cohorts of midlife women. Journal of Personality and Social Psychology, 69(3), 544-557.

Holland, P. T. (1993). Which comes first, cause or effect? In G. Keren & C. Lewis (Eds.), *A handbook for data analysis in the behavioral sciences: Methodological issues* (pp. 273-282). Hillsdale, NJ: Erlbaum.

Kerpelman, J. L., Shoffner, M. F., & Ross-Griffin, S. (2002). African American mothers' and daughters' beliefs about possible selves and their strategies for reaching the adolescents' future academic and career goals., *Journal of Youth & Adolescence, Vol 31(4),* 289-302.

Krippendorf, K. (1980). *Content analysis: An introduction to its methodology.* Beverly Hills: Sage Publications.

Kroger, J. (1993a). The role of historical context in the ego-identity formation process of late adolescence. *Youth and Society, 24,* 363-376.

Kroger, J. (1993b). On the nature of structural transition in the ego-identity formation process. In J. Kroger (Ed.), *Discussions on ego ego-identity (*pp. 205-234). Hillsdale, NJ: Lawrence Erlbaum Associates.

Kroger, J. (2000). *Ego-identity development: Adolescence through adulthood.* London: Sage.

Marcia, J. E. (1966). Development and validation of ego ego-identity status. *Journal of Personality and Social Psychology, 3,* 551-558.

Marcia, J. E. (1980). Ego-identity in adolescence. In J. Adelson (Ed.), *Handbook of Adolescent Psychology* (pp. 159-187). New York: John Wiley & Sons.

Markova, I. (1990). Causes and reasons in social development. In G. Butterworth, and P. Bryant (Eds.), *Causes of Development: Interdisciplinary Perspectives* (pp. 186-211). New York, NY: Harvester Wheatsheaf.

Markus, H. & Nurius, P. (1986). Possible selves. *American Psychologist, 41(9),* 954-969.

Markus, H. R. & Herzog, A. R. (1992). The role of the self-concept in aging. *Annual Review of Gerontology and Geriatrics, 11,* 110-143.

Robinson, B. S., Davis, K. L., & Meara, N. M. (2003). *Motivational attributes of occupational possible selves for low-income rural women. Journal of Counseling Psychology, 50(2),* 156-164.

Stewart, A. J., & Healy, J. M. (1989). Linking individual development and social changes. *American Psychologist, 44(1),* 30-42.

Stewart, A. J. (1994). The women's movement and women's lives: Linking individual development and social events. In A. Lieblich & R. Josselson, (Eds.), *Exploring ego-identity and gender: The narrative study of lives* (pp. 230-250). Thousand Oaks, CA: Sage Publications.

Tomlinson-Keasey, C. (1993). Opportunities and challenges posed by archival data sets. In D. C. Funder, R. D. Parke, C. Tomlinson-Keasey, & K. Widaman (Eds.), *Studying lives through time: Personality and development* (pp. 65-92). Washington, DC: American Psychological Association.

In: Possible Selves: Theory, Research and Application   ISBN 1-59454-431-X
Editors: C. Dunkel and J. Kerpelman, pp. 141-161   © 2006 Nova Science Publishers, Inc.

Chapter 8

POSSIBLE SELVES AS JOINT PROJECTS

Sheila K. Marshall and Richard A. Young
University of British Columbia
José F. Domene
Trinity Western University

ABSTRACT

Rather than conceptualizing possible selves as an individual venture of processing social information, this chapter presents the view that possible selves are social endeavors. We describe how the adoption, construction, revision, or abandonment of potential roles and characteristics can be studied as joint projects which are series of mid- and long-term goal-directed actions undertaken by two or more individuals. A theoretical approach to joint projects that is congruent with the goal-directed and socially embedded nature of possible selves is presented along with an overview of a methodology that has been designed to investigate joint projects. The utility of the theoretical and methodological approach for studying possible selves is discussed.

Possible selves are meaningful future self-representations (Markus and Nurius, 1986). Research on the regulatory function of possible selves (e.g., Oyserman and Markus, 1990; Hooker and Kraus, 1992) has advanced understanding of how the self-system guides actions. However, the processes by which people construct their repertoire of potential images remains understudied resulting in a lack of significant conceptualization supported by empirical evidence.

Possible selves emerge from images within proximal social environments and experiences (Trommsdorff, 1986; Markus and Nurius, 1986). Despite the social nature of possible selves that is presented at the level of theory, in the empirical literature the acquisition and modification of possible selves is more often conceptualized as an individual venture of processing social information (e.g., Hooker, Fiese, Jenkins, Morfei, and Schwagler, 1996; Segal, DeMeis, Wood, and Smith, 2001). While recent efforts have been made to understand how possible selves emerge in interpersonal relationships (e.g.,

Kerpelman and Pittman, 2001), the bulk of research has paid little attention to how the proximal environment and social experiences serve to support the construction of possible selves.

This chapter adopts the view that possible selves are social endeavors and describes how the adoption, construction, revision, or abandonment of potential roles and characteristics can be studied as joint projects. Joint projects are series of mid- and long-term goal-directed actions undertaken by two or more individuals (Young, Valach, and Collin, 1996). We postulate a theoretical approach to joint projects that is congruent with the goal-directed and socially embedded nature of possible selves. Additionally, we provide an overview of a methodology that has been designed to investigate joint projects and demonstrate its utility for studying possible selves. The theoretical approach and methodology will provide a foundation for understanding the construction of possible selves in proximal social contexts.

ACTION THEORY

The theory of action in which we are embedding our alternative view of possible selves is based mainly on the work of von Cranach and his colleagues (von Cranach, Kalbermatten, Indermühle, Gugler, 1982) and applications that have been made of that work in applied fields of psychology and the social sciences, including family studies and nursing (e.g., Valach, Young, and Lynam, 1996; Young, Valach, and Collin, 2002; Young et al., 2001). Valach, Young, and Lynam (2002) have provided a broad discussion of the conceptualization and method action theory. This approach to action has its sources in works such as Mead (1934), Parsons (1937/1968) and Schuetz (1932/1967). As well, it is part of recent efforts (Brandtstädter and Lerner, 1999; Gollwitzer and Bargh, 1996) and is compatible with notions such as activity theory (Wertsch, 1998; Vygotsky, 1986/1934).

Action theory is more of a conceptual approach than a highly predictive theory in the traditional sense. One may even consider it an epistemology or a language for conceptualizing how people live their lives. It is primarily concerned with processes across time and addresses how people engage themselves in their daily lives. In action theory, much of human behavior is considered as goal-directed, intentional action. Writing this chapter as well as reading it, working with others in a research group, and taking the bus are but four examples of the myriad number of actions in which people engage in action on a daily basis. This theory offers three perspectives on action: social meaning, internal processes, and manifest behavior. One can readily perceive that working in a research group has social meaning. This action can be readily understood by the participants, by observers, as well as by those who know of its occurrence from afar. It is socially meaningful to such an extent that governments, foundations, and individuals will support the work of research groups without close observations of the processes in which they engage. Once rooted in this social meaningfulness, these processes in which the researchers are engaged serve to construct (socially) the very meaningfulness in which they are rooted. Conversely, the social meaningfulness of an action is a necessary condition in most cases of the others' participation in that action. The social meaningfulness of action is also tied to its goals.

A second perspective on action is that action represents and encapsulates the internal cognitions of the actors, including cognitions that are used to steer the action and emotions that are used to energize it. One can readily appreciate how internal cognitions and emotions regulate and steer individual actions. Caring about this topic may energize each of the co-authors to contribute to this chapter. Sharing those feelings tacitly or explicitly among the co-authors allow the joint project of writing this chapter to go forward. A third perspective on action is that it can be seen as manifest behavior. There are specific, observable behaviors that people are engaged in during action. One can imagine the observable behaviors that are involved in writing this chapter, including consultation among the co-authors, editing the text and so on. These three perspectives provide an integrated view with molar processes of social relevance, intermediate systems of intrapersonal processes and finally, the micro level of observable behavior. We have alluded to the processes and corresponding functions of these perspectives. The process of social meaning functions to regulate action at the social level, internal processes serve to steer and energize action, and manifest behavior has a self-regulatory function, that is, we continue with, modify and change our behavior as we engage in it.

Action theory incorporates the notion of hierarchical goals across time. When particular goals are considered in relation to each other and across time, some coalesce, and subsume other goals. One may consider the hierarchical organization of action across time as a project. Projects include imagined and/or communicated end states or desired processes. One can imagine a project as involving actions that are considered as connected to each other and as having some priority in relation to actions that may not be as well organized. For example, it is not uncommon to think of a research study as a project. Most research studies involve a series of steps across time. These projects have goals that are decided at the beginning of the project and emerge during its course. The social meaning of the project is concomitant with these goals and represented in the cognitive steering, the emotional energizing, and the particular behaviors in which the researchers engage. The project may begin before all members of the research team are assembled and may continue after some have left the research team. The project also fits within a unique hierarchy of actions and projects that each member of the research team holds. The example of a research project may conjure up the notion of goals that are rational and completely set in advance. This is not the case of project as we propose it in action theory. Even in the case of the research project, we understand that new goals can emerge as the research is in progress and proceed in intuitive ways that can lead to previously unanticipated discoveries.

In action theory, motivation can be understood as the energizing of action that arises in connecting action with superordinate goals and processes (projects). In other words, a project, incorporating superordinate goals, can have considerable motivating influence. Motivation for particular actions increases as a function of their relationship to projects.

The language of action theory is particularly applicable to both individual and joint or group action. When one considers particular actions, focusing on the individual may be sufficient. However, when one considers superordinate goals, extended across time (that is, a project) then group action is an appropriate focus. This focus represents a shift in the traditional individualist approach of Western psychology. The contribution of action theory is to continue to address human processes and include the group as the locus of that address.

Possible selves construction as action. Possible selves have previously been described as consistent with action theoretical perspectives (e.g., Brandtstädter, 1998; Little, 1999) because possible selves operate as motivational resources. Potential selves motivate behavior when the valuation of future representations activates the pursuit of desirable goals and the avoidance of feared images (Oyserman and Markus, 1990). Extant literature views the motivational function of possible selves as intentional self-development or action (Brandtstädter, 1998). Unfortunately, the emphasis on motivation and self-development has overlooked the construction of possible selves; the construct has been the starting point for describing intentional self-development within action theoretical perspective. Advancement of research on possible selves requires employment of a theoretical framework that describes the formation and modification of possible selves. We propose that action theory is consistent with the uptake, modification, construction, maintenance, or abandonment of potential self-images.

The starting place for describing the construction of possible selves is an understanding of what we mean by self. Linking to historical action theory perspectives (James, 1961/1892; Mead, 1934), self is viewed as a social phenomenon that emerges out of social interactions. Self, as a motivated system (Mischel and Morf, 2003), is constructed through experiences in the interpersonal world and contributes to the shaping of proximal social environments (Tesser, 2002) within the bounds of affordances and constraints. As a facet of the self, the repertoire of meaningful future images is derived from interactions with the social environment. In turn, the regulatory function of possible selves contributes to selective and constructive activities that fit with intentions and the social environment.

One feature of the self, as we have described the construct, is the ability to imitate, explore, and try on various social roles and characteristics. Individuals' adoption of social roles and characteristics within the social realm contributes to possible selves. A range of goal-directed actions associated with trying out potential images have previously been described. For example, the exploration of social roles in the immediate environment as feasible potential images, efforts to integrate social feedback that is relevant to future self-construals (e.g., Oyserman, Terry, and Bybee, 2002), or discussing potential scenarios with a peer (e.g., Young et al., 1999) are goal-directed actions. These actions contribute to the uptake, alteration, or abandonment of possible selves.

Not all actions related to possible selves involve change. Individuals are likely to seek some stability of future self-views in order to maintain the sense that self persists over time (e.g., Erikson, 1968; Chandler, 1994). Maintenance of possible selves over time involves actions such as self-verification. Self-verification is a process by which individuals maintain consistent self-perceptions by eliciting congruent information about self-perceptions from the social setting (Swann, 1987). Self-verification varies according to the importance and certainty of the future image (Kerpelman and Pittman, 2001). Images are likely to be abandoned (yet another type of action) when their import is low or when discrepant information initiates movement toward exploring or constructing alternate potential selves.

Action theory is employed here to explain the uptake, shaping, maintenance, or abandonment of possible selves. These actions involve the immediate social setting. Theoretical links to the social setting are accomplished by describing how intentional behavior can be construed as joint action.

POSSIBLE SELVES CONSTRUCTION AS JOINT ACTION

Envisioned selves have been proposed to emerge from images within individuals' proximal social environments and experiences (Markus and Nurius, 1986). Personally relevant social experiences such as parenting (Hooker et al., 1996) have been found to influence the construction and modification of potential self-views. Additionally, social feedback and information from the environment contribute to alterations of present possible selves or willingness to consider alternative possible selves (Kerpelman and Pittman, 2001). The influence of social experiences on possible selves is indicative of the relevance of conceptualizing the uptake, shaping, retaining, or discarding of images as joint action between two or more people rather than individual activities.

We propose that the shaping of possible selves can be *joint* actions because individuals are unlikely to engage in the adoption, modification, maintenance, or abandonment of images in social isolation. Potential images are more likely to be co-constructed with other significant individuals such as family members, friends, or peers. Experimental research by Kerpelman and Pittman (2001) supports the idea that possible selves can be construed as joint action. Their protocol provided participants with feedback about future career and family roles. The feedback was given to the research participants who were accompanied by a partner (dating partner or same sex friend) to the laboratory. The focal participant and partner were left alone for five minutes to review feedback provided by an experimenter. Results indicated that individuals' responses to their partners' reactions to the feedback contributed, under certain circumstances, to the participants' modification of future self-construals. Similarly, when Young et al. (1999) observed adolescent dyads engaged in career conversations, three broad future-oriented goals emerged: interpersonal issues for the future (marriage, travel plans), educational planning, and career selection. These goals are congruent with joint possible selves.

POSSIBLE SELVES CONSTRUCTION AS PROJECT

Actions are short-term events and do not adequately reflect the construct of possible selves or to the process of adopting, shaping, or discarding potential images. Individuals take up, modify, decide and act on imagined futures over a mid- to long range period of time. Goal-oriented and intentional actions that link into series of coordinated and meaningful sets over time are what have been referred to as *projects* (Little, 1983, 1989, 1999; Cochran, 1992). Project recognizes the time-oriented and intentional actions of possible selves. However, if actions related to the construction, adoption, modification, maintenance, or abandonment of possible selves are carried out with other individuals in the proximal social environment, then possible selves projects are joint projects. Young and colleagues (2001) describe intentional coordinated actions of two or more individuals, such as a parent and adolescent child, over a mid-range period of time as joint projects. We propose that possible selves projects emerge from the joint action and goal-directed language of dyads.

We have focused on describing the construction, maintenance, modification, and abandonment of possible selves within an action theoretical perspective. In order to advance research in this area, we describe a methodology that can be employed to study how possible selves emerge in the everyday language of conversations between socially connected individuals such as parents and their adolescent children or marital dyads.

METHODOLOGY

Rationale

Extant assessment protocols do not capture future selves as they emerge in actions and everyday language of individuals' conversations with others. Focusing on the motivational function and content of possible selves, most assessment protocols access images as they are currently construed (e.g., Hooker et al., 1996; Oyserman and Markus, 1990). Some self-rating instruments (e.g., Cross and Markus, 1991) are scored to evaluate the balance between expected and feared future selves while other self-reports provide information about the content of future self-contruals (e.g., Segal et al., 2001). In contrast to these assessment protocols, the research methodology that we propose for examining possible selves has the advantage of tapping possible selves as they naturally occur. The procedures presented below allow the enactment of possible selves to be revealed by explicitly examining the actions that occur in conversations between socially connected pairs of people.

It has been proposed that potential selves emerge through individuals' reflection on the social feedback and information that is received from their environment (e.g., Kerpelman and Pittman). The protocol that we present is able to tap both the person's reflexive processes (through the self-confrontation procedure, daily logs, and monitoring telephone calls), and the kinds of feedback and environmental information that is presented to them (tapped through observation of joint conversations, daily logs, and monitoring telephone calls (see Valach, Young, and Lynam, 2002 for an extensive discussion of the method).

Finally, possible selves are theorized to be mutable over time, as these images are the facet of self-knowledge that is most sensitive to changing life circumstances (Markus and Nurius, 1986). Changes in potential selves over time can be captured by our methodology because people's actions, reflections, and the salient feedback that they receive are monitored over a period of six months rather than being captured at a particular moment. These innovative features of our research methodology facilitate an examination of the acquisition, modification, abandonment of hoped-for and feared possible selves as enacted in everyday living. The procedures enable us to account for the dynamic nature of possible selves in a way that has not always been possible in previous research.

Data Collection

The research protocol associated with action theory assesses the actions and goal-directed language of pairs of socially connected people (e.g. a couple, a parent and child, two friends) engaged in a joint project over a medial length of time. A period of six months, while arbitrary, has proven to be sufficient to reveal changes that occur in people's possible selves (e.g. Domene et al., 2003). Information is gathered from each dyad using multiple techniques, allowing participants' possible selves to be viewed from the perspectives of manifest behavior, internal processes, and social meaning. Specifically, the protocol utilizes interviews, observation of conversations, a self-confrontation procedure, participant self-report logs, and periodic telephone monitoring, all occurring in a structured sequence.

After participants are recruited and screened, they undergo a multi-part initial interview. This begins with a "warm-up" period, involving both members of the participant dyad and two interviewers. Participants are asked general questions about themselves, including their present interests, thoughts about the future, and involvement in each others' lives. The purpose of this warm-up is to increase participants' comfort with the research setting and recording equipment, and to prime them to be thinking about their future. Following the warm-up, the dyad is invited to engage in a 10 to 15 minute conversation in the absence of the interviewers. While the interviewers suggest that they talk about what they see for their futures, participants are provided the freedom to generate and direct the course of the conversation themselves. The self-generated and self-directed nature of the conversation allows the dyad to communicate using their natural, on-going style of interaction, and provides an opportunity for the themes that are most salient to the participants themselves to emerge. Appendix A displays a transcription of the first few minutes of a conversation between a mother and adolescent female.

Immediately afterwards, each member of the dyad will separately engage in a "self-confrontation procedure," with one of the interviewers. The self-confrontation involves the participant watching and commenting on his or her internal processes during the conversation. Participants are asked to describe the thoughts and the feelings that were occurring for them during each segment of the conversation. They pause the video-replay whenever something comes to mind. In addition, if a minute of tape passes without the participant making a comment, the interviewer will pause the tape and directly elicit information regarding the participant's thoughts and emotions at that time. Self-confrontation permits participants' internal processes to be accessed in a way that facilitates recall (i.e. having them review themselves on tape) and maintains privacy (i.e. being able to comment on what they were "really" trying to think or accomplish, without having to be concerned about what the other member of the dyad might hear). Appendices B and C display small portions of the self-confrontations in response to the conversation displayed in Appendix A.

Information from this first round of data collection is then subjected to an initial data analysis to generate a narrative description of each participant's opinions and their intent in the conversation, and to tentatively identify a joint project in which the dyad is engaged (see "data analysis" for details). The project includes goals or envisioned end-states that dyad members are working towards and, therefore, is reflective of their possible selves. These summaries are then written in chronological order, using the participants' own words as much as possible, in order to facilitate recognition by the participants when it is presented back to them in a subsequent interview.

The second interview begins with a presentation of each participant's tentative narrative descriptions to him or her individually, in order to elicit feedback regarding the accuracy of the analysis, and to correct any errors in interpretation. Participants and interviewers then engage in a group discussion to allow participants to share their narratives with each other, and delineate a joint project to focus upon. This includes clarifying the nature of the project by embedding it in specific actions (e.g., "if the project is working, we will be talking more openly with each other, and will sometimes go out for the evening without taking our children with us"). The joint project that is selected needs to be one in which the dyad is already engaged on an on-going basis, rather than something new that is derived from their involvement in the research.

For the following six months, participants complete log entries about their daily project-related activities. Information recorded in the log includes a description of the activity, their internal reactions at the time, and their intended goals for that action. Each member of the dyad is asked to complete their own log, and to respect the privacy of the other participant's records. In addition, the interviewers maintain regular telephone contact with participants, to discuss their progress towards their joint projects, and assess for changes that may be occurring in their possible selves. A final interview occurs at the end of the monitoring period. At this time, participants engage in another joint conversation and self-confrontation procedure, addressing the progress that they have made towards their joint project. Additionally, a short, semi-structured individual interview is conducted during self-confrontation, to re-assess participants' possible selves in light of the actions that they have taken over the six months, and to follow up on any other pertinent issues that emerged during the monitoring period.

DATA ANALYSIS

Information from all three meetings, the self-report logs, and telephone monitoring reports undergo a systematic form of content analysis. Particular attention is paid to the two joint-conversations, which are analyzed using the method for qualitative content analysis of action developed initially proposed by von Cranach and colleagues (1982) and refined over several research studies (e.g., Young, Valach, Dillabough, Dover, and Matthes, 1994; Young et al., 1999; Young et al., 2001). The procedure involves working from smaller to larger levels of analysis. First, the "expressions" and "functional steps" of the conversation are identified. Expressions are the actual manifest behavior that can be observed in the individual sentences and phrases of the conversation (e.g. asking a question, or making a statement). Functional steps are the intentional means by which each participant moves towards their goals, the purpose or function of the actions that they are engaging in (e.g. asking a question *to challenge the child's previous statement*, or asking a question *to elicit more information from the spouse*). It is then possible to identify the "goals" of each participant over the course of the conversation. Goals are what the participant hopes to accomplish through the expressions and functional steps (e.g. challenging the child's previous statement *to promote an alternative viewpoint*, or challenging the child's previous statement *as a way to exert control*). Goals are assessed within socially meaningful units that are usually shorter segments of the conversation, and can change over the course of the dialogue. Finally, each participant's "intentional framework"- his or her overall purpose or goal for the conversation in its entirety- is identified. It should be noted that, while the joint-conversation is the primary unit for analysis, information from the self-confrontation procedure (and possibly even the warm-up, if relevant) are incorporated into the process, in order to increase the accuracy of coding the latent content of the material. Self-confrontation information is particularly valuable for identifying the goals, and making the links between goals and the functional steps / expressions.

In the first round of analysis, information derived from this procedure is used to generate the narrative descriptions of the actions and goals for each participant in the initial conversation, and to tentatively identify on-going projects in which the dyad is engaged. (This is the information presented back to the participants for feedback in the second interview). In the second round of analysis, data from the conversations and self-confrontations are supplemented by information from the self-report logs, telephone monitoring and final semi-structured interview. Content analysis, with a similar action theory orientation as the analysis of the conversations, is employed to gain a broader understanding of the nature and shifts in participants' possible selves, as they worked towards their projects.

Consistent with the constructivist paradigm used, analysts would allow categories and themes to emerge naturally from the data, rather than attempting to fit the data into a pre-existing framework. This process of analysis allows for the identification of the constructs that are the most salient for each dyad, rather than focusing upon researchers' preconceptions of what is important. After the analysis of material from every dyad is completed, the identified constructs can be examined across the group in its entirety, with similarities between families and aspects that were unique to a particular dyad both being identified.

MAINTAINING THE RIGOR OF THE ANALYSIS

This method of gaining a systematic, qualitative understanding of possible selves incorporates a number of measures to ensure that a high level of rigor is maintained over the course of data analysis. These measures meet existing standards for conducting qualitative research in the health and psychological sciences (e.g. Elliott, Fischer and Rennie, 1999; Krefting, 1991; Lincoln and Guba, 1985):

1. *Audit trail.* Descriptions of all potential participants, written record of the analysis process, video recording of all interviews, and logs of the content of telephone contacts combine to form detailed audit trail of how the results and conclusions were reached. This permits outsiders to examine the research process and understand the train of logic leading to the conclusions that were made.
2. *Consensus.* Any discrepancies in the coding and categorization of data are discussed by the entire group until consensus regarding the appropriate interpretation is reached. This process is similar to the notion of inter-rater agreement in quantitative research (Young et al., 2001). Working towards consensus is performed at all levels of analysis, to guard against the possibility that a single researcher's preconceived expectations will systematically distort the information that is generated.
3. *Member checking.* This commonly utilized method of establishing the credibility of qualitative research involves bringing research materials and conclusions back to the original participants to ensure that the researcher has accurately captured their point of view. Presentation of the narratives and tentative joint-projects to participants after the first round of analysis reflects this member-checking process.
4. *Triangulation.* Information from observation, interview, self-report logs and the self-confrontation procedure are all used to formulate an understanding of possible selves. In effect we have data from the three perspectives of action discussed earlier in this

article, that is, manifest behavior, internal cognitions, and social meaning. This convergence of multiple sources provides a check against the possibility that findings are the result of a particular data collection technique, or way of phrasing a question. In addition, when similar patterns of findings are present across different forms of data collection, the credibility of those results is strengthened.

WHAT THIS METHODOLOGY MIGHT REVEAL ABOUT POSSIBLE SELVES

In the next section we describe how this theoretical perspective and methodology might advance research on possible selves. The methodology can be employed with socially connected pairs of individuals such as partners making the transition to parenthood, parents and their adolescents, marital partners, or friends. The emergence of categories and themes from the data will allow for the identification of the constructs that are salient for the dyads. It is important, however, for researchers to inform themselves of theoretical frameworks and research that will sensitize them to the data so that the systematic and rigorous system of analysis is maintained.

It is critical that the analysis of data focus on action rather than the content (anticipated roles or characteristics) of the possible selves. This is because action theory directs attention to the question "How do dyads anticipate future selves of one or both members and then direct interpersonal behavior accordingly?" While the content of the images emerging from conversations is not irrelevant, the theoretical orientation behind our methodology indicates that the emergent categories should reflect actions associated with the uptake, modification, maintenance, or abandonment of possible selves. We provide the following examples to illustrate how such actions might emerge from the data. To orient these descriptions, the organizational characteristics and functions of individual self-construals are used as a framework to guide analysis of joint possible selves projects.

Salience. Salience of a potential image is the relative importance assigned to a self-view in comparison with other future self-evaluations. Assessments of salience in joint possible selves projects should be focused on the salience in the dyad. Recall, the project is between two individuals so the level of analysis is the dyadic relationship rather than the individual. At the dyadic level, there will be two salience hierarchies (one for each partner) linked by the joint project. Analysis of how the salience of possible selves emerges in joint possible selves projects will contribute to understanding interpersonal regulation of the uptake, construction, or abandonment of images. For example, a dyad that is characterized by balanced salience would be one in which the individuals concur on the importance of an image relative to other images under consideration. Actions associated with the possible self should differ for dyads with an imbalance of salience. Dyads that are balanced in salience likely engage in exploration, modification, or abandonment of the potential image. When there is an imbalance in the salience, the low salience partner is likely to disengage from the project while the high salience partner tries to convince the low salience partner to increase the salience of the image. In this case, joint actions will likely involve strategies associated with interpersonal influence. This latter situation is exemplified by a parent-adolescent dyad in our study of family career projects in early adolescence. The parent wanted to pursue an image for her adolescent son (high salience) that was not interesting or important to the son (low salience). The parent tried to engage the adolescent in several conversations about a potential image and, when the adolescent did not respond, the parent resorted to offering rewards. The parent's actions included strategies to increase the salience for the son so that it would be congruent with the parent's salience. The adolescent was not interested in the image but was interested in the rewards offered by the parent. The parent tried to guide the adolescent toward considering the potential image and the adolescent followed the parent's guidance in order to receive the reward but never adopted the possible self. The adolescent's actions included strategies for maintaining current future self-construals, obtaining rewards, and ensuring that the parent did not "win". In this case, the strategic attempts to regulate the uptake and maintenance of future self-construals highlight how salience of images undergirds dyadic action related to possible selves.

Analysis of dyadic salience of potential roles and characteristics might provide key information regarding social pressures, constraints, and reward systems associated with future images and social settings. Of interest is not the degree of congruence but how the degree of congruence engenders certain actions.

CLARITY

Clarity of self-construals is the confident expression of clear, stable, and internally consistent self-beliefs (Campbell et al., 1996). Analysis of clarity might involve assessment of dyadic actions to gain or reduce clarity. We found that some parent-child dyads purposefully engage in exploration of various possible selves that are not entirely clear or stable because one individual in the dyad is in early adolescence. For these dyads, the exploration of possible future roles is purposely kept vague because the parents and adolescents believe that achieving greater clarity and certainty will result in premature acceptance of a future self that might diminish other opportunities for growth. In the same data set, other dyads gather information and even try out roles to gain clarity as part of the joint project. For example, one parent supported the adolescent's inquiry into the possible self of actor. The parent helped the adolescent attend acting lessons and take part in theatre productions. At night, when the adolescent returned from lessons or the theatre, the parent and adolescent would converse about the latter's experiences. These conversations involved discussion of experiences and information sharing that enabled the dyad to clarify what a career in acting entails.

It is possible that the clarity of the image is problematic for one or both individuals. Research on dyads facing an ambiguous or problematic future might illuminate this issue. For example, we are beginning research on transition to adulthood projects between young adults and their parents. A portion of the sample will be families in which the young adult has been diagnosed with schizophrenia. It is expected that joint actions in these dyads may be directed toward achieving greater clarity of future selves because of the ambiguous future associated with not being certain about the course of the illness or the social response (e.g., whether employers will not accommodate disability requirements, Akabas, 1994) to persons living with this type of problem. Research on the joint actions associated with clarity of possible selves may illuminate how social circumstances influence dyads' efforts to seek or avoid clarity.

MALLEABILITY

Malleability of possible selves is evident in longitudinal naturalistic observations (Hooker et al. 1996) and interventions (Oyserman et al., 2002) and shorter term experimental research (Kerpelman and Pittman, 2001). These assessments of individual change contribute to understanding the malleability of possible selves and allude to how social relationships contribute to the modification of envisioned images. The protocol we have presented for assessing joint possible selves projects allows for detection of change since the data is collected over a period of six months. The protocol allows us to observe not only modification of possible selves but the abandonment of images, a process not assessed by most other methodologies.

It is important to track not only the malleability of the dyads' potential images but the reasons for change and actions associated with initiating, facilitating, or preventing change. Of importance is tracking whether changes in a hoped-for image are in concert with a dreaded or feared future image within the same domain. Following changes in linked hoped-for and feared selves will contribute to understanding how the motivational features of possible selves are maintained over time.

Malleability includes the abandonment of possible selves. A longitudinal research design facilitates observation of how potential self-construals are discarded from the repertoire of possible selves. Additionally, the self-confrontation and logs permit access to the phenomenological experience of such changes. Monitoring dyads' abandonment of certain future images contributes to understanding how repertoires of possible selves are altered (rather than focusing on transformation of a single image) and what social resources are recruited during the transformation process.

TEMPORAL ORIENTATION

Inherent in the concept of possible selves is time. The temporal orientation of possible selves emerge in conversations and actions. The degree of similarity in focus towards the future may vary between the individuals in the dyad. Some dyads may be oriented to a similar future time while other dyads contain one individual focused on a distant future while the other individual is concerned with more imminent prospects. How dyads coordinate the time orientation and the meaning underlying any differences or similarities is of central interest. For example, the possible self of one mother-daughter dyad was the award of a scholarship in a few years. The daughter was focused on the distant prospects of the scholarship while the mother was more concerned about the more immediate future of maintaining and even improving grades at school in order to obtain the scholarship. Coordination of the future image emerged as the mother feeling she had to push her daughter to become more responsible and organized to make sure her grades remained high, and the daughter responding by paying some attention to her grades. The discrepancy in time orientation did not lead to explicit attempts to change the future image. Rather, the mother engaged in efforts to close the gap by challenging the daughter's current behaviors while the daughter focused on the distant future of the scholarship.

Various factors are likely to be associated with how dyads coordinate the temporal orientation of possible selves. For example, imminent transitional events such as the transition to parenthood or marriage might influence the temporal characteristics of the project. Coordination of the temporal orientation over time may also change so it may be critical to consider, within the notion of the malleability of an image, whether the focus toward the future is altered.

SUMMARY

The conceptualization of possible selves presented in this chapter departs from some of the established research approaches in the area. Rather than a primarily individual approach to potential self-construals, action theory is employed to describe the construction of possible selves as projects between socially connected individuals. The action theoretical perspective is the foundation for a protocol that is useful for studying the emergence of joint possible selves projects. The various sources of data facilitate access to manifest behavior, internal processes, and social meaning associated with the construction of potential self-construals. The longitudinal design supports examination of change and stability of the possible selves project.

The theory and methodology described in this treatise provide a useful framework for studying possible selves across an array of populations and social circumstances. We are currently examining how parents and their early adolescent children construct possible selves and are beginning work with parents and their young adult children. It would be helpful to expand this work beyond parent-child dyads and investigate couples making the transition to marriage or parenthood to understand how possible selves emerge among adult members of families. The proposed approach could also be employed with dyads in which one or both members have experienced a significant change, such as loss of employment or onset of a chronic illness, to understand the social (re)construction of anticipated future images.

Features of the conceptualization and methodology may be used to advance research on possible selves. Future investigations may consider aspects of the proposed procedure for studying possible selves as amenable to other methodologies, including quantitative approaches. There are various methods that will tap into manifest behavior, internal processes, and social meaning. Convergence of findings emerging from various methodologies will contribute to consolidating and strengthening the conceptualization of the construction of possible selves.

Action theory provides a framework that is consistent with the social nature of possible selves. Research from this perspective will facilitate understanding of the social construction of possible selves and how potential self-construals shape interpersonal relationship dynamics. Taken together, the theoretical perspective and methodology have the potential to advance research on possible selves by focusing on the uptake, shaping, and abandonment of images and highlighting the interconnected nature of future self-construals.

REFERENCES

Akabas, S. H. (1994). Workplace responsiveness: Key employer characteristics in support of job maintenance for people with mental illness. *Psychosocial Rehabilitation Journal, 17,* 91-101.

Brandtstädter, J. (1998). Action perspectives on human development. In R. M. Lerner (Ed.) *Handbook of Child Psychology: Theoretical Models of Human Development* (Vol. 1, 5th ed., pp, 807 - 863). New York: Wiley.

Brandtstädter, J., and R. M. Lerner (Eds.) (1999). *Action and self-development: Theory and research through the life span.*Thousand Oaks, CA: Sage.

Campbell, J. D., Trapnell, P. D., Heine, S. J., Katz, I. M., Lavallee, L. F., and Leman, D. R. (1996) Self-concept clarity: Measurement, personality correlates, and cultural boundaries. *Journal of Personality and Social Psychology, 70,* 141-156.

Chandler, M. (1994). Self-continuity in suicidal and non-suicidal adolescents. *New Directions for Child Development, 64,* 55-70.

Cochran, L. (1992). The career project. *Journal of Career Development, 18,* 187-198.

Cranach, M. von, Kalbermatten, U., Indermühle, K., and Gugler, B. (1982). *Goal-directed action* (M. Turton, Trans.). London: Academic Press. (Original work published 1980).

Cross, S., and Markus, H. (1991). Possible selves across the lifespan. *Human Development, 34,* 230-255.

Domene, J.F., Young, R.A., Marshall, S. K., Arato-Bollivar, J., Hayoun, R., Marshall, E.G. (2003, May). *Aspects of possible selves revealed in "Family Career Development Projects."* Poster session presented at the annual conference of the Western Psychological Association, Vancouver, BC.

Elliott, R., Fischer, C.T., and Rennie, D.L. (1999). Evolving guidelines for publication of qualitative research studies in psychology and related fields. *British Journal of Clinical Psychology, 38,* 215-229.

Erikson, E. H. (1968). *Identity: youth and crisis.* New York: Norton.

Gollwitzer, P. M., and Bargh, J. A. (Eds.) (1996). *The psychology of action: Linking cognition and motivation to behavior.* New York: Guilford.

Hooker, K., Fiese, B. H., Jenkins, L., Morfei, M. Z., and Schwagler, J. (1996). Possible selves among parents of infants and preschoolers. *Developmental Psychology, 32,* 542-550.

Hooker, K. and Kraus, C. R. (1992). Possible selves and health behaviors in later life. *Journal of Aging and Health, 4,* 390-411.

James, W. (1961). *Psychology: the briefer course.* New York: Harper and Row. (Originally published 1892).

Kerpelman, J. and Pittman, J. (2001). The instability of possible selves: identity processes within late adolescents' close peer relationships. *Journal of Adolescence, 24,* 491-512.

Krefting, L. (1991). Rigor in qualitative research: The assessment of trustworthiness. *American Journal of Occupational Therapy, 45,* 214-222.

Lincoln, Y.S., and Guba, E.A. (1985). *Naturalistic inquiry.* Beverly Hills, CA: Sage.

Little, B. (1983). Personal projects: A rationale and methods for investigation. *Environment and Behavior, 15,* 273-309.

Little, B. (1989). Personal project analysis: Trivial prusuits, magnificent obsessions, and the search for coherence. In D. M. Buss and N. Cantor (Eds.), *Personality psychology: Recent trends and emerging directions* (pp. 15-31). New York: Springer.

Little, B. (1999). Personal projects and social ecology: Themes and variations across the life span. In J. Brandtstädter and R. M. Lerner (Eds.), *Action and self-development: Theory and research through the life span* (pp. 197-221). Thousand Oaks, CA: Sage.

Mead, G. H. (1934). *Mind, self, and society.* Chicago: University of Chicago Press.

Markus, H. R., and Nurius, P. (1986). Possible selves. *American Psychologist, 41*, 954-969.

Mischel, W., and Morf, C. C. (2003). The self as psycho-social dynamic processing system: A meta-perspective on a century of the self in psychology. In M. R. Leary and J. P. Tangney (Eds.) *Handbook of self and identity* (pp. 15-43). New York: Guilford Press.

Osyerman, D., and Markus, H. R. (1990). Possible selves and delinquency. *Journal of Personality and Social Psychology, 59*, 112-125.

Parsons, T. (1968). *The structure of social action.* New York: Free Press (original work published 1937).

Schuetz, A. (1967). *The phenomenology of the social world.* London: Heinemann (original work published 1932).

Segal, H. G., DeMeis, D. K., Wood, G. A., and Smith, H. L. (2001). Assessing future possible selves by gender and socioeconomic status using the anticipated life history measure. *Journal of Personality, 69*, 57-87.

Tesser, A. (2002). Constructing a niche for the self: A bio-social, PDP approach to understanding lives. *Self and Identity, 1*, 185-190.

Trommsdorff, G. (1986). Future time orientation and its relevance for development as action. In R. K. Silbereisen, K. Eyferth, and G. Rudinger (Eds.), *Development as action in context* (pp. 121-136).

Valach, L., Young, R. A., and Lynam, M. J. (1996). Family health promotion projects: An action-theretical perspective. *Journal of Health Psychology 1*, 49-63.

Valach, L., Young, R. A., and Lynam, M. J. (2002). *Action theory: A primer for applied research in the social sciences.* Westport, CT: Praeger.

Vygotsky, L. S. (1986). *Thought and language* (Trans. and ed. Alex Kozulin), Cambridge, MA: MIT press (original published 1934).

Wertsch, J. V. (1998). *Mind as action.* New York: Oxford University Press.

Young, R. A., Antal, S., Bassett, M. E., Post, A., DeVries, N., and Valach, L. (1999). The joint actions of adolescents in peer conversations about career. *Journal of Adolescence, 22*, 527-538.

Young, R. A., Valach, L., and Collin, A. (1996). A contextual explanation of career. In D. Brown and L. Brooks (Eds.), *Career choice and development* (3rd ed., pp. 477-512). San Francisco; Jossey-Bass.

Young, R. A., Valach, L., and Collin, A. (2002). A contextual explanation of career. In D. Brown (Ed.), *Career choice and development* (4th ed., pp. 206-250). San Francisco; Jossey-Bass.

Young, R. A., Valach, L., Dillabough, J., Dover, C., and Matthes, G. (1994). Career research from an action perspective: The self-confrontation procedure. *Career Development Quarterly, 43*, 185-196.

Young, R.A., Valach, L., Ball, J., Paseluikho, M.A., Wong, Y.S., DeVries, R.J., McLean, H., and Turkel, H. (2001). Career development in adolescence as a family project. *Journal of Counseling Psychology, 48*, 190-202.

APPENDIX A, PARENT-ADOLESCENT CONVERSATION

P1:   So how are things?

A1:   Fine.

P2:   Good. Ok. You have hairdresser, author and a teacher. Tell me the way that you want to put them. Your very first, your very first choice.

A2:   Well, like after college or whatever, probably what I'll do first for a little while 'cause then I can ....

P3:   Ok, then what.

A3:   Um. Teacher.

P4:   Ok, then what? Author?

A4:   I don't think I'm going to be an author.

P5:   You don't think so 'cause you could be an author on the side. You know what I mean? You could have a day job during the day or go to school during the day and at night you can actually write a book at night. Understand?

A5:   Yeah.

P6:   Yeah. You know, while you're watching TV or whatever and hopefully we'll get a computer soon and then you can just open up a thing on the computer, start writing a book. Hairdresser I don't know. Because a hairdresser doesn't get paid a lot. And um, I mean a book doesn't get paid a lot either unless the book is out there to be sold. It has to go through a lot of stages. Right. And I want something more stable for you. But if you get into hairdressing and I know that you are awesome at hair. I really, really do, but if you want to look into cutting hair that's cool but again you could have a second job not as your main. You're not going to be able to live off of it.

A6:   Yea, I know.

P7:   Ok. I want better for you.

A7: Well it's like. There's like nothing out there.

P8: But if you do decide that as a career and do nothing else you are going to be stuck there because you are going to be busy, so busy cutting hair and trying to get more hours in that you aren't going to have time to find a better job. That's what I think. I don't want you to, you know, I don't know if [politician]'s going to be around then 'cause if he is, I don't know. Does that bother you?

A8: What?

P9: What I just said. (mumble) You would make an awesome teacher. Kids would adore you.

A9: Yeah?

P10: You get lots of benefits. I don't know if you will like, you know, by the time you're ready to become a teacher because of, again, as I mentioned, [politician], whether there will be schools at all, the way things are going but anyway um, I think that would be cool because you get holidays, half decent pay. And you'd be so good at it specially with kids. I think you teaching like grade 1 or 2. No maybe they'd have to. You'd want them to know how to read and write, right? So grades 3 and up?

A10: Probably.

P11: Yeah. Grade 1s are kind of slow. Oh I guess that's all on tape. They're little babies. Or kindergarten teacher where you just play all day.

A11: No.

P12: No. You'd want to teach them stuff, right?

A12: Yes.

P13: I knew that.

A13: But every teacher has an outline and I want to do stuff that I want to do.

P14: So you would want to do your own outline.

A14: Yeah.

P15: Yeah. Well why wouldn't you?

A15: Because.

P16: The school board steps in and

A16: Yeah.

P17: Yeah there are curriculums that you have to follow. What time time you go to bed last night?

A17: I don't know.

P18: Just curious. So that American Pie #2. You probably shouldn't have been watching that.

APPENDIX B, PARENT SELF-CONFRONTATION

I1:   Okay. [pause] Is this the beginning of the conversation ?

P1:   Yeah. It's when you guys left the room I spit my gum out.

I2:   Oh, okay. [pause] Okay, you can hear that ?

Transcript of videotape

P3:   'kay, stop.

I3:   Yes.

P4:   I don't want her to be a hairdresser at all.

I4:   Okay.

P5:   [laughter]

I5:   Okay. [incomprehensible]

P6:   That's what I was, that's what I was thinking, I'm like – no, because I've had aunts who have done it and it's, it's a no-end, it's a, it's a no-end, once you're in, you're in and you're stuck and, I mean, I don't mind her doing the – it's not like I'm telling her "no, forget it, it's out of the question". Do it as a second job, do it, you know, after hours,

I6:   Mmmmhmmm

P7:   Um, you know any courses she wants to take on hair, fine, no problem.

I7:   Okay.

P8:   She wants to learn how to do all this, great, but not as a career.

I8:   Does she know how you feel about this ?

P9:   I told her.

I9:   Okay.

P10: I think, I think I told her.

I10: Okay. Like, in here, or

P11: Yeah.

I11: Oh, okay. Okay. And so, you have a big concern about what if she ends up as a hairdresser, what is the, what are the other what ifs that come into it ?

P12: I mean, if she does, she does, right ?

I12: But ?

P13: Well, then she's gonna, she's gonna realize that it, she's gonna be working hard for her money. Not that she's not going to be working hard at other places, but you know, we're talking standing on your feet all day, and cutting hair, and people going "oh I don't look like Jennifer Aniston". And crap like that, that I don't think she should.

Appendix C, Adolescent Self-confrontation

A1:   Okay.

I2:   So. Is that alright ?

A2:   Yup.

I3:   Alright. [pause] [incomprehensible]

Transcript of videotape

I4:   Okay, so what were you thinking about during that first minute ?

A3:   Well, we were just starting to um, to talk about um, our future, and what I'm going to do, like the 3 things that I want to be.

I5:   Mmmhmm.

A4:   Like, an author, a hairdresser, and uh, a teacher.

I6:   Right.

A5:   And we were just starting about hairdressing.

I7:   Right. And so's you were saying, putting them in order and that one was first, and

A6:   Yeah. And then my Mom was saying that it would probably be best if you do hairdresser as the side job because it's not that, uh, it's not that huge, it's not that big.

I8:   Right. And how do you feel about that?

A7:   Well, it's probably a good idea.

I9:   Mmmm.

A8:   Because then I could like um, well, I could maybe be an author and be a hairdresser,

I10:   Mmmmhmmm.

A9:   Cause it doesn't take like that much very, like, very much to write a book.

I11:   Okay.

A10:   And so I could just make it take very long but only have like half a day to work on it.

I12:   Mmmmhmmm.

A11:   And the other half for being a hairdresser.

I13:   So, a way of combining, sort of, is it, do you, are you enjoying sort of having your Mom make these suggestions? Is that working for you?

A12:   Yeah.

I14:   Yeah ? Anything else about that minute?

A13:   Well, um, we talk about like ideas, and this helps me get a good picture in my head of what I'm gonna do.

I15:   Oh, okay.

A14:   And so that I can plan ahead before I actually do it.

I16:   Right. So you're liking this conversation with your Mom.

A15:   Yeah.

I17:   Well, good. Alright. We'll watch the next minute.

In: Possible Selves: Theory, Research and Application   ISBN 1-59454-431-X
Editors: C. Dunkel and J. Kerpelman, pp. 163-186   © 2006 Nova Science Publishers, Inc.

Chapter 9

USING Q METHODOLOGY TO STUDY POSSIBLE SELVES

Jennifer L. Kerpelman
Auburn University

ABSTRACT

Q-sort methodology offers a viable alternative for the examination of possible selves, permitting assessment of the relative importance of a large array of potential future outcomes. In the first half of this chapter, the development of a Q-sort, its implementation, and the steps used to analyze Q-data are discussed. Examples from prior studies that have employed Q-sort methodology to examine possible selves are then summarized. The second half of this chapter introduces a new measure, the 99 item PSQ-sort. The PSQ-sort contains possible selves that link to human, economic and social capital, important resources for adaptation in adulthood. Results from pilot testing this new measure with an all female, Caucasian college sample, and an African American high school sample of male and female adolescents are provided. Interesting patterns were found for each of the groups, and both similarities as well as differences between the groups are noted. The chapter concludes with directions for future research using the PSQ-sort.

Possible selves are beliefs about who one might become in the future (Markus and Nurius, 1986), and are highly salient when a person is considering potential or impending life transitions. For adolescents, these transitions can include changes such as finishing high school, starting a first full time job, beginning college, entering marriage or becoming a parent. As adolescents consider these transitions, they think about what they will be like in their new roles. Imagining oneself in the future helps to guide decisions in the present, and has been shown to motivate current behavior in areas of school persistence and academic achievement (Anderman, Anderman, and Griesinger, 1999; Leondari, Syngollitou, and Kiosseoglou, 1998; Oyserman, Gant, and Ager, 1995), career expectations and development (Chalk, Meara, and Day, 1994; Curry, Trew, Turner, and Hunter, 1994; Meara, Day, and Chalk, 1995), and delinquency (Oyserman and Markus, 1990; Oyserman and Saltz, 1993; Stein, Roeser, and Markus, 1998).

The methods used for assessing possible selves typically take the form of checklists or listings (e.g., Markus and Nurius, 1987; Oyserman, Gant, and Ager, 1995; Oyserman and Markus, 1990). The checklist method involves providing a large array of possible selves from which the respondents select those selves that are hoped for, expected, and/or feared. The respondents also may indicate how likely each self is, and when they expect to attain it. In contrast, the listing methodology has respondents generate the possible selves they imagine for themselves. In a few instances, the generation of possible selves has been acquired through group discussions (e.g., Curry et al., 1994), or short essays (e.g., Leondari et al., 1998; Ruvolo, and Markus, 1992).

Although these methods have been useful in learning about the kinds of possible selves individuals expect, hope for and fear, they do not permit assessment of the "relative" importance among the full set of possible selves a person imagines. The relative importance of different possible selves matters because *how* adolescents organize their possible selves has implications for the extent to which these future-oriented beliefs guide current behavior. For example, two adolescents may agree that the possible selves of parent, teacher, athlete, musician, and entrepreneur are all hoped for. When asked to consider the rank ordering of these, "musician" may be one adolescent's most hoped for self and "parent" may be the least hoped for among the 5 selves, whereas for the other adolescent, "parent" may be the top ranked future self. These adolescents' current behaviors may look substantially different given their priorities among their hoped for selves. Consider an even larger array of possible selves that cover a broader range of domains, such as career, family, friendships, and lifestyle. Rank ordering a set of 40 or more possible selves representing these domains becomes complicated. In order to assess relative importance among a large set of possible selves, this requires a methodology that permits the respondent to compare every item and to decide which are more hoped for (expected or feared) than others. "Q methodology" (Brown, 1993; McKeown and Thomas, 1988; Stephenson, 1953) offers a promising approach for understanding variation in the salience of a person's set of possible selves. This approach "encompasses a distinctive set of psychometric and operational principles that, when combined with specialized statistical applications of correlational and factor-analytical techniques, provides researchers with a systematic and rigorously quantitative means for examining human subjectivity" (McKeown and Thomas, 1988, p.7). Q methodology, therefore, offers a viable alternative for understanding how adolescents conceptualize the relevance of possible selves within a large set of items representing their future potential.

The purpose of this chapter is to describe and illustrate the efficacy of Q methodology for examining adolescents' possible selves. The first section addresses the development of the items for a Q-sort and its administration. Next, the analyses used to examine the Q-data are detailed. Finally studies using Q methodology to examine adolescents' possible selves are reviewed.

Q-SET CONSTRUCTION AND ADMINISTRATION OF THE Q-SORT

Constructing the sort. Q methodology involves having a person sort a set of items, where each individual item is written on a single card. The set of items represent a concept of interest, such as possible selves. When constructing a Q-set it is important to consider what the central purpose is for the sort; that is, how the sort will be used to elucidate the concept of interest. Typically one uses a Q-sort to explore the meaning of a concept in greater depth. Concepts that lend themselves best to Q methodology are those for which a range of subjective viewpoints are held across people, and where understanding these varying viewpoints will lead to greater conceptual clarity.

There are a number of approaches for developing a Q-set. Items can be generated from theory, from past empirical research, from an expert panel, or from samples drawn from the population of interest. The purposes for which the Q-set will be used determines, in part, the kinds of items selected. For example, if the research focus is future career expectations, an entire Q-set of career items could be generated. In contrast, if the focus is possible selves in multiple domains (e.g., marriage, career, and parenthood), then items representing each of these domains would need to be developed. The desired number of items ranges from 60-100 (McKeown and Thompson, 1988), however smaller or larger Q-sets can be used effectively.

Administering the sort. A common procedure for administering a sort is to have the sorters consider the items in terms of being most to least like them or their views. A sorter is given the set of items and told to make 3 piles (like me, not like me, neutral/undecided). Once the items have been sorted into these initial piles, the items are placed into an array with a preset number of columns where each column has a set number of slots (see Appendix A for an example Q-sort array). The participant can begin by placing the items from the "Like Me" pile into the "Most Like Me" column and moving inward until all of the cards have been placed. Next, the person sorts the items from the "Not Like Me" pile, beginning with the "Least Like Me" column, again moving inward until all the cards have been placed. What remains are the items in the "Neutral/Undecided" pile to be sorted into the middle columns of the array. In the example array shown in Appendix A, a person places his or her top 10 most expected possible selves in the left most column; his or her 10 least expected possible selves are placed in the right most column. All of the other possible selves fill in the remaining columns moving from the left (more like) to the right (less like). Although a quasi normal distribution often is used, this is a convention rather than a statistical requirement (McKeown and Thompson, 1988).

If fewer than 60 items are used, variability can be increased by using a mediated ranking procedure (Thompson, 1980) where the placement of each item is rank ordered after the items have been organized by column. That is, the participant is asked to place them in order where the top item is the most descriptive and the bottom item is the least descriptive of what that column represents. For example, if there are 6 items in the "most like me" column, while all six items are most like the participant, the item at the top of the column is considered to be the most descriptive of all, the second item is the next most descriptive, and so forth.

ANALYSIS OF THE Q-DATA

The first step in preparing the Q-sort data for analysis is to record on a code sheet each column placement score for each of the items in the Q-sort (see Table 1). In the example, placement scores range from 9 to 1, where 9 represents items placed in the "most like me" column, 1 represents items placed in the "least like me" column, and 5 represents items placed in the neutral column. The example sort has a total of 64 items and the distribution of cards into the nine columns is 5, 6, 7, 8, 12, 8, 7, 6, 5. Once the data have been logged on the code sheet, they can be entered into a data file for statistical analysis. The Q-set items label the variables across the top, and the location scores for each person's sort are then entered. Next, the dataset is transposed making the respondents the variables to be analyzed (see Table 2). Specifically, the transposition involves transforming the dataset so that the participants label the columns and the Q-set items label the rows, making it possible to analyze the data according to each person's full set of responses to the Q-sort. Thus, the goal of Q-analysis is to group "like people" who are similar in how they sorted the Q-set items.

Table 1 Possible Selves Q-sort Code Sheet

Item 1	Item 2	Item 3	Item 4	Item 5	Item 6	Item 7	Item 8
2	1	5	3	9	7	4	3
Item 9	Item 10	Item 11	Item 12	Item 13	Item 14	Item 15	Item 16
6	1	6	7	4	5	9	3
Item 17	Item 18	Item 19	Item 20	Item 21	Item 22	Item 23	Item 24
3	8	8	4	6	2	6	2
Item 25	Item 26	Item 27	Item 28	Item 29	Item 30	Item 31	Item 32
4	4	9	1	5	3	5	3
Item 33	Item 34	Item 35	Item 36	Item 37	Item 38	Item 39	Item 40
5	8	8	6	2	1	6	8
Item 41	Item 42	Item 43	Item 44	Item 45	Item 46	Item 47	Item 48
7	5	3	7	9	5	6	9
Item 49	Item 50	Item 51	Item 52	Item 53	Item 54	Item 55	Item 56
5	4	5	5	7	5	7	8
Item 57	Item 58	Item 59	Item 60	Item 61	Item 62	Item 63	Item 64
4	2	7	5	4	6	2	1

After the data are prepared, they are subjected to factor analysis, which involves the calculation of the correlations among all the possible pairs of Q-sorts and then factor analyzing them (Kerlinger, 1986; Thompson, 1980). The size of each person's loading on each factor represents the association of that individual's Q-sort with the "way of thinking" associated with each factor (Brown, 1993; McKeown and Thomas, 1988).

Table 2 Example of the Transposed Dataset

	Person 1	Person 2	Person 3	Person 4	Person 5
Item1	6	2	8	1	7
Item2	3	5	4	6	2
Item3	9	7	9	4	7
Item4	1	3	2	5	6
Item5	7	5	8	2	9
Item6	5	8	6	9	4
Item7	4	7	5	6	1
Item8	6	1	5	2	5
Item64	9	3	7	7	8

CONSTRUCTING COMPOSITE SORTS

After completing the factor analysis, the last step is to create "composite Q-sorts" from those individuals who load highest on a factor and do not cross load on other factors. Participants who have sorted the Q-sort items similarly will load significantly on the same factor; the higher a person's factor loading the more that person is consistent with the underlying meaning of that factor (Kerlinger, 1986).

For each person to be included in the composite sort, a weight is calculated (Brown, 1993; Mckeown and Thomas, 1988). A spreadsheet is useful for calculating these weights and the final location value for each item of the composite sort (see Appendix B). The formula for calculating the factor weights is $w = f/(1-f^2)$, where the weight is equal to the factor loading of an individual divided by 1 minus the square of the factor loading. After calculating the weights for each person, each person's placement score for each of his or her items in the sort is multiplied by his/her factor weight. These weighted scores then are summed across people for each item, creating the last column in the spreadsheet (i.e., the final location score for each item of the composite sort). Once the final location scores are calculated, these scores along with their respective item numbers can be sorted in descending order to create the composite sort for each factor. For the example sort with 64 items, the five items with the highest location scores would comprise the items in the "most like me" column (i.e., column 9); the next six highest location scores would identify the items in column 8 and so forth. Once created, the composite sorts can be compared to determine which items most differentiate the groups. According to Brown (1993) a difference of two or more columns is considered to be significant. These differences help to elucidate the distinct ways of thinking that each group represents.

PAST RESEARCH USING Q METHODOLOGY
TO STUDY POSSIBLE SELVES

Shoffner and Kerpelman (2005) designed a 41 item possible selves Q-sort derived from the Possible Selves Questionnaire (Markus, 1987). The Q-sort was used with a sample of 51 rural, female adolescents (ages 14-16) and included items representing the domains of personal attributes (e.g., intelligent, creative, selfish), life roles (e.g., hair stylist, high school graduate, married), and life circumstances (e.g., rich, famous, on welfare). The adolescents sorted these items twice, the first time in terms of their "expected" selves, and the second time in terms of their "feared" selves. The sorting array consisted of nine columns with the following distribution: 3,4,4, 6,7,6,4,4,3. The goals of this study were to identify the rural female adolescents' most salient expected and feared possible selves, and to determine whether there were subgroups within the sample that differed in their "thinking" about expected and feared possible selves.

The same items were used for both the expected and feared sorts, only the instructions varied. For the expected sort the adolescent was asked to arrange the items in terms of the extent to which they reflected who she expected to become. For the feared sort, the adolescent was asked to arrange the items to show the extent to which she feared becoming each of the possible selves comprising the sort. After sorting the items into columns, the adolescent used the mediated ranking procedure. Q-factor analysis resulted in three groups for the expected possible selves, and three groups for the feared possible selves. The composite Q-sorts were constructed and then examined to determine items that clearly differentiated the three groups.

For expected possible selves, one group was comprised of girls who most expected to be religious, married, and mothers, and who had few most expected selves in the career domain. A second group included girls who did not strongly expect to be religious, married or mothers, and focused primarily on most and least expected career selves. Finally, the third group was comprised of girls who expected to be married but not mothers and who anticipated a career in the medical field. The comparisons of the groups indicated that their expected possible selves in the areas of parenting, marriage and career roles had different strengths and valences. These findings support previous research that indicates female adolescents vary in how they prioritize their anticipated work and family roles (Curry, et al., 1994), with some placing family roles as more expected than career roles, others placing priority on career, and still others placing marriage and career over parenthood (Kerpelman and Schvaneveldt, 1999). The value of a religious self also was noteworthy in how it distinguished the three groups.

For feared possible selves, the adolescents also fell into three groups: those who viewed careers as neutral and marriage and motherhood as least feared possible selves, those who considered multiple career options as least feared possible selves and marriage and motherhood as somewhat feared possible selves, and those who most feared divorce, as well as science/math careers and were neutral regarding marriage and motherhood. When examining feared possible selves, girls appeared again to focus on marriage and/or motherhood, with the three groups varying on whether they viewed this aspect of their future selves as somewhat feared, not feared or neutral. For some girls, becoming a mother was a highly feared possible self. Viewing motherhood as a most feared possible self has implications for how these girls may proceed in their exploration of future family roles. For other girls, expressing fear for particular types of careers (e.g., science/math) also is consistent with past research addressing female adolescents' fear or rejection of higher status, male dominated, career options (Curry et al, 1994).

Another study using the same Q-sort (Kerpelman, Shoffner, and Ross-Griffin, 2002) focused on only African American adolescents (N=22) and their mothers. Different instructions were used for the sorting of the items. For this study, the adolescents and their mothers were asked to complete the Q-sort together in terms of what they expected for the daughter's future. The mother-daughter pairs were asked to discuss each item and decide together the extent to which it was expected for the daughter in the future. Thus, unlike the previous study that focused on only the adolescent's perspective, the Q-sorts that resulted from this study represented the shared views of the mother and daughter.

Analysis of the Q-data revealed that there were two groups of mother-daughter pairs. The first group placed higher expectations on the daughters' possible selves that reflected personal attributes, whereas the second group emphasized possible selves pertaining to life circumstances. The second group also had stronger expectations for the daughters' possible selves in the career domain.

When the adolescents and their mothers were interviewed about the strategies they were using to help attain the daughters' desired educational and career possible selves, it was found that the group 1 adolescents emphasized maintaining good grades and getting work experience; whereas the group 2 adolescents placed greater emphasis on saving money and filling out scholarship applications. The group 1 mothers viewed their daughters as more internally driven and self-disciplined; the group 2 mothers viewed their daughters as needing greater assistance and direct supervision. Mothers from both groups were engaged in a range of strategies for assisting their daughters' efforts to reach educational and career goals, and to some extent these strategies were consistent with how they viewed their daughters' possible selves. Thus, beliefs about the adolescent's possible selves had implications for what the mother and daughter were doing to work toward them. Linking possible selves and the strategies for obtaining them are important given that greater consistency between goals and plans may increase the likelihood of realizing preferred possible selves (Oyserman, Bybee, Terry, & Hart-Johnson, 2004) .

Across the two studies using the 41 item Q-set, distinctly different ways of thinking about possible selves emerged. In addition, the different purposes of the studies (and the different instructions for sorting the items) resulted in different outcomes. Together these studies add to what is understood about how adolescents (and parents) view the relative importance of a set of varied possible selves in terms of expectations and fears.

THE 99 ITEM POSSIBLE SELVES Q-SORT (PSQ-SORT)

Although the 41 item Q-set used in the previous research examining adolescent girls' possible selves was found to be useful, it was limited in the range of possible selves that might be part of adolescents' anticipated adult lives. The need for a more detailed Q-sort led to the development of the 99 item Possible Selves Q-sort (PSQ-sort; Kerpelman, Pittman, Lamke, and Sollie, 2005; see Appendix C). The PSQ-sort is comprised of items that tap adolescents' expectations for their possible selves in three primary domains, human, social, and economic capital, known to be important for adult adjustment. These items were generated based on both the possible selves and human/social capital literatures. In addition, small groups of undergraduate students responded to earlier sets of items and revisions were made to the Q-set based on these initial trials. Lastly, the PSQ-sort was pilot-tested with larger groups of college and high school students.

The final version of the PSQ-sort contains 46 items that reflect selves related to human capital (e.g., I will have job in which I can be artistic or creative, I will be a researcher or scientist; I will take lessons to develop my talents/skills); 27 items that reflect selves related to social capital (e.g., I will be a best friend, I will be a churchgoer, I will be a member of one or more organized groups); and 26 items that reflect selves related to economic capital (e.g., I will have savings in the bank, I will own my own home, I will take regular vacations). The adolescent is instructed to think about the kind of person s/he will be in his or her late 20s and to sort the items in terms of how much they will be like him or her in the future. The Q-sort array contains nine columns with the following distribution: 10, 11, 11, 11, 13, 11, 11, 11, 10.

The PSQ-sort was tested with two samples, a college sample (N=105 female young adults between the ages 18-24 who were primarily Caucasian and Human Sciences majors) and a high school sample (N=57 African American adolescents in grades 9-12; 22 male, 35 female). Analyses of the college and high school sample Q-sorts were conducted separately. Each analysis yielded 17 factors, five of which contained three or more individuals who loaded significantly ($>=.60$) and cleanly (i.e., did not cross load on any of the other 16 factors). To form the composite sorts representing the "thinking" of each of the groups, the top five individuals who loaded highest and cleanest on that factor were used. For factors with less than five people, all of those who loaded significantly and cleanly were used to construct the composite sort. Once the composites were created, the most and least expected possible selves for each group were examined. In addition, each group was compared to every other group in its column placement of the items. In order to ensure that the differences identified clearly distinguished the differences among the groups, a column difference of four or more (i.e., the items were placed four or more columns apart in the two composite sorts being compared) was used. This more conservative criterion was selected because it would ensure that an item that was highly important (or highly unimportant) to one group would be either neutral or highly unimportant (or highly important) to the other group. Thus, the groups were truly different in their thinking about these possible selves' items. After examining the most extreme items for each group, and the items for which each group was significantly higher or lower than some or all of the other groups, a description of each group was developed.

College sample. For the college sample, Table 3 shows each group's "most" and "least" expected selves. When attempting to understand the thinking of a group, it is useful to first examine the descriptions that fall into the extreme ends of the sort. Looking at these items offers a general idea of what matters most to each group. However, this does not fully address how the groups are distinct from one another. One way of examining group distinctions is to compare differences among each group's most salient selves (i.e., those placed in column 9, "most like me") by constructing a graph for each group that depicts where the other groups placed these 10 items. Although the groups had a lot of similarity in what they viewed as highly important, there are several places where the groups differed substantially. The figures depict these graphs for groups 2 and 4.

Table 3 Most and Least Like Selves for College Student Groups

Group	Like Me in the Future	Not Like Me in the Future
1(n=5)	C1. I will be a parent. C2. I will be a spouse. C12. I will be a churchgoer. B18. I will give money to a place of worship. A23. I will feel happy doing the job I choose. A4. I will work with children/teens. A11. I will have a teaching job. A24. I will have a job that allows me to help people. A42. I will have formal education beyond high school. B7. I will have savings in the bank.	B20. I will have enough money to buy my spouse a car. A13. I will be a researcher or scientist. B16. Making ends meet every month will be a big challenge. A27. I will have a job with the government. A22. I will have a job that will permit me to make a lot of money. A6. I will travel a lot in my job. A19. I will have a job in sports/athletics. A31. I will operate machinery for my job. A10. I will work in law enforcement. A45. I will be in the military.
2(n=5)	A12. I will work in the medical or health field. A42. I will have formal education beyond high school. A16. I will do work that involves saving lives and/or protecting people. C1. I will be a parent. C2. I will be a spouse. C4. I will have a close relationship with one or more of my family members. B2. I will own my own car. A24. I will have a job that allows me to help people. A23. I will feel happy doing the job I choose. C21. I will have good friends I can trust and feel supported by.	A19. I will have a job in sports/athletics. A33. I will have a job that involves entertaining people. A11. I will have a teaching job. A2. I will have a desk job. A10. I will work in law enforcement. A40. I will be a salesperson. C25. I will play in a band. A9. I will work with food. A1. I will drive vehicles for my job.
3(n=4)	C4. I will have a close relationship with one or more of my family members. C22. My parents will support me in the goals I have for myself. A42. I will have formal education beyond high school. C27. I often will have people visiting me at home. C26. I will be a pet owner. C21. I will have good friends I can trust and feel supported by. A17. I will work in the business field. C6. I will be a best friend. A23. I will feel happy doing the job I choose.	C14. I will sing in a choir. C7. I will be a community leader. A33. I will have a job that involves entertaining people. A13. I will be a researcher or scientist. A16. I will do work that involves saving lives and/or protecting people. A7. I will have a job in which I am physically active. A39. I will have a paid job I can do from my home. A38. I will be a stay-at-home parent. A45. I will be in the military. A19. I will have a job in sports/athletics.
4(n=3)	A23. I will feel happy doing the job I choose. A30. I will have a job that involves religion. C2. I will be a spouse. C12. I will be a churchgoer. C21. I will have good friends I can trust and feel supported by. A24. I will have a job that allows me to help people. C1. I will be a parent. A34. I will have a job that helps to change society. C5. I will form long-lasting friendships with co-workers. C8. I will be a Sunday school teacher.	A25. I will have a job that does not take a long time to master. A9. I will work with food. A10. I will work in law enforcement. B9. I will have a lot of clothes. A2. I will have a desk job. A45. I will be in the military. A38. I will be a stay-at-home parent. B11. I will have a lot of jewelry. C20. I will join a country club. A13. I will be a researcher or scientist.

Table 3 Most and Least Like Selves for College Student Groups (Continued)

Group	Like Me in the Future	Not Like Me in the Future
5(n=4)	A24. I will have a job that allows me to help people. A42. I will have formal education beyond high school. A4. I will work with children/teens. B7. I will have savings in the bank C6. I will be a best friend. C11. I will be a community volunteer. B2. I will own my own car. A23. I will feel happy doing the job I choose. B24. I will donate money to charity. C21. I will have good friends I can trust and feel supported by.	C19. I will volunteer at my child's school. A45. I will be in the military. A38. I will be a stay-at-home parent. B21. I will buy my child(ren) nice clothes. B26. I will purchase one or more of the ff: childcare, yard care, housecleaning. C1. I will be a parent. C18. I will help organize social activities for my child. B3. I will own a second home. A19. I will have a job in sports/athletics. A31. I will operate machinery for my job.

Most Expected Items for College Group 2:
Balance-oriented

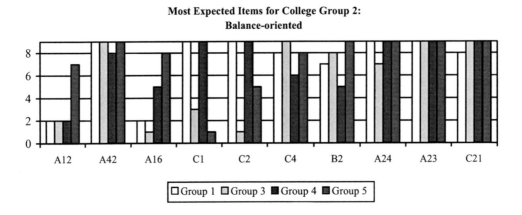

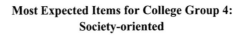

Most Expected Items for College Group 4:
Society-oriented

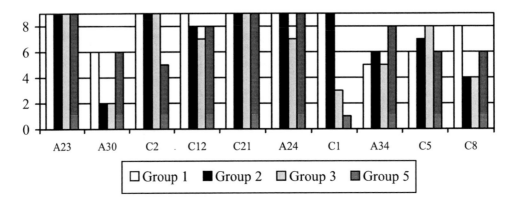

Looking across the most expected selves for group 2, it can be seen that this group was notably higher than groups 1,3, and 4 in desiring a job in the medical/health field (A12). Group 2 also was higher than groups 1,3 and 4 with regard to doing work that involves saving lives/protecting people (A16), and was higher than groups 3 and 5 in the desire to be a parent (C1) and spouse (C2). An examination of the most expected selves for group 4 shows that this group was considerably higher than the other groups, especially groups 2 and 3 in expecting a job that involves religion (A30). This group also strongly expected to have a job that helps to change society, where all of the other groups (except group 5) were neutral on this item. Thus, it can be seen that using this procedure helps to identify how those items that are highly salient to one group vary in salience across the other groups. A similar comparison across groups could be used with the "least like me" items.

To more fully understand the group profiles, however, it was necessary to compare all of the item placement locations. Table 4 shows the results of the column comparisons across the five groups. Looking across the rows shows the items for which a group is higher in expectation than the other groups; looking down the columns shows the items for which a group is lower in expectation than the other groups. For example, group 1 is higher in expectation than group 2 with regard to: (A8) having an artistic or creative job, (A11) having a teaching job, and (A38) being a stay-at-home parent. Group 1 is lower in expectation than group 2 for (A6) traveling a lot in job, (A12) working in medical/health field, (A16) having work that involves saving lives/protecting people), (A22) making a lot of money, (A29) having a highly skilled job, and (A32) having a job that involves taking risks. After completing an examination of each group's most and least expected selves and how the groups compared in terms of their column placements, it was possible to label and describe each of the groups generated by the Q-factor analysis procedures.

The first group was labeled "Traditional-oriented" because they highly valued traditional and conservative roles, emphasizing family, church and traditionally female careers, and rejecting predominantly male-oriented jobs and responsibilities. They had significantly higher expectations (i.e., four or more columns different) than several other groups for wanting to be stay-at-home parents and engaged in child-centered activities, such as: volunteering at my child's school, arranging social activities for my child and buying my child nice clothes. They also were significantly lower than some of the other groups in the expectation that they would have jobs that demanded a lot of their time or would take them away from their families (e.g. traveling, having a highly skilled job, having a job in the medical/health field), and they were not interested in being the family breadwinner.

The second group was labeled "Balance-oriented" because its members emphasized employment, involvement in family, and being connected to the social network. This group was significantly more likely than several of the other groups to expect employment in the medical/health field and to be involved in saving lives and protecting people. They expected to make a lot of money and to be invested in their parental and spousal roles. They were not interested in low skill jobs, or those that required teaching or being artistic/creative.

Table 4 Significant Differences Between the College Sample Q-Groups

	Group 1	Group 2	Group 3	Group 4	Group 5
Group 1 Traditional-oriented		A8, A11, A38	A4, A11, A38, B21, C1, C14, C18, C19	A38, B9, C20	A38, B21, C1, C18, C19
Group 2 Balance-oriented	A6, A12, A16, A22, A29, A32		A12, A16, B21, C1	A12, A22, B9	A22, A35, B21, C1
Group 3 Connection-oriented	A2, A14, A17, A22, A29, A37	A2, A17, A37		A2, A17, A36, B8	A17, A35, B26
Group 4 Society-oriented	A6, A19, B20, C17	A8, A11, A19, A30, C8	A7, A11, A19, A30, C1, C8, C17		A19, B26, C1, C17
Group 5 Child Free-oriented	A6, A12, A14, A16, A27	A2, A8, A27, A41, B23, C11	A4, A12, A16, A27, C14	A2, A12, A27, B9	

Given their strong interest in being connected with family and friends, the third group was labeled "Connection-oriented." Almost all of their highly rated items involved social capital. They expected to be close with their parents and other family members, as well as to have good friends. The occupation of greatest interest was in the business field. Although they were strongly interested in becoming spouses, they believed it was somewhat unlikely that they would be parents, and if they were, they would not be stay-at-home parents. This group also favored having a desk job and working with computers more than other groups did.

The fourth group was labeled "Society-oriented" because they strongly emphasized reaching out to others, being socially involved, having strong religious involvements in both their professional and personal lives, and making an impact on society. This group placed a notably low emphasis on economic capital, especially elements representing wealth (e.g., having a lot of jewelry, joining a country club, having a lot of clothes). They expected to be wives and mothers, but they did not anticipate being stay-at-home mothers. Compared to all the other groups, they were more interested in being involved in sport related activities. They also were less interested than some of the other groups in working in the medical/health field.

The last group was labeled "Child Free-oriented" because of their strong emphasis on not becoming parents (column 1) and their neutral interest in becoming a spouse (column 5). This group was not nontraditional, however, in their career goals. They also valued being involved in their communities and having a strong friendship network, and were higher than some of the other groups in their interest in working in the medical/health field or having a job with the government.

Looking across these groups, it is clear that meaningful variation existed in how these college women were imagining their possible selves. There also was substantial similarity across the groups. All the groups were comprised of members who expected to be happy in their jobs (A23), to have a job in which they could help people (A24), to have savings in the bank (B7), and to have good friends that they could trust and feel supported by (C21).

HIGH SCHOOL SAMPLE

Examination of the five groups found with the high school sample Q-sorts also showed some interesting ways that adolescents were thinking about their possible selves. The same procedures used to compare the college sample were used with the high school sample. Table 5 depicts each group's highest and lowest scoring possible selves. More striking group differences in most and least expected selves were seen for the high school sample than for the college sample. In the "most like" column, some groups placed greater emphasis on the human capital items, whereas others placed greater emphasis on the economic or social capital items. In the "least like" column, the groups varied in the social and human capital they least expected. None of the groups, however, placed economic capital items in their "least expected" column, and in general were more focused on obtaining economic capital than the college sample was.

The example figures show the comparison of the "most like" items (column 9) for groups 2 and 3 with the other groups' placement of those items. Clearly group 2 differs from the other groups in terms of expecting a job in the sports/athletics field (A19), as well as a job that involves entertaining people (A33). Group 3 had a stronger expectation than the other groups for becoming a spouse (C2), and was higher than most groups in the expectation of receiving financial support from parents (B15). Group 3 also was higher than several groups (especially group 5) in expecting to be involved in lessons to develop talents and skills (A44).

Table 6 shows the column comparisons across the five groups. As with the college student sample, items that were four or more columns apart were considered to be significantly different between the two groups being compared.

The first group (primarily females) was labeled "Career-oriented" given the high priority placed on having a fulfilling and challenging job and the secondary emphasis on family roles and social connections. The Career-oriented group was stronger than some of the other groups in terms of wanting to work in the medical or health field, wanting to have a job in which they could help people, and having a job that required a lot of time, had a variety of tasks, and involved taking risks. Both marriage and parenthood were placed closer to the neutral column for this group.

The second group (primarily males) was labeled "Sports Star-oriented" because of the strong expectation placed on having a sports career and a career involving entertaining people, as well as on economic wealth. This group was considerably stronger than other groups in the expectation of being involved in sports and hobbies and being able to purchase expensive over cheap clothes.

Table 5 Most and Least Like Selves for High School Student Groups

Group	Like Me in the Future	Not Like Me in the Future
1(n=5)	A14. I will have a job that requires a lot of my time. A29. I will have a highly skilled job. A26. I will have a job that has a wide variety of tasks. B7. I will have savings in the bank. A23. I will feel happy doing the job I choose A24. I will have a job that allows me to help people. A22. I will have a job that will permit me to make a lot of money. B14. I will be earning money to cover my living expenses. B2. I will own my own car. A42. I will have formal education beyond high school.	A40. I will be a salesperson. C13. I will play team sports. A19. I will have a job in sports/athletics. A9. I will work with food. A33. I will have a job that involves entertaining people. A11. I will have a teaching job. A45. I will be in the military. A10. I will work in law enforcement. A38. I will be a stay-at-home parent. A46. I will work with animals.
2(n=5)	A19. I will have a job in sports/athletics. B9. I will have a lot of clothes. B14. I will be earning money to cover my living expenses. B22. I will buy nice presents for my family. C4. I will have a close relationship with one or more of my family members. B1. I will own my own home. B7. I will have savings in the bank. C21. I will have good friends I can trust and feel supported by. A21. I will have a job in which I get to use my hands. A33. I will have a job that involves entertaining people.	C25. I will play in a band. C9. I will be a tutor or mentor. A12. I will work in the medical or health field. A11. I will have a teaching job. A5. I will work with nature. A34. I will have a job that helps to change society. A2. I will have a desk job. C8. I will be a Sunday school teacher. A46. I will work with animals. C14. I will sing in a choir.
3(n=4)	B21. I will buy my child(ren) nice clothes. B19. I will wear expensive clothes. C21. I will have good friends I can trust and feel supported by. A44. I will take lessons to develop my talents/skills. B22. I will buy nice presents for my family. B1. I will own my own home. C2. I will be a spouse (a husband or a wife). B7. I will have savings in the bank. B10. My home will have nice furniture. B15. My parents will provide me with financial resources if I need their support.	A46. I will work with animals. C25. I will play in a band. A26. I will have a job that has a wide variety of tasks. A31. I will operate machinery for my job. C17. I will volunteer to coach a sport. A19. I will have a job in sports/athletics. A32. I will have a job that involves taking risks. A6. I will travel a lot in my job. C20. I will join a country club. A5. I will work with nature.
4(n=3)	C24. I will have family members, other than my parents, who will give me support. C21. I will have good friends I can trust and feel supported by. A28. I will have a job with a clearly defined daily routine. C22. My parents will support me in the goals I have for myself. B5. I will take regular vacations. A3. I will have a job of high importance and respect. B22. I will buy nice presents for my family. C4. I will have a close relationship with one or more of my family members. C27. I often will have people visiting me at home. A44. I will take lessons to develop my talents/skills.	C8. I will be a Sunday school teacher. C17. I will volunteer to coach a sport. A9. I will work with food A24. I will have a job that allows me to help people. A25. I will have a job that does not take a long time to master. A39. I will have a paid job I can do from my home. C13. I will play team sports. A31. I will operate machinery for my job. A4. I will work with children/teens. C19. I will volunteer at my child's school.

Table 5 Most and Least Like Selves for High School Student Groups (Continued)

Group	Like Me in the Future	Not Like Me in the Future
5(n=3)	B2. I will own my own car. B9. I will have a lot of clothes. B10. My home will have nice furniture. B21. I will buy my child(ren) nice clothes. A22. I will have a job that will permit me to make a lot of money. A42. I will have formal education beyond high school. B11. I will have a lot of jewelry. A37. I will work with computers. B1. I will own my own home. A10. I will work in law enforcement.	A44. I will take lessons to develop my talents/skills. A5. I will work with nature. C17. I will volunteer to coach a sport. C8. I will be a Sunday school teacher. A1. I will drive vehicles for my job. C7. I will be a community leader. A19. I will have a job in sports/athletics. A30. I will have a job that involves religion. A28. I will have a job with a clearly defined daily routine. C14. I will sing in a choir.

Most Expected Items for High School Group 2:
Sports Star-oriented

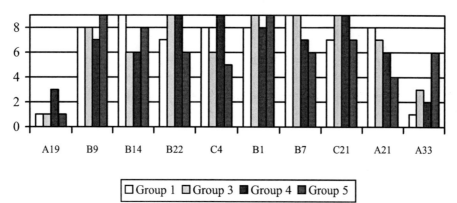

Most Expected Items for High School Group 3:
Family and Security-oriented

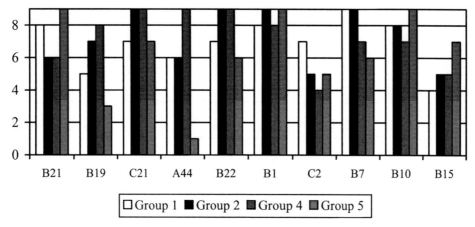

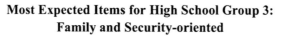

A strong emphasis on providing for their families and having support from family and friends was seen for the third group which was named "Family and Security-oriented." Compared to the other groups, this group was less interested in traveling with their jobs or having jobs that would require a lot of their time or taking risks. This was the only group that did not place any "career" items in the "most like" column.

Group 4 conveyed a primary interest in life outside of work and was labeled "Personal Life-oriented." Half of their "most like" items focused on relationships and they also indicated that they expected to take regular vacations and to spend time developing their talents and skills. With regard to employment, they were higher than other groups in desiring a job that involved being artistic/creative, yet having a clearly defined routine and involving thinking and problem solving. Having the support of their family and friends was a high priority.

Table 6 Significant Differences Between the High School Sample Q-Groups

	Group 1	Group 2	Group 3	Group 4	Group 5
Group 1 Career-oriented		A12, A16, A24, A26	A12, A14, A26, A32	A12, A14, A24, A42, B24, C19	A26, A28, A32, A44, C12
Group 2 Sports Star-oriented	A19, A33, C13		A6, A14, A19, A33, A43, C13	A19, A25, A33, A42, A43, B4, B12, B24, C13	A19, A21, A44, B12, C13, C23
Group 3 Family and Security-oriented	A9, A18, B15	A9		A9, A24, A25, A39, B12, B20, B24, C2, C19	A18, A44, B12, B19, C23
Group 4 Personal Life-oriented	A8, A10	A2, A20	A6, A20, A28, A32, B18, C20		A8, A28, A32, A44, B3, B19, C3, C23
Group 5 Economic-oriented	A9, A10, A27, A33, A41	A2, A4, A10, A12, A27, A34, A37, A41	A6, A10, A12, A14, A27, A37, A43	A4, A9, A12, A24, A25, A41, A42, A43, C11, C19	

The final group was labeled "Economic-oriented," given that seven out of the 10 "most like" items were economic capital. This group was open to working in areas that other groups rejected, such as working with food, in law enforcement, or with the government. They less expected to have a job that had a clearly defined routine or involved taking risks compared to some of the other groups. They also were lower than other groups in their expectation that they would receive their parents help should they encounter obstacles.

The groups that emerged for the high school sample were considerably different from one another in their visions of their futures. Some emphasized challenging or exciting careers, others focused on economic capital, and still others were concerned most about family and social relationships. Like the college sample, however, there also were aspects of possible selves that mattered for the majority of the groups, such as having savings in the bank (B7), feeling happy in their jobs (A23), owning a home (B1) and a car (B2), having jobs that would permit them to make a lot of money (A22) and having good friends whom they could trust and would support them (C21). Interestingly, some of these same items also were highly important for the college sample.

APPLYING THE COMPOSITE SORTS TO THE FULL SAMPLE

The composite sorts constructed for the college and high school samples can be thought of as "criterion sorts" derived from a group of interest. In essence they offer different "ways of thinking" that individuals in the sample share to some extent. Specifically, correlations for each participant with each of the "criterion" sorts can be calculated. This is accomplished by using the transposed dataset (in which each person serves as a variable and represents his/her unique way of thinking based on his/her Q-sort). The composite (i.e., criterion) sorts are added to this dataset as additional "items" that can be correlated with each person's sort, determining the similarity of each person's thinking with each of the criterion sorts. For the college student sample, the mean correlations ranged from .42 to .59 (sd = .12 to .18; rang e= -.03 to .91); the strongest associations were with the Traditional-oriented group closely followed by the Balance-oriented group. For the high school sample, the mean correlations ranged from .27 to .40 (sd= .17 to .19; range = -.17 to .73); the strongest associations were with the Career-oriented group, followed by the Sports Star-oriented group. The high school and college samples also were correlated with each other's "criterion" Q-sorts. The college students' mean correlations with the high school students' criterion Q-sorts ranged from .21 to .49 (sd = .10 to .13; range = -.04 to .75). The high school students' mean correlations with the college students' criterion Q-sorts ranged from .14 to .35 (sd =.12 to .16; range = -.17 to .73). Among the college student sorts, the high school students correlated highest with the Balance-oriented group, and among the high school student sorts, the college students correlated most with the Career-oriented group.

Calculating correlations for each participant with each of the criterion sorts makes it possible to examine how each sample member's thinking is related to the kinds of thinking uncovered by the Q-analysis, regardless of whether the sample member was used to create any of the composite sorts. Thus, even though many of the participants in a given sample often are not used to calculate the composite sorts (due to cross loadings or low loadings), it is possible to create scores for each person based on his or her correlation with each criterion sort. These correlation scores, therefore, represent how similar each person's thinking is to each of the different types of thinking identified by the Q-analysis, and can be related to other variables of interest, such as academic achievement, career planning, self-efficacy, or delinquency as a means for determining how the different types of thinking are associated with other attitudes or behaviors.

SUMMARY AND CONCLUSIONS

The goals of this chapter were to present the utility of using Q methodology for examining possible selves and to provide both a description of how to use this methodology, as well as offer examples of its use in studies examining possible selves. The value of Q methodology for understanding possible selves lies in the ability to identify different ways of thinking about possible selves. Q methodology allows for identification of the varied ways that adolescents structure their possible selves and the implications of understanding this structure for adolescents' current behaviors.

Results from two studies that incorporated a 41 item possible selves Q-sort supported the viability of this method for investigating the relative importance of adolescents' possible selves. A new 99 item possible selves Q-set (PSQ-sort) also was introduced and the results of pilot testing the sort with a college and a high school sample were detailed. A wide range of thinking about possible selves emerged, and although there was some overlap, the college and high school samples were quite different in their thinking about themselves in the future. Differences between the groups may have been the result of age, race, or social class, as well as due to other personal and contextual factors that differed between the high school and college student samples. Observing both intergroup and intragroup differences points to the importance of using methodologies that permit assessment of different ways of thinking about possible selves. These alternative ways of thinking have implications for the steps taken by adolescents, as well as by those who wish to support them, as they move toward their future goals.

Q methodology can be useful for examining the multitude of ways that adolescents think about their possible selves and identifying how these different types of thinking vary by demographic, personality, and social context variables. In addition to addressing group differences, changes over time in the ways adolescents' structure their possible selves could be observed through longitudinal work. As adolescents mature and move closer to the transition to adulthood, the ways they think about their possible selves may become more closely tied to the actual roles they will be assuming. Having adolescents construct Q-sorts across multiple time points during which the salience of their possible selves would be expected to change will permit elucidation of how and why the adolescents' structuring of their possible selves is modified. It will be important to learn from adolescents their reasons for (re)organizing their possible selves as they do. Interviews could be conducted that ask adolescents to describe why certain sets of possible selves are more or less expected (hoped for or feared), their plans for attaining (or avoiding) these selves, as well as whether they anticipate encountering any obstacles and how these obstacles might be overcome.

Examination of possible selves also can be broadened to others in the adolescent's social network. For example a parent or a close friend could complete the Q-sort on the focal adolescent. This would permit additional perspectives on the adolescent's possible selves and may be useful in explaining others' roles in supporting or hindering an adolescent's efforts to attain possible selves. The parent's or peer's Q-sort could be correlated with the adolescent's sort, as well as with the "criterion" groups that emerge from the Q-analysis of a sample.

Together, these different uses of Q methodology should facilitate greater understanding of the highly subjective images that people have of their future potential. This approach provides an alternative for capturing unique information about possible selves that is not available using traditional methodologies.

REFERENCES

Anderman, E. M., Anderman, L. H., and Griesinger, T. (1999). The relation of present and possible academic selves during adolescence to grade point average and achievement goals. *The Elementary School Journal, 100,* 3-17.

Brown, S. R. (1993). A primer on Q methodology. *Operant Subjectivity, 16,* 91-138.

Chalk, L. M., Meara, N. M., and Day, J. D. (1994). Possible selves and occupational choices. *Journal of Career Assessment, 2,* 364-383.

Curry, C., Trew, K., Turner, I., and Hunter, J. (1994). The effect of life domains on girls' possible selves. *Adolescence, 29,* 133-150.

Kerlinger, F. N. (1986). Chapter 32: Q Methodology (p. 507-522). In *Foundations of Behavioral Research* (3rd ed.) New York: Holt, Rinehart and Winston.

Kerpelman, J. L., Pittman, J.F., Lamke, L.K., and Sollie, D.L. (2005). The Possible Selves Q Sort (PSQ-sort). *Unpublished measure.* Auburn University, Alabama.

Kerpelman, J. L., and Schvaneveldt, P. L. (1999). Young adults' anticipated identity commitments to career, marital, and parental roles: Comparisons of men and women with different role balance orientations, *Sex Roles 41(3-4),* 189-217.

Kerpelman, J. L., Shoffner, M. F., and Ross-Griffin, S. (2002). African American mothers' and daughters' beliefs about possible selves and their strategies for reaching the adolescents' future academic and career goals. *Journal of Youth and Adolescence, 31,* 289-302.

Leondari, A. Syngollitou, E. Kiosseoglou, G. (1998). Academic achievement, motivation and possible selves. *Journal of Adolescence, 21(2),* 219-222.

Markus, H., and Nurius, P. (1986). Possible selves. *American Psychologist, 41,* 954-969.

Markus, H. and Nurius, P. (1987). Possible selves: The interface between motivationand the self-concept. In Yardley, K. and Honess, T. (Eds.), *Self and Identity: Psychosocial Perspectives.* (pp. 157-172). John Wiley and Sons Ltd.

McKeown, B., and Thomas, D. (1988). *Q Methodology.* Series: Quantitative Applications in the Social Sciences. Newbury Park, CA: Sage Publications, Inc.

Meara, N. M., Day, J. D., and Chalk, L. M. (1995) Possible selves: Applications for career counseling. *Journal of Career Assessment, 3,* 259-277.

Oyserman, D., Gant, L., and Ager, J. (1995). A socially contextualized model of African American identity: Possible selves and school persistence. *Journal of Personality and Social Psychology, 69(6),* 1216-1232.

Oyserman, D., and Markus, H. R. (1990). Possible selves and delinquency. *Journal of Personality and Social Psychology, 59(1),* 112-125.

Oyserman, D., and Saltz, E. (1993). Competence, delinquency, and attempts to attain possible selves. *Journal of Personality and Social Psychology, 65(2),* 360-374.

Oyserman, D., Bybee, D., Terry, K., & Hart-Johnson, T. (2004). Possible selves as roadmaps. *Journal of Research in Personality, 38,* 130-149.

Ruvolo, A.P. and Markus, H. R. (1992). Possible selves and performance: The power of self-relevant imagery. Special issue: Self-knowledge: Content, structure, and function. *Social Cognition, 10 (1)*, 95-124.

Shoffner, M.F., and Kerpelman, J. L. (2005). Examining the possible selves and careerdevelopment of rural adolescent girls through the use of Q-methodology. *Unpublished Manuscript*, University of North Carolina at Greensboro.

Stein, F. S., Roeser, R., and Markus, H. R. (1998). Self-schemas and possible selves as predictors and outcomes of risky behaviors in adolescents. *Nursing Research, 47(2)*, 96-106.

Stephenson, W. (1953). *The Study of Behavior: Q-Technique and Its ethodology*. Chicago: University of Chicago Press.

Thompson, B. (1980). Comparison of two strategies for collecting Q-sort data. *Psychological Reports, 47*, 547-551.

APPENDIX A
The Possible Selves Sorting Board

Most Like Me in the Future				Neutral				Least Like Me in the Future

APPENDIX B

Spreadsheet Entries for Calculating the Composite Q-sorts (*Example shows information for the first 25 items only*)

Item #	LOC P1	Factor Loading P1	LOC P2	Factor Loading P2	LOC P3	Factor Loading P3	LOC P4	Factor Loading P4	LOC P5	Factor Loading P5	Weight P1	Weight P2	Weight P3	Weight P4	Weight P5	Final Location
1	2	0.84	3	0.83	2	0.83	2	0.83	2	0.82	2.85	2.67	2.67	2.67	2.50	29.39
2	3	0.84	3	0.83	3	0.83	2	0.83	3	0.82	2.85	2.67	2.67	2.67	2.50	37.41
3	5	0.84	3	0.83	3	0.83	3	0.83	3	0.82	2.85	2.67	2.67	2.67	2.50	45.79
4[a]	**9**	**0.84**	**6**	**0.83**	**9**	**0.83**	**9**	**0.83**	**9**	**0.82**	**2.85**	**2.67**	**2.67**	**2.67**	**2.50**	**112.24**
5	2	0.84	1	0.83	2	0.83	6	0.83	2	0.82	2.85	2.67	2.67	2.67	2.50	34.72
6	1	0.84	3	0.83	1	0.83	2	0.83	1	0.82	2.85	2.67	2.67	2.67	2.50	21.36
7	4	0.84	4	0.83	4	0.83	5	0.83	4	0.82	2.85	2.67	2.67	2.67	2.50	56.11
8	8	0.84	6	0.83	6	0.83	7	0.83	5	0.82	2.85	2.67	2.67	2.67	2.50	86.03
9	2	0.84	2	0.83	3	0.83	4	0.83	3	0.82	2.85	2.67	2.67	2.67	2.50	37.23
10[b]	**2**	**0.84**	**1**	**0.83**	**1**	**0.83**	**1**	**0.83**	**1**	**0.82**	**2.85**	**2.67**	**2.67**	**2.67**	**2.50**	**16.21**
11	9	0.84	7	0.83	9	0.83	7	0.83	9	0.82	2.85	2.67	2.67	2.67	2.50	109.57
12	2	0.84	2	0.83	1	0.83	5	0.83	3	0.82	2.85	2.67	2.67	2.67	2.50	34.56
13	1	0.84	5	0.83	1	0.83	2	0.83	1	0.82	2.85	2.67	2.67	2.67	2.50	26.70
14	4	0.84	5	0.83	1	0.83	2	0.83	1	0.82	2.85	2.67	2.67	2.67	2.50	35.26
15	1	0.84	5	0.83	3	0.83	2	0.83	5	0.82	2.85	2.67	2.67	2.67	2.50	42.05
16	2	0.84	5	0.83	1	0.83	2	0.83	2	0.82	2.85	2.67	2.67	2.67	2.50	32.06
17	3	0.84	1	0.83	4	0.83	2	0.83	2	0.82	2.85	2.67	2.67	2.67	2.50	32.24
18	3	0.84	2	0.83	4	0.83	2	0.83	4	0.82	2.85	2.67	2.67	2.67	2.50	39.92
19	1	0.84	1	0.83	2	0.83	1	0.83	3	0.82	2.85	2.67	2.67	2.67	2.50	21.03
20	3	0.84	4	0.83	4	0.83	3	0.83	5	0.82	2.85	2.67	2.67	2.67	2.50	50.42
21	2	0.84	3	0.83	2	0.83	2	0.83	2	0.82	2.85	2.67	2.67	2.67	2.50	29.39
22	3	0.84	3	0.83	3	0.83	2	0.83	3	0.82	2.85	2.67	2.67	2.67	2.50	37.41
23	5	0.84	3	0.83	3	0.83	3	0.83	3	0.82	2.85	2.67	2.67	2.67	2.50	45.79
24	9	0.84	6	0.83	9	0.83	9	0.83	9	0.82	2.85	2.67	2.67	2.67	2.50	112.24
25	2	0.84	1	0.83	2	0.83	6	0.83	2	0.82	2.85	2.67	2.67	2.67	2.50	34.72

[a]Example of a "most like" item.
[b]Example of a "least like" item.Appendix C.
P1-P5 refer to the data for persons 1-5.
LOC refers to where each person placed the item on his/her sort.

APPENDIX C
POSSIBLE SELVES Q-SET

A1. I will drive vehicles for my job.

A2. I will have a desk job.

A3. I will have a job of high importance and respect (high prestige).

A4. I will work with children/teens.

A5. I will work with nature.

A6. I will travel a lot in my job.

A7. I will have a job in which I am physically active.

A8. I will have a job in which I can be artistic or creative.

A9. I will work with food.

A10. I will work in law enforcement.

A11. I will have a teaching job.

A12. I will work in the medical or health field.

A13. I will be a researcher or scientist.

A14. I will have a job that requires a lot of my time.

A15. I will have a job in which I can be my own boss.

A16. I will do work that involves saving lives and/or protecting people.

A17. I will work in the business field.

A18. I will work in a job that helps people improve their appearance.

A19. I will have a job in sports/athletics.

A20. I will have a job that requires a lot of thinking and problem solving.

A21. I will have a job in which I get to use my hands.

A22. I will have a job that will permit me to make a lot of money.

A23. I will feel happy doing the job I choose (It will be fun).

A24. I will have a job that allows me to help people.

A25. I will have a job that does not take a long time to master.

A26. I will have a job that has a wide variety of tasks.

A27. I will have a job with the government.

A28. I will have a job with a clearly defined daily routine.

A29. I will have a highly skilled job.

A30. I will have a job that involves religion.

A31. I will operate machinery for my job (excluding computers).

A32. I will have a job that involves taking risks.

A33. I will have a job that involves entertaining people.

A34. I will have a job that helps to change society.

A35. I will have a job that requires a lot of precision.

A36. I will hold a management position.

A37. I will work with computers.

A38. I will be a stay-at-home parent.

A39. I will have a paid job I can do from my home.

A40. I will be a salesperson.

A41. I will have more than one job at the same time.

A42. I will have formal education beyond high school.

A43. I will spend a lot of time doing one or more hobbies.

A44. I will take lessons to develop my talents/skills.

A45. I will be in the military.

A46. I will work with animals.

B1. I will own my own home.

B2. I will own my own car.

B3. I will own a second home.

B4 I will own a second car.

B5. I will take regular vacations.

B6. I will have financial investments (examples: mutual funds, bonds).

B7. I will have savings in the bank.

B8. I will have a lot of electronic equipment (e.g., stereo, DVD, computer, and more).

B9. I will have a lot of clothes.

B10. My home will have nice furniture.

B11. I will have a lot of jewelry.

B12. I will choose to have more expensive things rather than cheap things.

B13. I will have to find a way to earn money to pay for my education/training.

B14 I will be earning money to cover my living expenses.

B15. My parents will provide me with financial resources if I need their support.

B16. Making ends meet every month will be a big challenge.

B17. My spouse will make plenty of money to support our family.

B18. I will give money to a place of worship.

B19. I will wear expensive clothes.

B20. I will have enough money to buy my spouse a car.

B21. I will buy my child(ren) nice clothes.

B22. I will buy nice presents for my family.

B23. I will travel abroad.

B24. I will donate money to charity.

B25. I will attend plays and concerts.

B26. I will purchase one or more of the ff: childcare, yard care, housecleaning.

C1. I will be a parent (a mother or a father).

C2. I will be a spouse (a husband or a wife).

C3. I will have a lot of close friends (high placement = a lot; middle placement = some; low placement = none).

C4. I will have a close relationship with one or more of my family members.

C5. I will form long-lasting friendships with co-workers.

C6. I will be a best friend.

C7. I will be a community leader (examples: PTA president, hold a local political office).

C8. I will be a Sunday school teacher.

C9. I will be a tutor or mentor (such as a "Big Brother/Big Sister).

C10. I will spend a lot of time with my friends.

C11. I will be a community volunteer.

C12. I will be a churchgoer.

C13. I will play team sports.

C14. I will sing in a choir.

C15. I will be a member of one or more organized groups.

C16. I will spend a lot of time with my neighbors (high placement = a lot; middle placement = some; low placement = none).

C17. I will volunteer to coach a sport.

C18. I will help organize social activities for my child (example: play days).

C19. I will volunteer at my child's school.

C20. I will join a country club.

C21. I will have good friends I can trust and feel supported by.

C22. My parents will support me in the goals I have for myself.

C23. My parents will help me when I encounter obstacles.

C24. I will have family members, other than my parents, who will give me support.

C25. I will play in a band.

C26. I will be a pet owner.

C27. I often will have people (family, friends, guests) visiting me at home.

In: Possible Selves: Theory, Research and Application ISBN 1-59454-431-X
Editors: C. Dunkel and J. Kerpelman, pp. 187-204 © 2006 Nova Science Publishers, Inc.

Chapter 10

POSSIBLE SELVES AS MECHANISMS OF CHANGE IN THERAPY

Curtis S. Dunkel and Daniel Kelts
Illinois Central College
Brian Coon
Central Illinois Center for the Treatment of Addictions

ABSTRACT

This chapter describes two studies that were designed to test elements of a model that was proposed concerning the relationship between possible selves and self change in a therapeutic setting. The model predicts that: (1) as individuals contemplate change they generate possible selves, (2) as they decide to pursue change they begin to try and validate their chosen possible selves, (3) as they pursue some possible selves they also eliminate other possible selves, and (4) when the possible selves are achieved they are integrated into the current self-concept. Participants in each study were administered a measure of possible selves and a measure of the stages of change. The results from the two studies support the majority of the propositions derived from the model and suggest that future research in the area may be fruitful.

OBJECTIVE OF THE STUDY

The primary purpose of therapy or treatment is to produce change, to assist someone into a more adaptive state of being. The research reported in this chapter was undertaken on the premise that, (1) successful and sustained change involves a change in the self-system (Stein and Markus, 1996), and (2) that this change in the self-system begins with and can be seen in the production, elimination, and validation of possible selves.

POSSIBLE SELVES AND THEIR THEORETICAL RELATIONSHIP TO MOTIVATION AND CHANGE

Possible selves are representations of the self in the future (Markus and Nurius, 1986). Possible selves represent not only one's aspirations, but also one's concerns for the future. It is thought that they provide a link, or bridge, from the present self to the future self. Possible selves mediate long-term motivation and supply direction for the achievement of a desired goal (Wurf and Markus, 1991). They are seen as the component of the self-system that moves a person to action and are thus essential for motivation (Markus and Ruvolo, 1989).

It is the self-system that is at the center of motivation and action (Markus and Ruvolo, 1989); "... the crucial element of a goal is the representation of the individual *herself* or *himself* approaching and realizing the goal. Without this representation of the self, a goal will not be an effective regulator of behavior" (p. 211). Within the self-system, *possible selves* are the component that instigates and maintains motivation; they are the "...blueprints for change and growth..." (Cross and Markus, 1991).

EMPIRICAL EVIDENCE FOR THE LINK BETWEEN POSSIBLE SELVES AND CHANGE

Wurf and Markus (1991) proposed that the role of possible selves in personal growth and change first involves the generation of possible selves and secondly the attempt to validate them. Research in the area of identity development supports the first tenet of this proposition; that change first involves the generation of possible selves (Dunkel, 2000; Dunkel and Anthis, 2001). Based on the findings of Cross and Markus (1991), that late adolescents generate a greater number of possible selves than adults, it was proposed that possible selves were an important element in the formation of an identity (Dunkel, 2000). Specifically, it was hypothesized that the production of possible selves was a mechanism used in the exploration of identity alternatives. This hypothesis was supported because it was found that individuals who were engaged in active identity exploration endorsed more possible selves on a possible selves checklist in comparison to individuals who were not exploring.

Bolstering the position that possible selves generation is a mechanism used in identity formation, a follow-up study (Dunkel and Anthis, 2001) using a longitudinal design and different measures showed that the number of possible selves generated fluctuates in tandem with the amount of identity exploration exhibited. Additionally, it was found that identity commitment solidifies one's possible selves as witnessed by the consistency of the possible selves generated across time.

Thus it appears that possible selves play an important role in changing the personal view of one's self. Possible selves allow individuals to explore identity alternatives by "trying on" different possibilities without full commitment. The contemplation of change, such as occurs in identity exploration, is positively associated with the number of possible selves produced. This association implies that not only is the generation of possible selves a step in change (Wurf and Markus, 1991), but the elimination of possible selves also plays a role in the change process.

The research reported in this chapter represents an initial attempt to extend the findings on identity to other areas of change in the self; specifically, change of the self in a therapeutic context. Although a number of studies have been conducted on the relationship between possible selves and health related behavior (e.g., Sherrill, Hoyle, and Robinson, 2003) this study represents an attempt to examine the process of change and how it relates to possible selves.

THE POSSIBLE SELVES MODEL OF CHANGE

Based on the theoretical description of change put forth by Wurf and Markus (1991), a model of change involving possible selves is proposed. To reiterate, Wurf and Markus (1991) proposed a two-fold process of change using possible selves in which the generation of possible selves is followed by an attempt to validate them. We propose two additional steps.

The first additional step is thought to occur between the generation and validation of possible selves. This additional step involves the process of making decisions about which possible selves to pursue. Possible selves can often be mutually exclusive or at least difficult to reconcile. For example, a college student may generate a number of possible selves related to their career path (Cross and Markus, 1991). However, once a student decides to pursue one career they are often making a decision not to pursue other possible careers. Thus the decision to pursue one possible self may in turn result in the elimination of other possible selves.

Imagine a college student faced with the task of declaring a major. When faced with this task the student decides to major in physics because she likes the idea of becoming a physics professor, but she may have also pondered the possibility of becoming an attorney or a clinical psychologist. It would be unrealistic for the student to decide to simultaneously major in physics, pre-law to become an attorney, and psychology to become a clinical psychologist. Making a mature, realistic decision means that alternative possibilities are eliminated.

This elimination is not necessarily abrupt. The student may continue to consider becoming an attorney or a psychologist an option. However, as she receives her Bachelor's degree with a major in physics, attends graduate school for physics, and is hired as a professor of physics the likelihood that she will also become an attorney or clinical psychologist becomes diminished. Most people understand this and will eliminate conflicting possible selves. Stated in general terms, as a decision is made to pursue one possible self and the attempts to validate that self increase, the likelihood that the alternative possible selves are eliminated increases.

The second addition to the two-fold process proposed by Wurf and Markus (1991) also involves the elimination of possible selves. It is thought that once the possible self is validated it is eliminated from the range of possibilities and incorporated into the repertoire of current selves. For example, if our fictional student does become a physics professor, the possible self of being a physics professor should be incorporated into her self-system as a current attribute and no longer seen as a future possibility.

Accordingly possible selves may still be generated concerning a domain in which the self has been achieved: updating of possible selves is an ongoing process. Once hired our fictional physics professor may generate a possible self of receiving tenure, or if she is unsatisfied with her occupational choice she may actually revisit the former possibilities of attorney or psychologist.

THE HYPOTHESIZED LINK BETWEEN THE POSSIBLE SELVES MODEL OF CHANGE AND CHANGE IN THERAPY

The Stages of Change

The stages of change are a component of a larger eclectic therapeutic model called the Transtheoretical Model (A full description of the model is beyond the scope of this chapter. For reviews see Prochaska and DiClemente, 1984; Prochaska, DiClemente, and Norcross, 1992; DiClemente, 1999). The Transtheorectical Model attempts not only to synthesize an array of therapeutic orientations but also to describe the levels, processes, and stages of change. The stages of change are the temporal element of the model, and are the focus of this chapter.

The stages of change are composed of five discernable stages that describe how people change behavior. The stages are thought to occur in the following order; precontemplation, contemplation, decision or preparation, action, and maintenance. Those in the precontemplation stage may either be unaware of having a problem that needs changing or may be aware of the problem but resist change. In the contemplation stage individuals are aware of the problem and are actively considering change. In the decision/preparation stage individuals have decided to change and are gearing up for action, which is the subsequent stage. The action stage is when steps are undertaken in order to change the problem behaviors. Finally, the maintenance stage is reached when behaviors have been changed and the problem has improved, but continued vigilance is needed to ensure continued success. If there is a difficulty with the maintenance stage and a relapse in the problem behavior occurs, a return to the contemplation stage is likely to occur (Prochaska and DiClemente, 1984). On the other hand, termination can occur if the likelihood for a relapse is low and the individual does not have to exert effort to avoid a relapse. The stages have successfully described change using samples of psychotherapy clients (McConnaughy, Prochaska, and Velicer, 1983); those in outpatient alcoholism treatment (DiClemente and Hughes, 1990), and those attempting smoking cessation (DiClemente, Prochaska, Fairhurst, Velicer, Velasquez, and Rossi, 1991).

POSSIBLE SELVES AND THE STAGES OF CHANGE

Figure 1 illustrates the hypothesized link between the number of possible selves generated and the stages of change. The ability to deny to oneself a problem that is obvious to others would not be possible without a refusal to engage in self-exploration. Thus consciousness raising is a therapeutic technique that is suggested to help a client begin self-examination and hopefully move to the stage of contemplation (Prochaska et al., 1992). From the proposed possible selves model of change, the lack of self-exploration seen in the precontemplation stage should also result in a limited number of possible selves.

As one enters the contemplation stage it is hypothesized that there is a corresponding increase in the number of possible selves generated. The research on identity formation showed that self-exploration is associated with a greater number of possible selves (Dunkel and Anthis, 2001), and it is thought that the contemplation stage involves a similar self-exploration process. For example, Prochaska et al. (1992) identify self-reevaluation, a kind of self-exploration in which the self and one's values and goals are reassessed, as a process that is often engaged in during the contemplation stage.

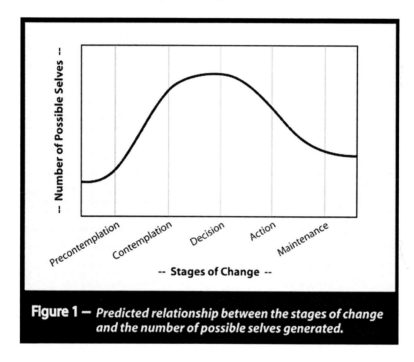

Figure 1 – *Predicted relationship between the stages of change and the number of possible selves generated.*

Next, it is thought that as a decision is made to pursue some possible selves, there is an increase in the likelihood that other possible selves (those that may interfere with the chosen possibilities) will be eliminated. Therefore, as the elimination of possible selves begins, the total number of possible selves held should decrease. Self-reevaluation begins to take a different tone. "Self-revaluation includes an assessment of which values clients will try to actualize, to act upon, and make real. Clients need to also assess which values they will let die." (Prochaska and DiClemente, 1984; p.54). It is predicted that the process of eliminating contradictory possible selves will begin in the decision/preparation stage, and the decrease will continue as commitment to the chosen possible selves, in the form of action as reflected in the action stage, increases.

Once change is established, it must be maintained. The maintenance stage is the last stage in of the stage of change model. As the process continues and goals are met, the list of possible selves will change accordingly. If the goal is not fixed, over time, as an individual continues to maintain their change, it becomes "second nature" and is converted into a component of the self-concept representing the current self.

The proposed curvilinear relationship between processes of change (the number of possible selves generated in the current research) and the stages of change is not new to stages of change research. Prochaska, Velicer, Guadagnoli, Rossi, and DiClemente (1991) found patterns of change in which the relationship between the processes of change (e.g., self-reevaluation) and stages of change resembled what they described as a mountain metaphor. Distinct processes were found to peak at different stages. The current approach differs slightly in that it is thought that possible selves continue to play a vital role throughout the stages, and that different means (production, elimination of alternatives, validation, elimination and integration) are used at each stage.

HYPOTHESES

Based on the proposed model and the methods used in the current study a series of predictions about the relationship between the stages of change and possible selves can be tested. Not all of the predictions based on the model can be tested given the limitations of the methods. The predictions were tested in terms of the addiction recovery process in Study 1 and non-specific non-residential counseling in Study 2.

Precontemplation will be negatively associated with the number of possible selves generated. Contemplation will be positively associated with the number of possible selves generated. Decision or Preparation is at the apex of possible selves generation. A greater number of possible selves should be generated at this stage in comparison to the maintenance stage. During this stage it is also predicted that the possible selves related to the problem behavior (i.e., abstinence in Study 1) become especially salient, and therefore more possible selves related to abstinence will be generated in comparison to the maintenance stage. Action will not be significantly associated with the number of possible selves generated. Maintenance will be associated with a fewer number of general possible selves generated, and a fewer number of possible selves specifically related to the problem (i.e., abstinence in Study 1) in comparison to the decision/preparation stage.

STUDY 1

Method

Participants
Data was collected from two groups of women. One group consisted of women who were residing in a long-term (> 6 months), residential facility for drug-addiction when the data was collected. This group will be referred to as the Tx group. Thirty-nine participants were in the Tx group with an age range from 19 to 59 (M=34.97, SD=9.06). The sample was composed of 18 Black, 17 White, 1 Hispanic, and 2 American Indian women, with one participant not answering the question regarding race. The length of stay ranged from 3 to 295 days with an average of 96 days (SD=78.68). The majority of the Tx group consisted of women who were court ordered to treatment and have had at least one prior treatment experience.

The second group consisted of women who responded "no" to the screening question, "Are you currently in any form of counseling?", and "yes" to the screening question, "Are you a recovering alcoholic/addict?" After answering "yes" to the second question they were asked, "How long have you been abstinent?" Women in this group were recruited from a group of volunteer lecturers visiting the treatment facility and students at the community college where the first two authors are employed. There were a total of 21 women in this group. The group was composed of 13 White, 7 Black, and 1 Hispanic with a range in age of 24-47 (M=37.76, SD=6.86). The self-reported length of continuous abstinence averaged 3.68 years with a range from 120 days to 15 years.

MEASURES

Possible Selves

Two open-ended possible selves questionnaires (OPSQ), one measuring hoped-for possible selves and one measuring feared possible selves, were administered to each participant. This format has been used extensively (e.g., Cross and Markus, 1991; Dunkel and Anthis, 2001; Frazier, Hooker, Johnson, and Kaus, 2000; Knox, Funk, Elliot, and Bush, 1998). The instructions for the two measures were based on those used by Cross and Markus (1991) in which a short description of possible selves is supplied prior to the administration of the questionnaire.

Two separate pages were supplied on which the participants were instructed to write down their hoped for and feared possible selves. Sixteen lines appeared beneath the instructions allowing the participants to write down one possible self per line. The hoped-for possible selves measure was always presented before the feared possible selves measure. It has been the experience of the first author that beginning with the feared selves measure is more likely to result in confusion on the part of the participant.

Although no specific hypotheses were stated that differentiated between hoped-for and feared possible selves, past research has consistently shown that they can yield different results and therefore should be kept separate (e.g., Oyserman and Markus, 1990; Sherrill et al., 2003). The possible selves measures were given to each group; Tx and recovery.

The use of the possible selves measure yielded the following variables for analysis: the number of possible selves (hoped-for and feared) and the number of possible selves related to abstinence (hoped-for and feared), and the balance of abstinence themed possible selves. Possible selves balance refers to having both feared (e.g., relapse) and hoped-for (e.g., stay clean) possible selves in the same domain (e.g., abstinence). It has been theorized that possible selves balance plays an important role in motivation (Oyserman and Markus, 1990). Although not central to the proposed hypotheses, given the theoretical importance of balance and ease of measurement it seemed reasonable to examine it as well.

A participant's number of possible selves was calculated by counting the number of lines used, where each line contained one possible self. The first and third authors judged the number of possible selves related to abstinence and these judgments were also used to measure balance. For abstinence related hoped-for possible selves, κ=.91, for abstinence related feared possible selves, κ= .81. Due to the greater experience of the first author with the possible selves construct, when disagreements between raters occurred, the first author's judgment was utilized.

Stages of Change

In addition to the possible selves measure the Tx group was administered a modified version of the Stages of Change Questionnaire (SCQ; McConnaughy, DiClemente, Prochaska, and Velicer, 1989). The SCQ is a 32-item, self-report, 5-point Likert-type measure that provides continuous scores for precontemplation, contemplation, action, and maintenance. Due to the structure of the treatment (e.g., long-term) and the type of clientele in the Tx group, the maintenance section of the SCQ was removed because it was thought to lack relevance. None of the clientele in the Tx group were in treatment to help maintain changes that had been accomplished, they were likely to have been court mandated to treatment and actively abusing drugs/alcohol if not in a controlled setting prior to admission. Therefore, instead of using the SCQ to measure maintenance in the Tx group, the recovery group was used as a proxy for maintenance. The recovery group exhibited the behavioral markers of the maintenance stage (all of the participants in the recovery group had been maintaining abstinence outside of a controlled treatment setting).

The internal consistency for each of the subscales was calculated and is as follows: precontemplation (α=.58), contemplation (α=.87), action (α=.88). The range of scores for precontemplation was 8-22 (M=12.02, SD=3.46), for contemplation the range was 33-40 (M=37.83, SD=2.14), and the range for action was 30-40 (M=36.24, SD=2.92).

Procedure

The research packets were administered in counter-balanced order to the Tx group in small groups (<15) by the first two authors. The OPSQ was given to the recovery group either at the treatment center, in a classroom setting, or participants were instructed to complete the measure at their leisure and return it when they had finished.

Planned Analyses

Stages of change research has utilized both continuous measures (McConnaughy et al., 1989) and approaches that fit participants into discrete categories based on behavioral factors or questionnaires (e.g., Prochaska, Velicer, DiClemente, and Fava, 1988; DiClemente et al., 1991). The current study utilizes both a continuous approach and a categorical approach.

Using a continuous approach, within-group correlational analyses were conducted using the Tx group's responses on the OPSQ and the SCQ. These analyses were used to test the predicted relationship between the precontemplation, contemplation, and action stages and the number of possible selves generated. One participant was removed from the within group sample because of outlying data on the SCQ. Her score for contemplation was 11.68 standard deviations below the mean and her score for action was 8.23 standard deviations below the mean.

Using a categorical approach, between-group analyses were conducted using a series of t-tests. One participant failed to complete the feared possible selves portion of the OPSQ and two participants failed to complete the feared possible selves portion of the OPSQ correctly (they continued to write down hoped-for selves) and therefore these three participants were not included in the analyses on feared possible selves.

As stated in Prochaska et al. (1992) when using the continuous measure (McConnaughy et al., 1989) those who score high in contemplation and action, with a higher score in contemplation are likely to be in the decision/preparation stage. Prochaska et al. (1992) reported that clients who are beginning treatment often match this pattern and are therefore thought to be in the decision/preparation stage.

Following the advised classification by Prochaska et al. (1992) participants who scored high on both measures, with a higher score on contemplation, were thought to reflect the decision/preparation stage. Twenty-six of the Tx group participants were classified into the decision/preparation stage based on this classification scheme.

RESULTS

Because Cross and Markus (1991) found that age was significantly related to the number of possible selves generated, prior to the analyses, correlations between age and the number of possible selves were conducted. The correlations were not significant and when adding age as a covariate the results were unchanged and therefore not reported.

Despite the previous finding that people in therapy often progress from contemplation to action, none of the correlations between time spent in Tx and the stages of change were significant; precontemplation (r=-.00), contemplation (r=-.16), action (r=.05).

WITHIN-GROUP ANALYSES

The results of the correlational analyses can be seen on Table 1. As predicted, the number of hoped for possible selves generated was positively correlated to the SCQ contemplation score, with the number of hoped for possible selves accounting for over 20% of the variance in the SCQ contemplation score. No other correlation between the SCQ scores and the number of possible selves generated (hoped for or feared) was significant. However, the correlation between precontemplation and the number of hoped for possible selves generated approached significance.

Table 1 Correlations between the Stages of Change and the Number of Possible Selves Generated

Possible Selves Stages of Change	Hoped-for	Feared
Precontemplation	-.28*	-.15
Contemplation	.46+	.06
Action	.19	.02

Note. N=38. +p<.01, *p<.09

BETWEEN-GROUP ANALYSES

The results of the *t*-tests examining the differences between the Tx group in the decision stage and recovery group representing the maintenance stage on the number of hoped-for, $t(46)=3.81, p<.001, \eta^2=.24$, number of feared, $t(43)=2.92, p<.01, \eta^2=.17$, number of hoped-for related to abstinence, $t(46)=2.60, p<.05, \eta^2=.13$, number of feared related to abstinence, $t(43)=3.56, p<.005, \eta^2=.23$, and the balance of abstinence themed possible selves, $t(43)=3.49$, $p<.005, \eta^2=.22$, were all significant. The means and standard deviations of the two groups on the possible selves indices can be seen on Table 2. As predicted, the Tx group in the decision stage generated a greater number of possible selves, both hoped for and feared, a greater number of possible selves specifically related to abstinence, both hoped-for and feared, and greater balance in the abstinence themed possible selves.

Table 2 Mean and Standard Deviations of the Possible Selves Measures by Group

Group *Possible Selves*	*Treatment*	*Recovery*
Total		
Hoped-for	12.30(2.88)	8.43(4.14)
Feared total	7.72(3.16)	4.95(3.17)
Abstinence related		
Hoped-for	1.48(1.16)	0.67(.97)
Feared	1.28(.89)	0.45(.61)
Balance	1.00(.65)	0.35(.58)

Note. Standard deviations are in parentheses.

DISCUSSION

Overall, the results of Study 1 suggest that the stages of change are systematically related to the number of possible selves generated.

Within-Group Analyses

The relationship between the stages of change and the number of possible selves generated was especially clear in the case of hoped-for possible selves. As predicted, the within-group analyses resulted in a positive correlation between contemplation and the number of hoped-for possible selves generated. This result supports the contention that the production of possible selves is a mechanism used in the contemplation or exploration of self-change.

The predicted relationship between precontemplation and the number of hoped-for possible selves produced was not significant. However, given the low reliability of the precontemplation subscale (α=.58), the correlation between the two variables (r=-.28) suggests that the hypotheses regarding the relationship between the number of possible selves generated and precontemplation should not be discarded without further research. In fact, r=-.38 when the correlation is recalculated and corrected for attenuation for the low reliability of the precontemplation subscale.

No significant relationships between the stages of change and the number of feared possible selves generated were found. Thus, it appears that the predicted relationships only held true for the hoped-for possible selves. It may be, given the participants' life circumstances, the feared possible selves were readily available and are therefore independent of the degree of contemplation expressed. The participants were well aware of the bad turns their futures could take; but that once they began to actively contemplate they could see the possible positive outcomes for their future as well.

Between-Group Analyses

The between-group analyses augmented the findings of the within-group analyses. Using a categorical approach it appears that the decision/preparation stage is associated with a significantly greater number of possible selves in comparison to the maintenance stage. Unlike the within-group analyses, the differences were found for both hoped-for and feared possible selves. The results lend support to the proposal that possible selves are eliminated when there is progression from the decision/preparation stage to the maintenance stage, although longitudinal methods would need to be used to verify this notion.

It was also found that the number of abstinence-specific possible selves generated was greater for the Tx group. This finding is consistent with the idea that abstinence related possible selves are eliminated from the possible selves repertoire during the maintenance stage. It is also thought that at this stage possible selves become integrated into the set of current selves. This prediction, however, was not testable using the current methods.

The greater number of abstinence specific hoped-for and feared possible selves also resulted in greater balance in the Tx group. If balance is an indication of motivation (Oyserman and Markus, 1990), than this finding suggests that the Tx group is at a heightened level of motivation for change in the area of abstinence.

STUDY 2

Despite the general support for our proposed integration of the possible selves model of change and the stages of change provided by Study 1, a number of factors limit the reliability and ability to generalize the results. These factors include the type and intensity of the therapy. The results from Study 1 could be specific to treatment for drug/alcohol addiction and/or an intensive residential treatment. Study 2 was undertaken in order to begin to address these two possibilities.

METHOD

Participants

All of the participants in Study 2 were women who were currently attending classes at a community college and participated in the study for course credit. One group was made up of participants who responded "yes" to the screening question, "Are you currently in any form of counseling?" This group consisted of 14 women. All of the women in this group were white and their age ranged from 19-55 (M=32.50, SD=12.82). It is assumed that the intensity of the therapy was less than the Tx group in Study 1 because the participants were attending college and therefore were not in a residential setting. Questions concerning the type of counseling engaged in were not asked[1].

The second group was comprised of participants who responded "no" to the screening question. This group consisted of 28 women; 22 white, 5 black, and 1 Hispanic, women with an age range of 18-69 (M=31.61, SD=10.33).

Measures and Procedure

The OPSQ used in Study 2 was identical to the one used in Study 1.

The opportunity to participate in the current study was announced in class. Volunteers were given a research packet including a consent form, instructions, a demographic questionnaire, and the OPSQ and were allowed to complete the forms at their convenience.

RESULTS AND DISCUSSION

As in Study 1 preliminary correlations were conducted between age and the number of possible selves generated. The calculations resulted in a significant correlation between age and the number of feared possible selves, $r(42)$=-.33, p<.05. As found by Cross and Markus (1991) age was inversely related to the number of possible selves generated. The correlation between age and the number of hoped-for possible selves generated was not significant.

Two t-tests were calculated to examine the possible differences between the counseling and no-counseling groups on the number of hoped-for, $t(40)$=2.36, p<.05, η^2=.12, and feared possible selves, $t(40)$<1, ns, generated. The means and standard deviations for the groups can be seen in Table 3. The counseling group generated significantly more hoped-for possible selves than the no counseling group; no differences were found for the number of feared possible selves generated. The results did not change when age was added as a covariate.

---

[1] Because we did not inquire about the reason for or type of counseling being received it is not possible to determine what number, if any, of the participants were in therapy for addictions. This is an obvious problem given our desire to examine the generation of possible selves in therapy other than therapy for addictions.

Table 3 Number of Possible Selves Generated by Group

Group Possible Selves	Counseling	No Counseling
Hoped-for	10.86(4.72)	7.82(3.67)
Feared	8.00(4.85)	6.50(3.94)

Note. Standard deviation in parentheses.

The results of Study 2 suggest that the generation of possible selves in therapy is not limited to residential treatment for drug addiction. Although Study 2 had methodological limitations (e.g., vague screening question, small N), the results indicate that the larger number of possible selves (at least hoped-for) generated by individuals in counseling is reliable and is consistent with the proposition that the generation of possible selves is a mechanism used when engaged in change.

GENERAL DISCUSSION

A review of the possible selves literature reveals that a growing body of research has used possible selves to predict health related outcomes and behaviors. Possible selves criteria been found to be predictive of depression[2] (Penland, Masten, Zelhart, Fournet, and Callahan, 2000), the engagement in health-protective behaviors in older adults (Hooker and Kaus, 1992), the use of cigarettes and alcohol consumption in adolescence (Aloise-Young, Hennigan, and Leong, 2001), and mammography screening adherence (Black, Stein, and Lovelan-Cherry, 2001). A recent empirical review of this literature by Sherrill et al. (2003) supports the idea that possible selves are a significant predictor of an array of health behaviors.

Based on the relationship between possible selves and behavior, other researchers have begun to develop interventions and possible selves therapy techniques to change behavior in such areas as adolescent school involvement (Oyserman, Terry, and Bybee, 2002), youth educational retention and improvement (see chapter 12 by Hock, Deshler, and Schumaker), career counseling (Meara, Day, Chalk, and Phelps, 1995; Wai-Ling Packard, 2003), identity issues (Nurius and Majerus, 1988), depression (Nurius and Berlin, 1994), substance abuse (Buirs and Martin, 1997) and child abuse (Nurius, Lovell, and Edgar, 1988).

While a number of theoretical papers have been written on the role played by possible selves in the process of health behaviors, therapy, and change (e.g., Stein and Markus, 1996; Wurf and Markus, 1991), empirical research is lacking. The research reported in this chapter is an attempt to begin to fill that void by examining the relationship between possible selves and a well established indicator of change (i.e., the stages of change). The studies reported in

---

[2] Allen, Woolfolk, Gara, and Apter (1996) also examined the relationship between possible selves and depression. They found null results. The discrepancy in the results between the two studies could be the possible selves criteria used as the predictor. Allen et al. used expected possible selves, while Penland et al. (2000) used positive and negative possible selves to predict depression criteria used as the predictor. Allen et al. used expected possible selves, while Penland et al. (2000) used positive and negative possible selves to predict depression

this chapter demonstrate a predictable and consistent relationship between the number of possible selves generated (most consistently for hoped-for possible selves) and the stages of change.

There is some indication that precontemplation is associated with fewer hoped-for possible selves. The correlation between the two measures within the Tx group in Study 1 approached significance, but was attenuated by the low reliability of the precontemplation measure. The avoidance of the problem seen in precontemplation is also an avoidance of the self. This lack of self-evaluation should limit the elaboration of the components of the self, including possible selves.

As predicted, in Study 1, contemplation was positively correlated with the number of hoped-for possible selves generated within the Tx group. As one contemplates personal change, by definition she is also contemplating the change of the self, what the self could be. She is actively generating possible selves.

Consistent with the findings on precontemplation, the relationship between contemplation and the number of possible selves generated was only found for hoped-for possible selves. The modal population of the treatment facility utilized in this study is women who have at least one prior treatment experience and are involved in the criminal justice system. A negative event (e.g., arrest) often precipitates entry into treatment and individuals (e.g., probation officers, treatment staff, family members) may continually remind the individual of what she may face (e.g., prison, lose of child custody) if she fails to complete treatment and stay abstinent. This may make feared possible selves quite salient. Therefore, for the Tx group feared possible selves may be readily available independent of the stage of change, and this may also explain why the Tx group had more feared possible selves than the recovery group.

The results of Study 2 suggest that the relationship between contemplation and the number of hoped-for possible selves generated is reliable. While it is not known what stage of change any of the counseling group participants were in; the general purpose of counseling is to produce change and this change appears to involve an increase in the number of possible selves generated.

Because SCQ does not include a scale (McConnaughy, et al., 1989) to measure the decision/preparation stage, the categorical approach to measurement recommended by Prochaska et al. (1992) was taken. Using this approach, the majority of Tx group participants were placed into the decision/preparation stage and comparisons were made between this group and a recovery group representing the maintenance stage.

It was anticipated that the decision/preparation stage would be at the apex of possible selves generation and once a decision is made to pursue a particular set of possible selves and action commences the number of possible selves are reduced. The results of Study 1 support this prediction because the Tx group generated a greater number of possible selves than the recovery group. This suggests that the junction between decision and maintenance involves a pruning of possible selves. The prediction that the action stage coincides with the attempt to validate the decided upon possible selves was not tested in these two studies and should be addressed in future research.

It was proposed that the maintenance stage includes the elimination of possible selves from the possible selves repertoire and that some of the selves that are removed are integrated into the concept of the current self. The proposition that possible selves are eliminated was tested and supported in Study 1.

The proposition that the possible selves that are pursued and met are integrated into the current concept of self was not tested and needs to be directly tested in future research. However, the results of Study 1 show not only a decrease in the overall number of feared and hoped-for possible selves generated from the decision to the maintenance stage, but also a decrease in the number of possible selves related specifically to abstinence. This finding suggests that the abstinence-themed possible selves were not only removed from the possible selves, but also integrated into a current self concept. It would seem odd that individuals who self-identify as recovering addicts (as witnessed by the "yes" answer to the screening question), do not have a self-concept that includes a current self of recovering addict.

IMPLICATIONS FOR CLINICIANS

The generation of possible selves during contemplation most likely would not occur for changes that are not somehow central to one's concept of self. If the problem is central to a person's identity, than changing the problem means a restructuring of the identity as well. This type of change was expected in the Tx group and was supported by the significant positive correlation between the two measures.

If on the other hand, the problem behavior is not central to the person's self-concept an individual may change the problem behavior without a restructuring of the identity and therefore may not generate a greater number of possible selves when contemplating change. Smokers could be a population in which both types of people could be found (those in which smoking is a central element of their self-concept and those in which it is a peripheral element). Individuals to which smoking is an important self-defining behavior should generate a greater number of possible selves when contemplating change than those to which smoking is not central to their view of themselves. Thus, for therapeutic purposes it may be useful to know the extent to which the problem is used for purposes of self-definition.

Supporting an earlier position stated by possible selves researchers (e.g., Stein and Markus, 1996), the results suggest that clients that are clearly in the precontemplation stage may benefit from tasks that require the generation of hoped-for possible selves. Asking clients to generate possible selves as a self-evaluation method may assist in movement to the contemplation stage. There are a number of possible tools that could be used to help the client generate possible selves including role-playing (Buirs and Martin, 1997), the adaptation of a possible selves interview (Hooker and Kaus, 1992), or the completion of a possible selves tree (see chapter 12 by Hock, Deshler, and Schumaker).

Prochaska et al. (1992) state that patients entering therapy are most likely to be in the decision/preparation stage. This is reflected in Study 1 by the Tx group's scores on the SCQ. In light of these findings, it appears that patients entering therapy may already have an array of possible selves, and that therapists must often assist patients in the elimination of possible selves. The process of possible selves elimination may be difficult for any number of reasons. Patients may have difficulty "letting go" of some possibilities that are no longer attainable, have an aversion to the difficult action needed to reach the possibilities, not have the self-efficacy necessary to strive for the possibilities, vacillate amongst any number of possibilities, simply hold on to "pipe dreams", or get frustrated when unrealistic goals are not met. This last possibility was identified as possible therapeutic problem by Stein and Markus (1996; p. 367) and described in the following passage:

> A high school dropout with a history of delinquent behavior may at the beginning of rehabilitation articulate a vision of himself as a wealthy, BMW-driving business executive. However, after a single semester of intense struggling and frustration in attempt to complete his GED, he may abandon his goal as "impossible for someone dumb like me" and reinvest in his delinquent identity. The unrealistic possible selves, in this case, rather than facilitating the initiation of behavioral change, may function to impede the goal-directed behavior and block the process of change

Possible selves that may pose similar problems were seen in some of the responses of the Tx group in Study 1. For example, one patient hoped for "the ideal Better Homes and Gardens life" and another hoped to become "an Olympic athlete".

LIMITATIONS

The two studies reported in this chapter represent an initial empirical examination of the role possible selves play in the process of change in therapy and adds to the growing body of evidence pointing to the importance of possible selves in change. However, the studies have several limitations including the inability to test a number of predictions posited by the proposed model, the assessment of change without the inclusion of the necessary element of time, and the always present possibility that the clinical participants were simply responding to the demands of the context.

Future research should address these limitations. New methods can be developed that allow for further testing of the proposed model. A longitudinal design can be employed, thus including the element of time and allowing for the examination of actual not just implied change. Extending external validity could also be accomplished by utilizing other groups; including men, adolescents, patients with different disorders, and patients receiving treatment in different modalities.

AUTHOR NOTE

We would like to thank James Barrett, and Pam Wilfinger for their assistance with data collection, Jeanne Metros for her assistance in creating the figure, and the volunteers for their time.

REFERENCES

Allen, L.A., Woolfolk, R.L., Gara, M.A., and Apter, J.T. (1996). Possible selves in major depression. *The Journal of Nervous and Mental Disease, 184(12),* 739-745.

Aloise-Young, P.A., Hennigan, K.M., and Leong, C.W. (2001). Possible selves and negative health behaviors during early adolescence. *Journal of Early Adolescence, 21(2),* 158-181.

Black, M.E.A., Stein, K.F., Lovelan-Cherry, C.J. (2001). Older women and mammography screening behavior: Do possible selves contribute? *Health Education and Behavior, 28(2)*, 200-216.

Buirs, R.S., and Martin, J. (1997). The therapeutic construction of possible selves: Imagination and its constraints. *Journal of Constructivist Psychology, 10*, 153-166.

Cross, S., and Markus, H. (1991). Possible selves across the life span. *Human Development, 34*, 230-255.

DiClemente, C.C. (1999). Motivation for change: Implications for substance abuse treatment. *Psychological Science, 10(3)*, 209-213.

DiClemente, C.C., and Hughes, S.O. (1990). Stages of change profiles in outpatient alcoholism treatment. *Journal of Substance Abuse, 2*, 217-235.

DiClemente, C.C., Prochaska, J.O., Fairhurst, S.K., Velicer, W.F., Velasquez, M.M., and Rossi, J.S. The process of smoking cessation: An analysis of precontemplation, contemplation, and preparation stages of change. *Journal of Consulting and Clinical Psychology, 59(2)*, 295-304.

Dunkel, C.S. (2000). Possible selves as a mechanism for identity exploration. *Journal of Adolescence, 23*, 519-529.

Dunkel, C.S., and Anthis, K.S. (2001). The role of possible selves in identity formation: a short-term longitudinal study. *Journal of Adolescence, 24*, 765-776.

Frazier, L.D., Hooker, K., Johnson, P.M., Kaus, C.R. (2000). Continuity and change in possible selves in later life: A 5-year longitudinal study. *Basic and Applied Social Psychology, 22(3)*, 237-243.

Hock, M.F., Deshler, D.D., and Schumaker, J.B. (2004). Enhancing student motivation through the pursuit of possible selves. In C.S. Dunkel and J.L. Kerpelman (Eds.), *Possible Selves: Theory, research, and application*. Huntington, NY: Nova.

Hooker, K., and Kaus, C.R. (1992). Possible selves and health behaviors in later life. *Journal of Aging and Health, 4(3)*, 390-411.

Knox, M., Funk, J., Elliot, R., Greene Bush, E. (1998). Adolescents' possible selves and their relationship to global self-esteem. *Sex Roles, 39*, 61-80.

Markus, H., and Nurius, P. (1986). Possible selves. *American Psychologist, 41*, 954-969.

Markus, H., and Ruvolo, A. (1989). Possible selves: Personalized representations of goals. In L.A. Pervin (Ed.), *Goal concepts in personality and social psychology* (pp. 211-241). Hillsdale, NJ: Erlbaum.

McConnaughy, E.A., DiClemente, C.C., Prochaska, J.O., and Velicer, W.F. (1989). Stages of change in psychotherapy: A follow-up report. *Psychotherapy, 26*, 494-503.

McConnaughy, E.A., Prochaska, J.O., and Velicer, W.F. (1983). Stages of change in psychotherapy: Measurement and sample profiles. *Psychotherapy: Theory, research, and practice, 20(3)*, 368-375.

Meara, N.M., Day, J.D., Chalk, L.M., and Phelps, R.E. (1995). Possible selves: Applications for career counseling. *Journal of Career Assessment, 3(3)*, 259-277.

Nurius, P.S., and Berlin, S.B. (1994). Treatment of negative self-concept and depression. In D.K. Granvold (Ed.), *Cognitive and Behavioral Treatment: Method and Applications* (pp. 249-271). Pacific Grove, CA: Brooks/Cole.

Nurius, P.S., Lovell, M., and Edgar, M. (1988). Self-appraisals of abusive parents. *Journal of Interpersonal Violence, 3(4)*, 458-467.

Nurius, P.S., and Majerus, D. (1988). Rethinking the self in self-talk: A theoretical note and case example. *Journal of Social and Clinical Psychology, 6 (3/4)*, 335-345.

Oyserman, D., and Markus, H. (1990). Possible selves and delinquency. *Journal of Personality and Social Psychology. 59*, 112-125.

Oyserman, D., Terry, K., and Bybee, D. (2002). A possible selves intervention to enhance school involvement. *Journal of Adolescence, 25*, 313-326.

Penland, E.A., Masten, W.G., Zelhart, P., Fournet, G.P., and Callahan, T.A. (2000). Possible selves, depression and coping skills in university students. *Personality and Individual Differences, 29*, 963-969.

Prochaska, J.O., and DiClemente, C.C. (1984). *The Transtheoretical Approach: Crossing Traditional Boundaries of Therapy.* Homewood, IL: Dorsey Professional Books.

Prochaska, J.O., DiClemente, C.C., and Norcross, J.C. (1992). In search of how people change: Applications to addictive behaviors. *American Psychologist, 47*, 1102-1114.

Prochaska, J.O., Velicer, W.F., DiClemente, C.C., and Fava, J. (1988). Measuring processes of change: Applications to the cessation of smoking. *Journal of Consulting and Clinical Psychology, 56(4)*, 520-528.

Prochaska, J.O., Velicer, W.F., Guadagnoli, E., Rossi, J.S., and DiClemente, C.C. (1991). Patterns of change: Dynamic typology applied to smoking cessation. *Multivariate Behavioral Research, 26(1)*, 83-107.

Sherrill, M.R., Hoyle, R.H., and Robinson, J.I. (2003, May). *Role of possible selves in self-regulation and behavior: Review and synthesis.* Poster presented at the annual meeting of the Midwestern Psychological Association.

Stein, K.F., and Markus, H.R. (1996). The role of the self in behavioral change. *Journal of Psychotherapy Integration, 6(4)*, 349-384.

Wai-Ling Packard, Becky. (2003). Science career-related possible selves of adolescent girls: A longitudinal study. *Journal of Career Development, 29(4)*, 251-263.

Wurf, E., and Markus, H. (1991). Possible selves and the psychology of personal growth. In D.J. Ozer, J.M. Healy, and A.J. Stewart (Eds.), *Perspectives on personality* (Vol. 3, 39-62). London: Jessica Kingsley.

In: Possible Selves: Theory, Research and Application
Editors: C. Dunkel and J. Kerpelman, pp. 205-221

ISBN 1-59454-431-X
© 2006 Nova Science Publishers, Inc.

Chapter 11

ENHANCING STUDENT MOTIVATION THROUGH THE PURSUIT OF POSSIBLE SELVES

Michael F. Hock, Donald D. Deshler, and Jean B. Schumaker
The University of Kansas

ABSTRACT

Enhancing the academic motivation and commitment of students who have lost the desire to engage in learning in a meaningful way is a major challenge for many teachers, counselors, and parents. In an effort to address this challenge, the Possible Selves Program was developed to nurture academic and personal motivation in elementary through post-secondary students. Program activities guide students through the process of thinking about their hopes, expectations, and fears for the future. The program includes activities that help students identify short and long-term goals that they value and to develop and pursue action plans that lead to goal attainment. Studies conducted with middle and high school students and university student-athletes indicate that Possible Selves can be effective in increasing the number of roles students identify as possible for them in the future and the number and diversity of career, learning, and personal goals they wish to achieve. Also, Possible Selves has resulted in higher academic performance, higher retention rates, and higher graduation rates for university student-athletes than for student-athletes in control conditions.

"I'm going to play professional football. Ever since I was a little kid my dream has been to be a great tailback. And that's what I think about all the time. Nothing else matters that much, especially school! Don't bother me about learning all this stuff. I just need to get by until I'm ready for the NFL."

8th Grade Student

THE CHALLENGE

The statement above may sound all too familiar to teachers, counselors, and parents. While having a hope or dream to enter a highly competitive career field is admirable, limiting the scope of possibilities to one area may not be entirely wise. For example, only 250 out of approximately 1,000,000 high school football players actually end up playing in the NFL (NCAA, 2001). The odds are 6,000 to 1 that the young athlete quoted above will actually play in the NFL. Thus, limiting one's goals, commitment, and effort to one domain may close the door to other equally rewarding experiences and careers, especially if the acquisition of skills, knowledge, and learning how to learn are foundational to entry into these other areas.

Teachers report that one of their biggest frustrations is the challenge presented by students who seem to be academically unmotivated (Bogner, Raphael, & Pressley, 2002; Davis & Wilson, 2001; Garber, 2002; Graves, 2001). They are frustrated by students who passively or overtly refuse to participate or engage in educational activities even when learning activities are well-designed and reflect scientifically proven practices (Jarvis & Seifert, 2002; Reyna & Weiner, 2001). They recognize that the effectiveness of instruction with students who are reluctant to commit time and energy to learning is limited at best and completely ineffective at worst. Additionally, the challenge presented by academically unmotivated students has significant implications for a nation committed to No Child Left Behind legislation (U.S. Department of Education, 2002) and improving student performance on high-stakes measures of academic competence. Closing the literacy performance gap for underprepared students who lack the personal commitment to learn essential skills and knowledge is an exceedingly difficult task. Borkowski, Day, Saenz, Dietmeyer, Estrada, & Groteluschen (1992) captured the essence of this point when they wrote,

> As we were teaching reading strategies, we noticed that many students failed to see how strategies were relevant to their long-range goals. In fact, we came to realize that students did not see many, if any, relationships between the things they were learning in school..., and their dreams and expectations for the future. (p. 15)

While every teacher has experienced first hand the central role that motivation seems to plays in the learning process, it is significant to note that volumes have been written on motivation theory and special issues of journals on academic motivation are common (Pressley & McCormick, 1995). The attention that has historically been given to motivation and the growing body of current research on the topic verifies what teachers have known for years: unless the motivation of students is deliberately accounted for in the instructional planning process and during actual instruction, outcomes will be less than optimal (Cruickshank, 1990). The American Psychological Association underscored the vital role that motivation plays in learning in its 1997 document entitled *Learner-Centered Psychological Principles: A Framework for School Redesign and Reform* by highlighting two areas of particular importance in the learning process that have emerged through research on motivation. First, motivation to learn is influenced by the individual's emotional stress, beliefs, interests, goals, and habits of thinking. For example, intense negative emotions (e.g., anxiety, panic, insecurity) and related thoughts (e.g., worrying about competence, fearing failure, etc.), generally detract from motivation and interfere with learning and contribute to low performance. Second, acquisition of complex knowledge and skills requires extended learner effort and guided practice. Without a learner's motivation to learn, the willingness to exert effort without coercion is unlikely. Thus, educators need to be concerned with facilitating motivation by using strategies to enhance learner effort and commitment to learning and to achieving high standards of comprehension.

The National Research Council 2000 volume entitled *How People Learn* further reinforces the direct linkage between motivation and the amount of time students are willing to spend learning. This work underscores the repeated finding that appears in the research literature that learners of all ages are more motivated when they can see the usefulness of what they are learning and when they can use the information they are learning will lead to something of significance for them and others. In short, when learning is effectively tied to future purposes and outcomes, motivation to set goals and invest the necessary effort to meet goals is enhanced (e.g., Pintrich & Schunk, 1996). Without this commitment, significant numbers of learners will be left behind.

Because of this crying need, research over the past decade has focused on the development of programs to help students become committed to taking part in the academic journey. The purpose of this chapter is to describe and discuss one such program, The Possible Selves Program (Hock, Schumaker, & Deshler, 2003). Thisprogram was designed to give teachers and counselors a tool for increasing the academic motivation and focus of students. In order to understand the Possible Selves Program, the foundational theory and research that underlies the program must first be reviewed.

ACADEMIC MOTIVATION

A great deal of knowledge about academic motivation has been acquired over the years. For example, we know that most students begin their formal school experience motivated to learn. In fact, they seem to have a natural desire to learn (Csikszentmihalyi & Nakamura, 1989; Pressley & Ghatala, 1989). Additionally, most students have high expectations for success. That is, when children are given an appropriate learning task, they have great confidence that they can do it (Pressley & McCormick, 1995).

Not only are younger children motivated to learn, they tend to remain motivated. Even when young learners encounter frustration and failure, they demonstrate remarkable resilience. They continue to work at being academically successful even in the face of failure, at least for awhile (Clifford, 1978; Pressley & Ghatata, 1989). However, for many learners, motivation and optimism begin to diminish with repeated failure. By the upper elementary grades, teachers begin to see "unmotivated" students (Stipek & MacIver, 1989). Teachers and parents begin to hear, "I don't want to do this. I don't care. I hate school. Don't bother me!" Once students begin to believe they cannot perform certain tasks or do well academically, teachers and counselors must take steps to rekindle the "motivational fires" that support instruction and learning success.

INCREASING ACADEMIC MOTIVATION

Several validated interventions have been shown to be effective with learners in certain situations and under specific circumstances with regard to enhancing academic motivation. For example, positive reinforcement (Brophy, 1981; Bandura, 1986; Lepper, Green, & Nisbett, 1973), communication of high expectations to students (Brophy, 1987; Pressley & McCormick, 1995), rewarding personal improvement (Ames & Archer, 1988), making academic tasks more interesting (Anderson, Shirey, Wilson, & Fielding, 1987), teaching attribution alternatives and self-advocacy (Bandura, 1982; Borkowski, Weyhing, & Carr, 1988; Reid & Borkowski, 1987; Carr & Borkowski, 1989), nurturing student hopefulness (Curry, Snyder, Cook, Ruby, & Rehm, 1997; Snyder, 1994; Snyder, Cheavens, & Sympson, 1997) and orchestrating success through cognitive and metacognitive learning strategy instruction (Borkowski, et al., 1992; Deshler & Schumaker, 1988; McCombs & Marzano, 1990) have been reported as being effective with regard to academically motivating students.

Many of theses motivational interventions are closely related to cognitive goal theory (Blumenfeld, 1992). Cognitive goal theory holds that much of student behavior, mastery, and performance is the outcome of the desire to attain individual goals (Seifert, 1995). Increasingly, academic motivation seems to be directly related to the pursuit of meaningful and specific goals (Bandura, 1997; Dweck, 1986; Nicholls, Cobb, Wood, Yackel, & Patashnick, 1990). Conversely, academic underperformance or resistance to academic engagement may be due, in large measure, to a lack of goals in the domain of learning. In remarks to an audience of educational practitioners, Richard Lavoie said that students are not so much unmotivated as they are not motivated to do what we want them to do (Tollefson, 1998). In other words, having goals not aligned with learning outcomes may be related to academic underachievement due to disinterest and lack of effort in course work perceived to be unrelated to personal goals (Blumenfeld, 1992; Davison-Aviles, Guerrero, Howarth, & Thomas, 1999).

In contrast, students who see learning as a way to acquire skills and knowledge that will increase competence in goal areas *they* value are more likely to put forth the effort needed to attain those goals (Bandura, 1982; Blumenfeld, 1992; Borkowski, et al., 1992; Dweck & Leggett, 1988). These students are often labeled intrinsically motivated and are said to be mastery oriented (Ames & Archer, 1988). That is, they are driven to put forth the effort necessary in academic situations because the reward they seek is directly related to what they personally value. In effect, the process and goal attainment related to learning is the reward (Deci, Hodges, Pierson, & Tomassone, 1992; Lepper, 1988; Maehr, 1989; Wehmeyer, Palmer, Agran, Mithaug, & Martin, 2000). On the other hand, *learning for the sake of achievement* is driven more by extrinsic factors (Dweck, 1986; Lepper, 1988). Students who are motivated to achieve to get a certain grade, for example, could be called extrinsically motivated. Unfortunately, if these students believe that high levels of achievement and performance are beyond their reach, they may disengage from learning. Thus, helping students think in terms of mastery goals that are related to what they personally value and that help them attain the future selves to which they aspire seems helpful.

Recently, conceptual thinking and research has tied goal attainment theory to the construct of hope. Rick Snyder (1994) and colleagues at the University of Kansas have developed hope theory that states, in part, that human action is goal directed, and the level of hope that one has for the future is the result of the interaction between willpower (agency) and way power (pathway) for goals. That is, if individuals have the willpower to put forth effort to reach a goal, and if they have a plan that will help them reach a goal, they will have high hope. Hope can also be measured, and more importantly, nurtured, in low-hope individuals (Babyak, Snyder, & Yoshinobu, 1993; Snyder, Harris, Anderson, Holleran, Irving, Sigmon, Yoshinobu, Gibb, Langelle, & Harney, 1991; Snyder, Sympson, Ybasco, Borders, & Higgins, 1996; Snyder et al., 1997). Having high hope is useful because research conducted by Snyder and associates has found high hope individuals are more successful in life. For example, they recover from accidents and illness faster, they perform at higher levels athletically, and they experience more academic success than low-hope individuals. Interventions related to helping students think about possible future selves with its focus on future hopes, expectations, and fears may be one way to nurture hope (Snyder, 1994).

Let's return to the student quote that opened this chapter. This student could very well be the product of motivationally undermining experiences. For example, at some point in his educational experience, his academic performance may have been constantly and publicly compared to the performance of his better performing peers to the point of ridicule. If a student such as this one seems academically unmotivated, unwilling to risk failure again, and focused on limited goals, a response focused on goal setting related to personally valued outcomes seems required if this student is to become "intrinsically motivated." A way must be found to surface the student's personal goals, and help the student create a pathway or plan for reaching the goals, thus making learning more meaningful. Based upon the body of knowledge about goal theory, educators need to recognize that students are motivated by personal goals and that having hope involves three critical elements. First, students must identify individual goals that are valued and attractive to them. Second, they must believe that the goals are attainable with reasonable effort. Finally, they must develop specific plans that lead to attainment of the goals (Levine, 2002; Seifert, 1995).

DEVELOPING POSSIBLE SELVES TO NURTURE STUDENT MOTIVATION

One way of helping students surface goals related to future learning involves the analysis of "Possible Selves." Hazel Markus, professor of psychology at Stanford University, has drawn recent attention to the term "Possible Selves." Markus said that *Possible Selves are ideas about what one might become in the future* (Markus & Nuris, 1986). Markus and her colleagues reported that ideas about one's self in the future can be very motivating. That is, individuals with clear ideas and goals about what they want to do, be, and be like seem more willing to put forth the effort needed to attain these hoped-for ideals. For example, a student who has identified becoming an emergency medical technician as a possible self is more likely to work hard to graduate from high school and get the necessary training for that career than a student who has never thought about a career. Additionally, Markus reported that some individuals will work just as hard to avoid the possible selves that they fear. For example, students who have thought about the possible self living on welfare with no money to support a family may be more likely to work hard in school to avoid that possible self than students who have not seriously considered such outcomes. In either case, possible selves can increase one's motivation to work hard to attain specific goals because possible selves are an essential link between self-concept and individual motivation (Cross & Markus, 1994; Leondari, Syngollitou, & Kiosseoglou, 1998; Markus & Nurius, 1986; Oyserman & Markus, 1990a; Oyserman & Markus, 1990b).

Several descriptive studies have been conducted that detail the nature of hoped for, expected, and feared possible selves for specific groups. For example, Markus and Nurius (1986) found that possible selves could be assessed in college students. That is, most, if not all, college students have some conceptual knowledge of what they hope, expect, and fear in the future. Additionally, there is a positive bias in these thoughts about possible selves. Most individuals identify more positive possibilities for the future than negative possibilities. Importantly, future possible selves are different than the current self and individuals believe they can change and attain hoped-for selves.

Similar findings were reported for youth between the ages of 13 and 16 years of age. Youths attending a public school had no problems explaining what their possible selves were, and their explanations were diverse in nature. This finding also held true for youths who had been adjudicated and placed in delinquency programs. However, the nature of the possible selves of the groups differed. The adjudicated youth were focused on feared possible selves more so than hoped-for or expected possible selves, suggesting less balance between positive and negative selves and a sense of hopelessness (Oyserman & Markus, 1990a). In another study designed to assess the relationship of possible selves and self-schema to performance, college students were classified as being schematic (good problem solvers) or aschematic (not-so-good problem solvers). While the performance on problem solving measures did not distinguish between the groups, those who were schematic and endorsed more positive possible selves enjoyed attacking problem-solving tasks and required less failure feedback than did the aschematic group (Cross & Markus, 1994). Other researchers have reported that the use of open-ended questionnaires seems to be an effective way to surface current and future possible selves (Anderman, Hicks, & Maehr, 1994; Day, Borkowski, Dietmeyer, Howsepian, & Saenz, 1994; Garcia, Lissi, Egan-Dowdy, Davila, Matula, & Harris, 1995), and that associations can be made between positive visions of one's self in the future and academic performance and deep processing or self-regulating strategy usage (Anderman, 1992; Anderman et al., 1994; Day et al., 1994; Leondari et al., 1998).

In a related study, Estrada (1990) developed an intervention designed to build awareness and bring clarity to the possible selves of Hispanic students in 2nd through 7th grade. The intervention consisted of career, family, leisure, and friends awareness activities, discussion of the relationship between possible selves and high school graduation, how to deal with negative feedback, and coping with failure. The effects of the intervention were described as moderate with most gains in the number and specificity of roles and goals identified as possible for the learner. Effects for increased self-efficacy and academic performance were not evident. The authors speculated that by providing parallel programs for parents and increasing parental support for student goals and action planning that the effects of the intervention will be enhanced.

THE POSSIBLE SELVES PROGRAM

Based on the research described above, the possible selves concept seems to be a promising one in terms of helping students become more motivated to learn. However, although several individuals have reported interventions based on the Markus possible selves concept, no one has developed a program that can be used by educators at all levels of schooling to enhance the academic motivation of students, especially those students who are having difficulty in school. As a result, the Possible Selves Program (Hock et al., 2003) was born. The Possible Selves Program is designed to increase student motivation by having students examine their future and think about goals that are important to them. Specifically, students participating in the program think about and describe their hoped-for possible selves (selves **they** would like very much to create; a wish or a dream), expected possible selves (selves **they** are fairly sure they can create), and feared possible selves (selves they wish to avoid). Once students describe their possible selves, they create a Possible Selves Tree (Borkowski et al., 1992; Day et al., 1994; Estrada, 1990), a drawn picture of a tree which has branches and other elements representing their possible selves. The tree is used as a metaphor to help students examine the key roles they will assume in life, their hopes, expectations, and fears for the future, and the overall condition of their "tree." In effect, students examine their personal tree and are challenged to evaluate and take action to nurture their tree so it can become a strong, well-balanced, beautiful tree. Finally, they set goals related to the actions they need to take to nurture their trees, make plans for reaching the goals, and then work toward those goals.

Researchers have suggested that once students have examined their possible selves (i.e., hoped for, expected, and feared), they are more inclined to believe that they can do well in school and in life (Day et al., 1994; Estrada, 1990; Hock et al., 2002a). In effect, they begin to view learning as a pathway to their hopes and expectations and as a way to prevent feared possible selves from materializing. Thus, learning becomes more relevant, and students increase their willingness to put forth effort and commit to learning.

There are six components in the Possible Selves Program. The first component, **DISCOVERING**, helps the student answer the question, "What are my strengths and interests?" During this phase, the teacher engages students in activities designed to help them identify areas in which they have interest and skills and feel good about themselves. The goal is to find an area in which each student has had positive experiences and about which is willing to share those experiences. For example, a student skilled at soccer or playing computer games will, in all likelihood, have much to talk about and share with others in this strength area. By finding an area about which the student feels positive, the "pump is primed," and the student becomes more willing to share information related to areas about which he or she may not feel so positive (e.g., learning).

THINKING is the second component of the program, and it is designed to help the student answer the question, "Who am I?" Here, the student completes a structured but open-ended interview with a teacher or counselor, either individually or as part of a group. In the interview, students are asked to identify words or phrases that describe them in targeted areas (as a learner, person, worker, and in a strength area). They are also asked to define their hopes, expectations, and fears for the future in each area. In this way, an outline of the current self and possibilities for the future is developed within each area. Sample interview questions are: What statements or words best describe you as a *learner*? What do you hope to achieve as a *learner*? What do you expect to achieve as a *learner*? What do you fear as a *learner*? The targeted areas and number of questions within the interview can be modified to fit the age and interests of the students (see page 30 for a sample Possible Selves Interview).

As the student responds to questions and describes himself or herself, the student writes down answers to the interview questions. Additional questions about the student's hopes, expectations, and fears for the future in at least three domains (learner, person, and worker (or an individually selected strength area) are asked, and these responses are also recorded. Figure 1 represents responses to questions from a first-year university student-athlete, a 6th grade student, and an 8th grade student.

Responses to: What do you Hope to achieve as a *learner*?		
University Student -Not to flunk out -get a 2.5 G.P.A. -be eligible to play sports -really want a Degree	8th Grade Student -have the grades to go to college -learn more science, history, reading	6th Grade student -graduate from high school -be a successful student -pass English
Responses to: What do you Hope to achieve as a *person*?		
University Student -be more responsible -take care of my responsibilities -take care of details as expected	8th Grade Student -earn lots of money -help out in the community -have self-respect -be trustworthy	6th Grade student -have lots of friends -have a decent home -be a good person

Figure 1

Once the interview has been completed, the third component of the Possible Selves Program is introduced. It is called **SKETCHING**. It helps the student answer the question, "What am I like and what are my possible selves?" During this activity, the student draws a Possible Selves Tree. The teacher begins by stating something like, "You've listed a lot of important information about yourself. Now, you're going to pull that information together by creating a Possible Selves Tree. The tree will have limbs that represent you as a learner, person, and worker (or in a strength area). It will have branches that represent your hoped-for and expected possible selves in those areas. You will represent your feared possible selves with dangerous conditions for your tree (lightning, termites, poison in the soil). You'll use the exact words you recorded in the interview to add branches and roots to the tree and the dangers around it. You can add to or modify the statements you made. Later, I'll ask you to evaluate your tree and tell me if it really represents the ideas you shared."

Next, the tree is drawn and evaluated, and preliminary goals are discussed concerning how to keep the tree strong, make it fuller, protect it from fears, and provide it with nourishment. In short, the student is asked to briefly think about the tree and ways to nurture it.

Figure 2 is an actual tree completed by a university student-athlete. Notice the unbalanced nature of the tree. The athletic limb is much fuller and contains branches with very positive hope statements. The learner limb is less full, and the words are not nearly as positive. The roots of the tree on the athletic side are deep and strong. On the other hand, the roots for the learner side are short and weak. Fears have been added to the picture as toxins in the soil that threaten the roots or as a strong wind able to break a limb off the tree.

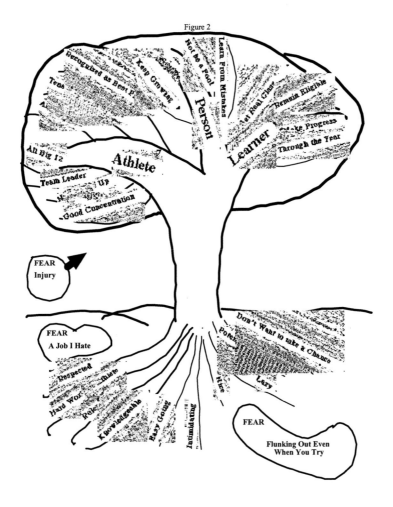

Figure 2

The fourth component of the program, **REFLECTING**, helps students answer the question, "What can I be?" It provides an opportunity for the student to evaluate the condition of his or her tree and set goals for the future. During this activity, for example, the student who drew the tree in Figure 2 would realize that nurturing in the learner and person areas is needed if balance and fullness are to be achieved. This reflection activity can include a discussion of how learning can support the total tree. Since athletic hopes will be lost without improved academic performance because the student cannot achieve in this area if he is academically ineligible to participate in sports, the student may be more inclined to commit time and energy to learning if the direct relationship is clarified. For example, if the student expresses the hope to remain eligible for sports, he might set goals to attend class regularly and earn a 2.50 in all his classes.

The fifth component, **GROWING**, helps the student answer the question "How do I get there?" It is utilized to get the student to start thinking about specific ways to nurture and "grow" his or her tree and attain identified goals. If, for example, a student identified the of hope for a career as the owner of a trucking business during the Reflecting component, the student and teacher can take the short and long-term goals that are necessary to attain this "possible self" and develop a plan to reach these goals. Hopefully, the student will discover (with teacher guidance) that learning how to problem solve, earning a high school diploma, learning business math skills, and learning different reading strategies in order to comprehend important material support the attainment of the student's hopes and expectations for the future. In addition, the student may discover that these same goals help the student avoid the "feared selves" that have been identified (e.g.. no job, no money, no friends). In short, during the Growing activities, a well-developed Action Plan is constructed by the student. The Action Plan will list a specific hope, a short-term goal underpinning the hope, the specific tasks that must be completed to reach the goal, and a timeline for completing all of the tasks. The action plan provides "pathway" to support the attainment of long-term goals and hopes for the future.

The sixth and final component is **PERFORMING**. It helps students answer the question, "How am I doing?" During this phase, the Possible Selves Tree, the goals established to "nurture" the tree, and the action plans are revisited regularly. Task completion is reviewed, goals and action plans are modified, goal attainment is celebrated, new goals are added, and hopes, expectations, and fears are continually examined. In addition, whenever the value of learning is questioned, the tree can be used to demonstrate how specific learning experiences and student effort contribute to the strength of the student's tree (i.e., future).

RESEARCH SUPPORTING THE POSSIBLE SELVES PROGRAM

A few studies have been conducted on the effects of the Possible Selves Program with university-level student-athletes and middle-school students. Two studies were conducted with freshmen university student-athletes, including student-athletes who were not well prepared for the academic demands of college. In the first study, 60 student-athletes were randomly assigned to one of three conditions (Hock, Schumaker, & Deshler, 2002a). For the control condition, 20 students received tutorial support from trained tutors and academic advising from athletic department counselors. Tutorial support consisted of unlimited access to subject-area and academic skills tutors as needed. Academic advising was delivered by athletic department counselors and consisted of bimonthly meetings during which students' academic progress was monitored and discussed. Counselors encouraged students to put forth effort and achieve success in their classes. The 20 students in the career-counseling condition received the same tutoring and counseling services as students in the control condition with the addition of six to eight hours of career-counseling activities over the course of a semester provided by staff associated with the university's Counseling and Psychological Services (CAPS). Specifically, these students were administered the Strong-Campbell Interest Inventory, and the results of the inventory were discussed with a CAPS counselor in one-to-one sessions. Students then explored possible careers using CAPS resources. The 20 students in the Possible selves condition received the same tutoring and counseling services as the control group, and they participated in the Possible Selves Program that consisted of the Thinking, Sketching, and Reflecting components (i.e., the students did not receive the

Discovering, Growing, and Performing components since they hadn't been conceptualized as part of the original intervention). The Possible Selves Program took about six to eight hours of time and was presented to students in one-to-one interactions with a sport counselor or other athletic department staff member. There were no statistically significant differences among the three groups' ACT scores, ethnicity, reading comprehension achievement scores, or gender.

The results of this study showed that, at the end of the first semester of the freshman year, students in the Possible selves condition scored significantly higher than students in the control group on measures of goal identification. That is, they identified more goals beyond the field of athletics as possible for them in life. Interestingly, the number of goals identified by students in the other conditions actually declined over the course of the first semester in the athlete and learner areas, while the possible selves group increased slightly or were maintained. Thus, freshman student-athletes at a mid-western Division 1 university reported fewer athletic and academic goals than they did on pretests administered at the beginning of their first semester at the university. Also, at the end of six years, the possible selves students had earned higher grade-point averages (GPAs) than the students in the other groups: The mean GPA for the possible selves group was 2.65. The mean GPA for the control group was 2.25 and the mean GPA for the career-counseling group was 2.41. Moreover, 75% of the possible selves group had graduated from the university, compared to 45% of the control group and 60% of the career-counseling group. The overall graduation rate for all students entering this university was 54%. Thus, student-athletes who participated in the Possible Selves Program graduated at a rate that was 21% higher than the general student population and 30% higher than student-athletes in the control group.

For another study, the original Possible Selves Program that was implemented in the first study was revised to include additional steps (Hock, Deshler, & Schumaker, 2002b). The two new steps included developing elaborate goal-directed action plans (Growing) and periodic monitoring and feedback on the completion of tasks and action plan goals (Performing). In this study, 32 freshmen student-athletes, matched for ACT scores, sport, gender, and high school GPA, were randomly assigned to either a control or an experimental group. Fifth-year student-athletes (hereafter called "peer mentors") were recruited and taught how to guide others through the Possible Selves Program. Two peer mentors were assigned to each group of four to six student-athletes who had been assigned to the experimental group. Each group met for one hour a week for 12 weeks during the fall semester. The peer mentors taught the possible selves lessons during that time. The control students met individually with sport counselors during the same time period and for the same number of hours.

Students in the Possible Selves Program significantly outperformed the control group on measures of role identification and goal setting in the areas of athletics, academics, and personal life. That is, the possible selves group identified significantly more roles for themselves as athletes, learners, and persons than did the students in the control group. Additionally, they identified more goals for themselves as athletes, learners, and persons, and the goals they identified were more specific than the goals identified by the control group. These differences were statistically significant. Finally, retention of students at the university was greater for the possible selves group than for the control group. Although students in both conditions still had one year left in a 6-year time period in which they might graduate at the time of this printing, 75% of the students in the possible selves group were on track to graduate or had graduated, and 56% of the students in the control condition were on track to graduate or had graduated. Thus, the retention results for the Possible Selves Program as taught by peer mentors with small groups of students are similar to the retention results of the original possible selves study where academic counselors and other athletic department staff members worked individually with students. Interestingly, the peer-mentored student-athletes in the second study identified significantly more roles and goals than did the counselor led possible selves students in the original study.

In a third study, using a quasi-experimental design, 52 middle-school students, including students with disabilities, participated (Hock, 2003). These students attended an urban school that serves a diversity of populations. Ten of these students were served in a self-contained special education classroom, and 21 students were served in an inclusive career-orientation class. These 31 students were the experimental group, whereas 21 students in another section of the same career-orientation course, taught by the same teacher, participated as a comparison group. Students in the experimental group participated in the Possible Selves Program over the course of the fall semester during approximately two class sessions each week for 12 weeks. The Possible Selves Program was revised from the second study to include the Discovering component. Students in the comparison class received the traditional career-orientation curriculum adopted by the school district. Results showed that the students who participated in the Possible Selves Program identified significantly more roles they hoped to play in the future than did students who participated in the traditional career orientation curriculum. Additionally, these students identified significantly more goals as learners and persons, and these goals were much more specific than the goals identified by comparison students. Finally, the experimental students and teachers reported that they were highly satisfied with the Possible Selves Program. Some students and teachers reported using goal and action-plan information resulting from the Possible Selves Program activities during IEP and transition conferences held at the school.

CONCLUSION

The Possible Selves Program shows promise as an intervention designed to enhance academic motivation and improve student performance across different instructional levels on key outcome measures. Specifically, students who participated in the Possible Selves Program identified more life roles and goals than did their peers, and these goals were significantly more specific in nature than the goals of other students. Additionally, university-level student-athletes earned higher GPAs over extended periods of time and graduated at a higher rate than did other student-athletes with similar profiles. Thus, the Possible Selves Program seems to be an effective intervention that increases the type, number, and specificity of goals students identify. In turn, these goals may be important in enhancing academic motivation and performance by making school experiences and learning activities relevant to students' hoped-for future possible selves. Once students begin to see the relevance of academic skills, knowledge, and effort as the means to attain what they have identified as important hopes for the future, commitment to learning may follow. Hopefully, the student described at the beginning of this chapter and others like him will hold on to their dreams of success as athletes, lawyers, doctors, business people, and rocket scientists and will also expand the vision of what is possible for them in the future to include goals for becoming good people, learners, family members, and workers. As a result, the outcomes that students achieve may be markedly enhanced in a way that makes a difference in the quality of their lives.

REFERENCES

American Psychological Association. (1997). *Learner-centered psychological principles: A framework for school redesign and reform.* Washington, DC: APA

Alderman, E.M. (1992). *The effect of personal and school-wide goals on deep processing strategies of at-risk, not at-risk and special education students.* Paper presented at the Society for Research on Adolescence, Washington, D.C.

Alderman, E.M., Hicks, L.H., & Maehr, M.L. (1994). *Present and possible selves across the transition to middle grade school.* Paper presented at the Society for Research on Adolescence, San Diego, CA.

Ames, C., & Archer, J. (1988). Achievement goals in the classroom: Students' learning strategies and motivational processes. *Journal of Educational Psychology*, 80, 260-270.

Anderson, R.C., Shirey, L.L., Wilson, P.T., & Fielding, L.G. (1987). Interestingness of children's reading material. In R.E. Snow & M.J. Farr (Eds.) *Aptitude, learning, and instruction, Volume 3: Conative and Affective Process Analysis* (pp. 287-299). Hillsdale, NJ: Erlbaum & Associates.

Bandura, A. (1997). Regulation of cognitive processes through perceived self-efficacy. Jennings, George-Harold (Ed), *Passages beyond the gate: A Jungian approach to understanding the nature of American psychology at the dawn of the new millennium.* (pp. 96-107). Needham Heights, MA: Simon & Schuster Custom Publishing.

Bandura, A. (1986). *Social foundations of thought and action: A social cognitive theory.* Englewood Cliffs, NJ: Prentice-Hall.

Bandura, A. (1982). Self-efficacy mechanisms in human agency. *American Psychologist*, 37, 122-147.

Babyak, M., Snyder, C.R., & Yoshinobu, L. (1993). Psychometric proprieties of the Hope Scale: A confirmatory factor analysis. *Journal of Research in Personality*, 27, 154-169.

Blumenfeld, P. C. (1992). Classroom learning and motivation: Clarifying and expanding goal theory. *Journal of Educational Psychology*, 84, (3), 272-281.

Bogner, K., Raphael, L., & Pressley, M. (2002). How grade 1 teachers motivate literate activity by their students. *Scientific Studies of Reading*, 6, (2), 135-165.

Borkowski, J.G., Day, J. D., Saenz, D., Dietmeyer, D., Estrada, T. M., & Groteluschen, A. (1992). Expanding the boundaries of cognitive interventions. In B. L. Wong (Ed.), *Contemporary Intervention Research in LD: An Interventional Perspective.* New York: Springer-Verlag.

Borkowski, J. G., Weyhing, R. S., & Carr, M. (1988). Effects of attributional retraining on strategy-based reading comprehension in learning disabled students. *Journal of Educational Psychology*, 80, 46-53.

Brophy, J. (1987). Socializing students' motivation to learning. In M.L. Maehr & D.A. Kleiber (Eds.), *Advances in motivation and achievement: Enhancing motivation*, Vol. 5, (pp. 181-210). Greenwich, CT: JAI Press.

Brophy, J. (1981). Teacher praise: A functional analysis. *Review of Educational Research*, 51, 5-32.

Carr, M., & Borkowski, J. G. (1989). Attributional training and the generalization of reading strategies with underachieving children. *Learning and Individual Differences*, 1, 327-341.

Clifford, M. M. (1978). The effects of quantitative feedback on children's expectations of success. *Journal of Educational Psychology*, 48, 220-226.

Cross, S. E., & Markus, H.R. (1994). Self-schemas, possible selves, and competent performance. *Journal of Educational Psychology*, 86(3), 423-438.

Cruickshank, D. R. (1990). *Research that informs teachers and teacher educators.* Bloomington, IN: Phi Delta Kappa.

Csikszentmihalyi, M. & Nakamura, J. (1989). The dynamics of intrinsic motivation: A study of adolescents. In R. Ames & C. Ames (Eds.), *Research on motivation in education: Vol. 3. Goals and Cognitions* (pp. 45-71). New York: Academic Press.

Curry, L. A., Snyder, C. R., Cook, D. L., Ruby, B. C., & Rehm, M. (1997). The role of hope in student-athlete academic and sport achievement. *Journal of Personality and Social Psychology*, 73, 1257-1267.

Davis, J. & Wilson, S. M. (2000). Principals' efforts to empower teachers: Effects on teacher motivation and job satisfaction and stress. *Clearing House,* 73, (6), 349-353.

Davison Avilés, R. M., Guerrero, M. P., Howarth, H. B., & Thomas, G. (1999). Perceptions of Chicano/Latino students who have dropped out of school. *Journal of Counseling & Development*, 77, 465-473.

Day, J. D., Borkowski, J. G., Dietmeyer, D. L., Howsepian, B. A., & Saenz, D. S. (1994). Possible selves and academic achievement. In L.T. Wineger & J. Valsinen (Eds.) *Children's development within social contexts: Metatheoretical, theoretical and methodological issues* (Vol. 2) Hillsdale, NJ: Erlbaum.

Deci, E. L., Hodges, M., Pierson, L., & Tomassone, J. (1992). Autonomy and competence as motivational factors in students with learning disabilities and emotional handicaps. *Journal of Learning Disabilities*, 25, (7), 457-471.

Deshler, D. D., & Schumaker, J. B. (1988). An instructional model for teaching students how to learn. In J.L. Graden, J. E. Zins, & M.L. Curtis (Eds.), *Alternative education delivery systems: Enhancing instructional options for all students* (pp. 391-411). Washington, DC: National Association of School Psychologist.

Dweck, C. S. (1986). Motivational processes affecting learning. *American Psychologist*, 41, (10), 1040-1048.

Dweck, C. S., & Leggett, E. L. (1988). A social-cognitive approach to motivation and personality. *Psychological Review*, 95, 256-273.

Estrada, M. T. (1990). *Improving academic performance through enhancing possible selves.* Unpublished master's thesis. University of Notre Dame, South Bend, IN.

Garber, S. H. (2002). *"Hearing their voices": Perceptions of high school students who evidence resistance to schooling.* Paper presented at the annual meeting of the American Educational Research Association, New Orleans, LA.

Garcia, T., Lissi, M. R., Egan-Dowdy, K., Davila, C., Matula, J. S., & Harris, C. L. (1995). *Gender and ethnic differences in college students' academic possible selves.* Paper presented at the annual meeting of the American Educational Research Association, San Francisco, CA.

Graves, D. H. (2001). *The energy to teach.* Westport, CT: Heinemann.

Hock, M. F. (2003). *Enhancing academic and personal goals with middle school students through the exploration of possible selves.* Manuscript in preparation.

Hock, M. F., Schumaker, J. B., & Deshler, D. D. (2003).*Possible selves: Nurturing student motivation.* Lawrence, KS: Lawrence, KS: Edge Enterprises, Inc.

Hock, M.F., Schumaker, J.B., Deshler, D.D. (2002a). *The role of Possible Selves in improving the academic focus and performance of university student-athletes.* Manuscript in preparation.

Hock, M. F., Deshler, D. D., & Schumaker, J.B. (2002b). *Nurturing possible selves in student-athletes through peer interactions: Surfacing academic, athletic, and personal goals.* Manuscript in preparation.

Jarvis, S., & Seifert, T. (2002). Work avoidance as a manifestation of hostility, helplessness, and boredom. *Alberta Journal of Educational Research*, 48, (2), 174-187.

Leondari , A., Syngollitou, E., & Kiosseoglou, G. (1998). Academic achievement, motivation and future selves. *Educational Studies*, 24 (2), 153-163.

Levine, M. (2002). *A mind at a time.* New York: Simon & Schuster.

Lepper, M. R. (1988). Motivational considerations in the study of instruction. *Cognition and Instruction*, 5, (4), 289-309.

Lepper, M. R., Greene, D., & Nisbett, R. E. (1973). Undermining children's intrinsic interest with extrinsic rewards: A test of the "over-justification" hypothesis. *Journal of Personality and Social Psychology*, 28, 129-137.

Maehr, M. L. (1989). Thoughts about motivation. In R. Ames & C. Ames (Eds.), Research on motivation in education: Vol. 3. *Goals and Cognitions* (pp. 299-315). New York: Academic Press.

Markus, H. & Nurius, P. (1986). Possible Selves. *American Psychologist*, 41, 954-969.

McCombs, B. L. & Marzano, R. J. (1990). Putting the self in self-regulated learning: The self as agent in integrating will and skill. *Educational Psychologist*, 25, 51-70.

National Collegiate Athletic Association. (2001). *A career in professional athletics.* Indianapolis, IN: Author.

Nicholls, J., Cobb, P., Wood, T., Yackel, E., & Patashnick, M. (1990). Assessing students' theories of success in mathematics: Individual and class differences. *Journal of Research in Mathematics Education*, 21, 109-122.

Oyserman, D. & Markus, H. R. (1990a). Possible Selves and delinquency. *Journal of Personality and Social Psychology*, 59, (1), 112-125.

Oyserman, D. & Markus, H. (1990b). Possible Selves in balance: Implications for delinquency. *Journal of Social Issues*, 46, (2), 141-157.

Pressley, M., & Ghatala, E. S. (1989). Metacognitive benefits of taking a test for children and young adolescents, *Journal of Experimental Child Psychology*, 47, 430-450.

Pressley, M., & McCormick, C. B. (1995). *Cognition, teaching, and assessment.* New York, NY: Harper Collins.

Reid, M. K., & Borkowski, J. G. (1987). Causal attributions of hyperactive children: Implications for teaching strategies and self-control. *Journal of Educational Psychology*, 79, 296-307.

Reyna, C. & Weiner, B. (2001). Justice and utility in the classroom: An attributional analysis of the goals of teachers' punishment and intervention strategies. *Journal of Educational Psychology*, 93, (2), 309-319.

Pintrich, P. R., & Schunk, D. (1996). *Motivation, in education: Theory, research, and application.* Columbus, OH: Merrill Prentice-Hall.

Seifert, T. L. (1995). Academic goals and emotions: A test of two models. *The Journal of Psychology*, 10, 543-551.

Snyder, C. R. (1994). *The psychology of hope: You can get there from here.* New York: Free Press of New York City.

Snyder, C. R., Cheavens, J., & Sympson, S. (1997). Hope: An individual motive for social commerce. *Group Dynamics: Theory, Research, and Practice*, 1, 1-12.

Snyder, C. R., Harris, C., Anderson, J. R., Holleran, S. A., Irving, L. M., Sigmon, S. T., Yoshinobu, L., Gibb, J. Langelle, C., & Harney, P. (1991). The will and the ways: Development and validation of an individual differences measure of hope. *Journal of Personality and Social Psychology*, 60,570-585.

Snyder, C. R., Hoza, B., Pelham, W.E., Rapoff, M., Ware, L., Danovsky, M., Highberger, L., Rubinstein, H., & Stahl, K. (1997). The development and validation of the Children's Hope Scale. *Journal of Pediatric Psychology*, **22**(3), 399-421.

Snyder, C.R., Sympson, S.C., Ybasco, F.C., Borders, T.F., M.A., & Higgins, R.L. (1996). Development and validation of the State Hope Scale. *Journal of Personality and Social Psychology*, 2, 321-335.

Stipek, D., & Maclver, D. (1989). Developmental change in children's assessment of intellectual competence. *Child Development*, 60, 521-538.

Tollefson, J. (1998, July). Focusing on what's best for students. *Strategram*, 10, (4), 1-7.U.S. Department of Education, Office of Elementary and Secondary Education. (2002). *No child left behind: A desktop reference*, Washington D.C.

Wehmeyer, M. L., Palmer, S. B., Agran, M., Mithaug, D. E., & Martin, J. E. (2000). Promoting causal agency: The self-determined learning model of instruction. *Exceptional Children*, 66, (4), 439-453.

POSSIBLE SELVES QUESTIONNAIRE

What words or phrases best describe you in these areas? Respond verbally or write down your responses to the questions. Remember, there are no right or wrong answers to the questions so respond honestly and to the best of your ability.

Section 1: Individual Strength

1. What's one thing that you are **really good at doing**?
2. What are some of the things you *hope to achieve* in this area?
3. What are some of the things you *expect to achieve* in this area?
4. What are some of your *fears* in this area?

Section 2: Learner

1.What words or phrases best **describe** you as a **learner**?
2.What are some of the things you *hope to achieve* as a learner?
3.What are some of the things you *expect to achieve* as a learner?
4.What are some of your *fears* as a learner?

Section 3: Person

1. What words or phrases best **describe** you as a **person**?
2. What are some of the things you *hope to achieve* as a person?
3. What are some of the things you *expect to achieve* as a person?
4. What are some of your *fears* as a person?

Section 4: Worker

1. What words or phrases best **describe** you as a **worker**?
2. What are some of the things you *hope to achieve* as a worker?
3. What are some of the things you *expect to achieve* as a worker?
4. What are some of your *fears* as a worker?

INDEX

D

E

H

I

M

N

O

P

Y